1860 POPULATION SCHEDULE
OF THE
UNITED STATES CENSUS

BLOUNT COUNTY, TENNESSEE

Transcribed from the Original

by

David Templin

and

Cherel Bolin Henderson

Heritage Books
2024

HERITAGE BOOKS

AN IMPRINT OF HERITAGE BOOKS, INC.

Books, CDs, and more—Worldwide

For our listing of thousands of titles see our website
at
www.HeritageBooks.com

A Facsimile Reprint
Published 2024 by
HERITAGE BOOKS, INC.
Publishing Division
5810 Ruatan Street
Berwyn Heights, MD 20740

Maryville, Tennessee
1981

International Standard Book Number
Paperbound: 978-0-7884-8763-7

FOREWORD

Blount County was divided into two roughly equal halves for the purpose of the 1860 census. Sam Wallace, a resident of the Rockford area, took the northern half, which consisted of Districts 8, 9, 11, 12, 13, 14, 15 and 16. The southern half of Blount County was covered by Hiram Heartsill and included Districts 1, 2, 3, 4, 5, 6, 7, 10 and 17. Part of what is today Loudon County was then Blount County and was included in the southern division.

The two enumerators had distinctly different styles of handwriting and of personal expression. The latter is particularly evident in the listing of occupations by Mr. Wallace. As is always the case in the transcription of a census, the handwriting is subject to the interpretation of the transcriber. In all cases where there is a question about the exact reading of a name or initial, the transcribers urge the reader to consult the microfilm copy of the original.

In Mr. Heartsill's handwriting, the middle initial is sometimes difficult to decipher. What appears to be a "L" could easily be a "S", "T", or "Y".

In several cases the post offices changed from one page to the next in the same district. We have tried to head a page the same as in the original. Mr. Wallace made no distinction as to where one district ended and another began, his only notation being made in the page heading. In some cases Mr. Heartsill made a notation as to where his districts began and ended.

For this transcription we have listed the name of the individual, his age, occupation, amount of real property, amount of personal property, and place of birth. In some cases people were listed with physical infirmities or as a pauper. We have listed these in parenthesis under the heading "Occupation". The color is listed only for blacks (bl) and mulattoes (mul). In cases where an individual had a name not easily recognizable as male or female, we have put the sex in parenthesis following the name. (m) = male, (f) = female. In a few cases Mr. Wallace made errors in listing the sex of an individual. Even though he was obviously in error, we have followed Mr. Wallace and listed the sex after the name, though we are reasonably sure that some one named Elizabeth was female, even if Mr. Wallace had written male after her name.

Included with this census is the 1860 Blount County Mortality Schedule, containing a list of the individuals in Blount County who died between June 1, 1859 and June 1, 1860. These names are not included in the index.

The transcribers are sure that this transcription will contain errors. In all cases we have tried to follow the enumerators, but as we pointed out on the previous page, in instances where there was doubt about the exact reading we were forced to use our own judgement. Again, let us suggest that in all cases where the reader has a doubt as to our interpretation, he should consult the original.

We wish to extend our thanks to the Blount County Public Library for the use of their film and microfilm readers. The records of Blount County are almost intact. Many of these records are available on microfilm or in print in the Blount County Public Library.

District 11   P. O.: Rockford

	Name	Age	Occupation	Real	Pers.	Birthplace
Page 1						2 June 1860
1	Sam WALLACE	50	Farmer	12,000	12,000	Tenn.
	Elizabeth	34				"
	Susanch REDER (f)	24			2,000	"
2	Jacob WRINKLER	25	Carpenter		200	"
	Narcissa	24				"
	Andrew	1				"
	Marion PATTERSON (m)	25	Chairmaker			N. Car.
3	Emerson WRINKLER	31	Carpenter	100	50	Tenn.
	Sarah	31				
	Sophronia	9/12				
4	Sophronia WRINKLER	50				
	Margaret	23				
	Jane	22				
	Elzena (f)	20				
	Elizabeth McCARTY	74				Va.
5	Agnes McNABB	59				Tenn.
	Mary	34				
	Adaline	26				
	Alexander	24	Painter			
	Catherine	21	Factory hand			
	Robert	18				
6	Wm. MARTIN (mwy)	25	Cabinet maker	250	150	Va.
	Victoria	19				
7	I. R. LOVE	37	Bookkeeper	250	14,783	Tenn.
	Eliza	24				
	Sam P.	5				
	James (C?)	4				
	Charles E.	2				
	Susan M.	3/12				
	Jane PEARSON	15	Indentured			
	Mary J. LOVE	35	Tutoress		1,200	
8	Will McCAMPBELL	31	Bookkeeper	750	100	
	Mary	30				
	Andrew	1				
9	A. WILLIAMS	28	Saddler	650	400	
	Mary	24				
	Rutelia (f)	4				
	Andrew	1				
	Jane McCAMPBELL	60				
	Andrew McCAMPBELL	20	Saddler	1,500		

District 11   P. O.: Rockford

	Name	Age	Occupation	Real	Pers.	Birthplace
	Page 2					2 June 1860
10	Thos. E. OLDHAM	30	Merchant	2,500	40,000	Ky.
	Georgia W.	25				Tenn.
	Carrick P. (m)	6				
	Luelder (f)	4				
	Mary K.	2				
	Infant (f)	4/12				
11	Frank SHOFFIER (mwy)	33	Stone mason		400	Prussia
	Mary	18				Tenn.
	James KIDD	22	Carpenter		75	
	Nancy Jane	20				
12	David WINE	40	Blacksmith		300	
	Elizabeth Jane	32				Va.
	Mariah	11				Tenn.
	Mary	10				
	William	8				
	Hester	5				
	David	2				
	Sam Porter	1/2				
13	Mary WEBSTER	39			75	N. Car.
	Mary Ann	22	Factory hand			"
	Nancy	17				"
	Margaret	15				"
14	Maj. H. STEPHENS	83	Pensioner			Va.
	Wm. STEPHENS	66		3,500	2,500	"
	Nancy STEPEHNS	74	Maiden			
	Scoto (?) (f)	70				
	Henry STEPHENS	25	Labourer	300		Tenn.
	Catherine	39			2,000	"
15	Alfred RODDY	40	Farm labourer		150	
	Elizabeth	43				
	Jane	15				
	Caroline	13				
	Susan	11				
	Andrew Jackson	9				
	Peter	7				
	Henrietta	5				
16	Jas. DEARMOND	27	Miller	160	150	
	Charlotte	27				
	Millard F.	4				
	James F.	2				
	Page 3					2 June 1860
	Sam Houston	1				

	Name	Age	Occupation	Real	Pers.	Birthplace
17	John Barker	35	Turner		200	England
	Martha Ann	25				Tenn.
	Mary	5				
	Sarah	2				
	Martha	6/12				
18	Wm. GARDNER	28	Machinist		400	Scotland
	Agnes	24				
	William	1				Tenn.
19	Philip HENDERSON	23	Card stripper		75	
	Tennessee	26				
	Arthur	21				
20	Henry HODGE	60	M. Miss. Baptist		150	
	Jane	49				
	Sarah	27	Reeler in factory			
	Delilah	25	Spinner			
	Henry I.	23	Card grinder			
	Mary	18	Spinner			
	Margaret	16	"			
	Harrey	15	Cotton picker			
	Charlotte	12	Miss			
21	Jas. KIDD	41	Labourer		150	
	Mary	41				N. Car.
	Harrey	16				Tenn.
	Betty Ann	13				
	Leander	12				
	Eliza Jane	5				
22	A. C. STANSBERRY	43	Fireman		100	N. Car.
	Mary Jane	41				
	Richard	13				
	Caroline	11				
	Monroe	7				
	J. Wesley	5				
	Sarah C. (twins)	3				
	Elizabeth S.	3				
	Eliza Jane	2				
23	Jefferson KIDD	28	Farmer		1,500	
	Mary Jane	22				
	Samuel	1				
	Jas. KIDD	26			600	

Page 4

	Milton KIDD	25	Labourer		600	Tenn.
24	David GODDARD	43	Farmer	3,800	1,050	
	Matilda	40				
	James A.	17				
	Eliza Jane	15				

District 11   P. O.: Rockford

	Name	Age	Occupation	Real	Pers.	Birthplace
	Wm. R.	14				
	Robt. W.	12				
	Margt. E.	10				
	Harry S.	8				
	Mary M.	6				
	John L.	4				
	Sam D. (twins)	2				
	Harriett A.	2				
25	Wm. McNABB	31	Carpenter	600	225	
	Susan R.	28				
	Charles P.	2				
	Wm. H.	10/12				
26	Emily SUANER	33	Weaver		50	N. Car.
	Eliza C.	15	Factory hand			Tenn.
	Nancy E.	12	" "			
	John L.	10	" "			
	Hester Ann	5				
27	Rev. John CALDWELL	38	N. S. Pres.	1,000	500	
	Mary	44				
	William	8				
	Rebecca ANDERSON	22		500	3,800	
	Isaack ANDERSON	19	Law student	3,500	600	
	Julia PEARSON	15	Indentured			
28	Dorothy BEARD	98				Va.
	Matilda	34	Factory hand		100	
29	Benj. LEWIS	58	Shoemaker	250	600	
	Sarah LEWIS	51				
	William	16				Tenn.
30	Frank LANTER	31	Farmer	2,000	500	Va.
	Mary Jane	25				Tenn.
	Charles	3				
	Margaret	2				
	Martha CALDWELL	15	Help			
31	Hu D. CALDWELL	50	Carpenter	100	250	Va.
	Matilda	60				"

Page 5   4 June 1860

	Name	Age	Occupation	Real	Pers.	Birthplace
	Mahala CALDWELL	44				Tenn.
	Lovenia	20				
	Joseph	17				
	James	6				

-4-

1860 U. S. CENSUS OF BLOUNT COUNTY, TENNESSEE

	Name	Age	Occupation	Real	Pers.	Birthplace
32	James BADGETT	65	Gentleman			N. Car.
	Susan BADGETT	55				" "
	Keron (f)	29				Tenn.
	Elizabeth	27				
	Mandy	23	Spinner			
	Harris	21	Labourer			
	Burrel	19				
	Josephine	15	Weaver			
	Rufus	12				
	Mat BADGETT	26	Dresser	1,800	1,500	
33	David DEARMOND	24	Labourer		75	
	Eliza Jane	22				
	Rebecca Ann	1				
34	Lewis KIDD	40	Labourer	100	75	
	Lydda	43				
	John	18				
	Elizabeth	16				
	Esther	14				
	Henry	12				
	Mary	9				
	Minerva	7				
	Alexander	3				
35	James HITCH	31	Farmer	2,000	800	
	Ellen	28				
	Lucinda	7				
	Eleven (f)	3				
	Maria	2				
	Andrew	6/12				
	Mary TUCK	11	Indentured			
	James ADDISON	11				
36	Henry JOINER	45	Blacksmith		100	
	Rebecca	48				Va.
	Mary	23	Warper			Tenn.
	Lucy	22	Spinner			
	William	11				
	Thomas	9				

Page 6   4 June 1860

	Name	Age	Occupation	Real	Pers.	Birthplace
	Griffeth	6				Tenn.
37	John GODFREY	47	Tenant		500	
	Lucinda	44				
	Alexander	20				
	Loreldy (?) (f)	17				
	Augustine	16				
	Sarah Ann	14				

District 11   P. O.: Rockford

	Name	Age	Occupation	Real	Pers.	Birthplace
38	William GIBBS	41	Tenant		400	
	Martha Jane	42				
	Montgomery	15				
	Zachary Taylor	13				
39	Sarah McGILL	38	Tenant		75	N. Car.
	Polly	27				Tenn.
	Susan	26	Weaver			
	Martha	22				
	Jane	19				
40	David CHANDLER	55	Farmer	15,000	9,050	
	Jane	32				Va.
	James	12				Tenn.
	Richard	10				
	Stephen	2				
41	James SINGLETON	38	Farmer	4,500	2,500	
	Caroline	36				
	Philander (m)	11				
	William	9				
	Rebecca	4				
	John	9/12				
42	John CHANDLER	47	Farmer	4,000	3,500	
	Cynthia Ann	38				
	William	14				
	Mary	12				
	Catherine	11				
	Richard	9				
	Sarah	7				
	Nancy	5				
	James	2				
43	Jas. TAYLOR	31	Farmer		1,100	
	Mary Ann	29				
	Hughs	8				
	Melissa	3				

Page 7   4 June 1860

	David	2				Tenn.
44	Robert SINGLETON	39	Farmer	3,000	3,000	
	Catherine	37				
	Bettie	16				
	Malinda	14				
	James	2				
45	Unoccupied					
46	Unoccupied					

	Name	Age	Occupation	Real	Pers.	Birthplace
47	Lewis WEST	49	Tenant	700	700	
	Martha	44				
	Nathaniel	21				
	Mary	18				
	William	16				
	Samuel	13				
	Esther	10				
	John	4				
	John REAGAN	90	(Pauper)			Va.
48	Holston RODDY	20	Tenant		100	Tenn.
	Nancy	17				
	Baby (m)	1/52				
49	Thos. HARDIN	27	Farmer	2,500	700	
	Candis	29				N. Car.
	Sarah	4				Tenn.
	Suella (?)	2				
	Baby	7/12				
	James ELLIOTT	17	Labourer			N. Car.
	Creyton HICKS	25	Carpenter			" "
50	Arch PASS	35	Tenant		100	" "
	Mary	37				Va.
	Margaret	14				Tenn.
	Nancy	12				
	John	10				
51	Hughs TAYLOR	39	Tenant		400	
	Nancy	31				
	Jackson	18				
	Nancy	16				
	Edney (f)	14				
	John	11				
	Rufus	10				
52	Mat TAYLOR	42	Farmer	3,000	700	

Page 8   4 June 1860

	Name	Age	Occupation	Real	Pers.	Birthplace
	Nancy	36				Tenn.
	Thomas D.	15				
	Hughs	13				
	William	11				
	Jane	5				
	Grinsfield (m)	3				
53	Johnson ROGERS	61	Cooper		50	N. Car.
	Polly Ann	49				Tenn.

District 11   P. O.: Rockford

	Name	Age	Occupation	Real	Pers.	Birthplace
54	William SCRIBNER	60	Carpenter		50	Maryland
	Charlotte	43				Tenn.
	Sarah	20				
	Henry	17				
	Nancy	14				
	Margaret	12				
	John	10				
	Mary	8				
	Susan	6				
	Martha	1				
55	Arch HITCH	36	Farmer	2,000	200	
	Eveline	25				
	James	7				
	John	5				
	William	2				
	Nancy J. BROWN	16	Help			
56	Joel VON	60	Miller			S. Car.
	Hannah	57				N. Car.
	Rebecca	15	(Pauper)			Tenn.
	Benj. VON	21	Miller		50	
	Martha	17				
	Mary Jane	10/12				
57	Will JAMES	26	Labourer		40	
	Margaret	17				
58	Henry THOMPSON	47			100	
	Elizabeth	41				N. Car.
	Jane	17				Tenn.
	Martha	13				
	Samuel	15				
	Eliza	12				
	Edward	8				
	Hannah	5				

Page 9   5 June 1860

	Name	Age	Occupation	Real	Pers.	Birthplace
59	James HADDOX	39		500	550	Tenn.
	Rebecca	44				
	Andrew	13				
	Mariah	11				
	Will TUCK	7	Indentured			
60	Ed KIDD	59	Tenant		200	Va.
	Malindy	43				Tenn.
	John	19				
	Franklin	17				
	Maria	15				
	Elzena (?) (f)	13				
	Lewis	11				

1860 U. S. CENSUS OF BLOUNT COUNTY, TENNESSEE

| District 11 | | | | | P. O.:Rockford |

	Name	Age	Occupation	Real	Pers.	Birthplace
	Sarah	8				
	Catherine	6				
	Ransome	3				
	Will KIDD	23	Labourer		75	
	Robt. KIDD	21	Labourer		100	
61	Isaack WAGNER	47	Blacksmith		150	N. Car.
	David	11				
	Margaret	10				
	Sophia	9				
	Polly SWEET	51	Housekeeper		25	
62	Rufus P. JOHNSON	27			250	Tenn.
	Matildy	26				
	James	5				
	William	2				
63	Ransome BADGETT	30	Farmer	2,500	5,000	
	David ANDERSON	55	Tenant			
	Polly	53				
	James	13	(Dumb & Idiot)			
64	Sam BALLARD	43	Farmer	1,000	500	
	Nancy BALLARD	41				
	Marcus	17				
	Samuel	15				
	Mary	11				
	Martha	10				
	Nancy	8				
	William	6				
	Ann	3				
65	Abigale BARNHILL	50	Tenant		75	

Page 10   5 June 1860

66	J. D. WRIGHT	62	Farmer	5,000	5,500	Tenn.
	Mary	12				
	James	12				
	Tilly WHITLOCK (m)	18	Labourer			
67	Andrew BALLARD	45	Tenant		80	
	Nancy	39				
	Nancy Ann	21				
	Louisa	18				
	Samuel	16				
	Whitson	13				
	Rebecca	10				
	Berthina (f)	4				
	Mary	11/12				

-9-

District 11   P. O.: Rockford

	Name	Age	Occupation	Real	Pers.	Birthplace
68	James BALLARD	27	Tenant		50	
	Martha Jane	21				
	Sarah	4				
	Isabella	1				
69	Esther PRICE	42			40	
	William	8				
70	Sarah JONES	62	Farmer	1,200	500	
	Nancy	26	Spinster			
	William JONES (mwy)	22	Labourer			
	Catherine	17				
71	Lewis JONES	26	Tenant		250	
	Nancy	20				N. Car.
	Sarah Ann	4				Tenn.
	Nancy	3				
	Lewis James Jefferson	5/12	(twins)			
	William Lea Epperson	5/12				
72	Samuel NEELY	57	Labourer		75	
	Elizabeth	52				
	William	15				
	John	13				
	Sarah	11				
	Mary	9				
73	Richard LEBO	43	Farmer	1,500	600	
	Amy	45				
	Prior	19				
	William	16				
	David	20				

Page 11   5 June 1860

	Name	Age	Occupation	Real	Pers.	Birthplace
	Sarah	14				Tenn.
	Housten	12				
	Maddison	10				
	Mary	6				
	David LEBO	73	Traymaker			
74	Isam LEBO	53	Farmer	1,500	1,500	
	Sarah	53				
	Mary	30				
	Susanna	20				
	Greenfield	18				
	Marquss	16				
	Rose Jane	15				
	Isaack	13				
	Richard (twins)	8				
	Dickson	8				
	Esnier (f)	7				

District 11   P. O.: Rockford

	Name	Age	Occupation	Real	Pers.	Birthplace
75	Arthur BOND	52	Tenant		50	
73	Sarah	57				
	John	24				
	Mary	20				
	William	17				
	Matildy	14				
	David	11				
76	J. S. GEORGE	42	Farmer	18,000	18,000	
74	Eliza	38				
	Samuel	17				
	Lucy	14				
	Josiah	10				
	Isaack	8				
	Burrell	5				
	Alice	2				
77	Daniel TAYLOR	66	Farmer	5,000	5,000	Va.
75	Martha	60				Tenn.
	Mary Jane	42				
	Francis (f)	40				
	Sarah	37				
	Richard	30	Labourer			
	Susanna	25				
	Melissa	21				
	Lucy	18				

Page 12   5 June 1860

	Name	Age	Occupation	Real	Pers.	Birthplace
78	William TAYLOR	34	Tenant		5,300	Tenn.
76	Susan	21				
	Martha	2/12				
79	Eliza RANKIN	42		1,000	4,000	
77	Milton	13				
80	Lew GIBBS	45	Tenant		75	
78	Elizabeth	26				
	Nancy	17				
	Samanthy	14				
	Wilson	10				
	Martha	7				
	John	5				
81	Will HARDEN	34	Farmer	4,500	3,000	N. Car.
79	Jane	26				Tenn.
	Sarah	1				
	John	5/12				
82	John SINGLETON	26	Tenant		1,500	
80	Martha	24				
	Jas.	2				
	Margaret	9/12				

District 11   P. O.: Rockford

	Name	Age	Occupation	Real	Pers.	Birthplace
83	Andrew McFADDEN	45	Farmer	1,800	1,900	
	Martha	33				
	William	9				
	John	8				
	David	7				
	Mary	5				
	Sarah	3				
	Eliza	2				
	Baby (m)	11/12				
84	Strong McFADDEN	50	Farmer	2,100	1,800	
	Jane McFADDEN	40				
	John BROWN	19	Indentured			
85	Alen TAYLOR	42	Farmer	2,000	800	
	Harriet	35				Maryland
	Rufus	18				Tenn.
	Catham (m)	15				
	Matilda	13				
	Susanna	10				
	Martha	6				
	Samanthy	4				

Page 13   6 June 1860

	Name	Age	Occupation	Real	Pers.	Birthplace
	Julia	2				Tenn.
86	Mary KIDD	50	Farmer	4,000	1,000	
	Minerva	29			400	
	Alexander KIDD	21	Tenant		200	
	Perry	20				
	Mary	15				
	Wesley JOHNSON	16	Labourer			
87	Ao__ HARRIS	46	Shoemaker	100	125	
	Mary	41				
	James	19				
	Sarah	18				
	Marshall	15				
	Elizabeth	7				
	Newman	5				
88	Ham HENSON	35	Tenant		200	N. Car.
	Leah	36				" "
	Winny	17				Tenn.
	Andrew HOLLOWAY (mwy)	24	Tenant			S. Car.
	Rosan (f)	18				Tenn.
89	James THOMPSON	68	Farmer	5,000	8,500	
	Martha THOMPSON	61				
	Martha	31				
	Elvira	30				
	Ann	28				
	Margaret	20				

	Name	Age	Occupation	Real	Pers.	Birthplace
90	Alexander THOMPSON	28	Tenant		600	
	Elizabeth	24				
	James	3				
91	Ed GEORGE	54	Farmer	15,500	7,700	
	Mary	40				
	Houston	13				
	Martha	11				
	Elizabeth	9				
	Barbary	6				
	Edward	4				
	Samuel	1				
	Thomas GIBSON	16	Labourer			
92	Will WRIGHT	44	Farmer	10,000	3,500	
	Ann	42				
	Nancy	14				

Page 14   6 June 1860

	Name	Age	Occupation	Real	Pers.	Birthplace
	Dorcus	7				Tenn.
	Mary	6				
	William	1				
93	John KIDD	38	Carpenter	250	150	
	Polly	47				
	Catherine	14				
	Henry	12				
	Emmons (m)	11				
94	Thos. McCAMPBELL	26	Waggoner	150	175	
	Mary Ann	29				
	Sophronia	5				
	Texana (f)	4				
	Leon	2				
	Ann	3/12				
95	Alen MITCHELL	48	Carpenter	300	550	
	Eliza MITCHELL	36				
	Harriet	17	Spinner			
	Catherine	16				
	Lucindy	15				
	William	14				
	Mary	6				
	David	3				
	Thomas	1				
96	Will MOSS	48	Cooper		250	Va.
	Hester MOSS	50				
	Sarah MOSS	24	Weaver			
	Priscilla	20	Wraper			Tenn.
	Sophia HENDERSON	60				Va.

District 11   P. O.: Rockford

	Name	Age	Occupation	Real	Pers.	Birthplace
__ 95	William HODGE	26	Factory hand	50	75	Tenn.
	Margaret	23				
	William	2				
97	William GARDNER, Sr.	60		1,000	60	Scotland
	Mary	58				
	Alexander GARDNER	21	Weaving master		100	
	James	19	Student of divinity			
98	David CALDWELL	52	Farmer	8,000	12,000	
	Elizabeth	46				
	Jane	24				
	Libby	19				
	Mary (?) (f)	12				

Page 15   6 June 1860

	Name	Age	Occupation	Real	Pers.	Birthplace
	Opelia	7				Tenn.
	Esther CALDWELL	54		2,000	300	
99	Samuel HAWPSON	24	Weaver		50	England
	Eliza	20				Tenn.
	Martha	11/12				
100	Thomas McCOLLOUGH	74	Farmer	10,000	2,300	Va.
	Thomas McCOLLOUGH, Jr.	32	Tenant			Tenn.
	Ann	27				
	Millard	5				
	Libby Jane	3				
101	GIBBS	71	Tenant	230		S. Car.
	Jane	62				Tenn.
	Ibby GIBBS (f)	48	Weaver			
	Sam	6				
	Thos. GIBBS	21	Labourer			
102	James MAYFIELD	38			100	
	Mary	38				
	Sarah	17				
103	Nat HARRIS	48	Tenant		150	
	Catherine	34				
	Elenor	13				
	John	11				
	Lucy	9				
	Betsy	7				
	Susan	4				
	James	1				
104	Elizabeth VINEYARD	40	Farmer	600	400	Va.
	James	14				Tenn.
	Ellen	12				

	Name	Age	Occupation	Real	Pers.	Birthplace
	Mary	10				
	William	8				
	Filpena (f)	7				
	John	5				
	Tabler	2				
	Letitia (f)	1				
105	Vance SWAGGERTY	24	Tenant		40	
	Sarah	19				
	Louisa	1/12				
	Nancy NORMAN	61	Help			
106	Andrew PORTER	28	Farmer	5,000	4,000	Va.

Page 16   7 June 1860

	Louisa PORTER	19				Tenn.
	Sam STOOPS	18	Labourer			
107	Emaline SWAGGERTY	29	Tenant		140	
	Marion (m)	18				
	Claiborne	15				
	Ann	13				
	Mary	5				
	William	1				
108	Porter McCOLLOUGH	50	Farmer	2,000	1,000	
	Christiana	49				
	Mary	18				
	Ann	14				
	Samuel	11				
	Esther	8				
109	Eliza HUMPHREY	25	Tenant		75	
	Nancy	24				
	Sarah	2				
	Ann	9/12				
110	William HOOD (mwy)	33	Tenant		75	
	Elizabeth	27				
	Syrena (f)	10				
	Francis (m)	8				
	Sarah	6				
111	And. HARRIS	51	Farmer	5,000	1,800	
	Sarah	29				Va.
	John	19				Tenn.
	William	5				
	Andrew	4				
	Harrey	3				
	Eliza	1				
	Benj. HARRIS	23			200	

	Name	Age	Occupation	Real	Pers.	Birthplace
112	John M. COFFIN	48	Farmer	21,250	53,800	
	Mary K.	40				
	Charles I.	20	Student			
	June E.	18				
	Susan A.	15				
	James W.	13				
	Richard W.	9				
	John M.	7				
	H. M. WILSON	11				

Page 17   7 June 1860

	Name	Age	Occupation	Real	Pers.	Birthplace
	James WILSON	9				
	Arch HOLBERT	63	Carpenter			Maryland
113	Augustus BADGETT	37	Farmer	8,500	10,750	Tenn.
	Catherine	36				
	Samuel	14				
	Sarah	13				
	John	10				
	Newman	6				
	Philander	2				
114	Fleming MAYS	45	Tenant		250	
	Jane	44				
	Joseph	12				
	David	10				
	John	8				
	Alexander	6				
	Elzenia (f)	4				
	Jas. MAYS (mwy)	19	Labourer		350	
	Sarah	17				
	Jane CALDWELL	60				
115	Peter RULE	48	Miller		600	Va.
	Mary RULE	46				Tenn.
	Minerva	25				
	Robt.	18				
	Andrew	15				
	Harriet	12				
	Sarah	7				
116	Robt. GODFREY	24	Miller		100	
	Serena	18				
	Augustine	7/12				
117	Elizabeth WHEELER	45	Farmer	100	75	
	Jasper	19				
	Joicey	16				
	Perry	14				
	Rachel	11				
	Mary	8				

1860 U. S. CENSUS OF BLOUNT COUNTY, TENNESSEE

District 11 P. O.: Rockford

	Name	Age	Occupation	Real	Pers.	Birthplace
118	Jordan WHEELER	29	Tenant		60	
	Elizabeth	29				
	Mary	7				
	James	3				
	Nancy	4/12				

Page 18 7 June 1860

	Name	Age	Occupation	Real	Pers.	Birthplace
119	And. McBATH	32	Farmer	5,000	8,000	Tenn.
	Jane McBATH	32				
	James	8				
	Lucindy	6				
	William	1				
	Eliza McBATH	30	(Idiotic)	500		
120	Will CRAWLY	24	Tenant		200	
	Margarett	24				
	John	2				
	Richard	9/12				
	Noah CRAWLEY	30	Labourer			
121	Rich. KIRBY	40	Farmer	5,000	7,000	
	Wright	9				
	Mary	4				
	Betsey HOPE	81				Va.
	Nancy LEA (black)	78	Nurse			
122	Sarah HENSON	51	Nitter		20	N. Car.
	Nancy J. HENSON	26	Hooker			Tenn.
	John	4				
123	Nathan GIBSON	25	Bird of passage			N. Car.
	Martha	31				
	Agnes	8				
	Elizabeth	5				Tenn.
	Bradford	2				
	Eli	1				
	James GIBSON	19	Bird of passage			N. Car.
	Amandy	21				Tenn.
124	Agnes GIBSON	57				N. Car.
	Elizabeth GIBSON	19	Hooker			
	Eliza	13				Tenn.
	Mary	5				
	John	1				
125	Ann BOWEN	42	Farmer	4,000	550	
	Alexander	15				
	Elizabeth	13				
	Lucindy	11				
	Hester RODDY (mwy)	18				
126	Margaret WHEELER	78	Farmer	4,000	100	
	Martha WHEELER	35				
	Lucy	blank				

-17-

District 11					P. O.: Rockford

	Name	Age	Occupation	Real	Pers.	Birthplace
Page 19						8 June 1860
127	Newton WHEELER	50	Tenant		50	Tenn.
	Phebe WHEELER	37				
	Caswell	15				
	Caroline	11				
	Christiana	9				
	John	7				
	Porter	4				
	Malissa	2				
128	Jas. KIRBY	48	Farmer	2,000	675	
	Margaret	49				
	Isabella	15				
	Syrena	9				
	Franklin	7				
	Preston RODDY (mwy)	21	Labourer		100	
129	Dr. W. S. PORTER	48	M.D./farmer	6,000	8,000	
	Phebe I. PORTER	34				
	Samuel	14				
	Robert	12				
	Ann	9				
	Jinny	6				
130	Calvin RODDY	39	Farmer	2,000	1,300	
	Sarah RODDY	40				
	Margaret	18				
	Massa (f)	16				
	Mary	14				
	Martha	9				
	Malindy	7				
	Barckly (m)	3				
	John BURDEN	6	Indentured			
131	Henry LINCONFELTER	30	Farmer	1,000	3,000	
	Phebe	36				
	Franklin	8				
	Jacob	3				
	Joseph	4/12				
	Will BAYLES	25	Labourer			
132	Thomas GODFREY (mwy)	22	Tenant		40	
	Catherine	23				
133	Nancy TIPTON	50			75	
	Emeline TIPTON	30				
	James	15				
Page 20						8 June 1860
	Clemantine	9				Tenn.
	William	3				
	Stephen CHILDRESS	61	Labourer			Va.

-18-

District 12   P. O. Rockford

	Name	Age	Occupation	Real	Pers.	Birthplace
134	R. J. WILSON	37	Manuftur	31,500	106,675	Tenn.
135	Elias HITCH, Sen.	40	Farmer	3,000	1,500	
	Jane	44				
	William	19				
	Mary	17				
	Mathew	14				
	Nancy	9				
	Archibald	7				
136	Payton MITCHEL	52	Tenant		400	Va.
	Catherine	54				Tenn.
	Perry	18				
	Mary	16				
	Sarah	14				
	Mary HENDERSON	60			100	
137	James SIMMS	24	Tenant		50	
	Elizabeth	22				
	William	2				
	Jane	1				
138	John H. DEARMOND	25	Tenant		800	
	Jane	25				
	Oliver	3				
	Robert	7/12				
139	Will BELLAW	67	Farmer, minister Mis. Baptist	4,000	6,000	N. Car.
	Susan	57				Va.
	Matildy SPRADLIN	27	Help			Tenn.
140	Harrey HOOKS	57	Farmer	3,100	700	
	Margaret	49				N. Car.
	Harrey	21				Tenn.
	Elizabeth HOOKS	25				
	Abigail	18				
	Margaret	16				
141	Jno. P. HOOKS	30	Farmer	2,000	700	
	Elizabeth	32				
	Robert	10				
	Albert	8				
	Adda	6				
	Okena (f)	4				

Page 21   District 12   P. O.: Rockford   9 June 1860

142	John HEADRICK	47	Cooper		30	Tenn.
	Susanah	46				N. Car.
	Sarah	19				Tenn.
	Alexander	18				

District 12   P. O.: Rockford

	Name	Age	Occupation	Real	Pers.	Birthplace
	Mary	17				
	Rebecca	16				
	George	13				
	Daniel	2				
143	Thomas SHARP	41	Farmer	4,000	3,000	
	Susannah	63				
	Nicholes	14				
	James	10				
	Evelen PARKS	22				
144	Sally PARKS	42			200	
	Mary	20				
	Thomas	19				
	Sarah	16				
145	Sam LANE	33	Tenant			
	Sarah	30				Ky.
	John	6				Tenn.
	Ruth	3				
	James	1				
146	Robt. CHANDLER	60	Farmer	2,500	1,300	
	Nancy	56				S. Car.
	Martha	19				Tenn.
	Rich D.	18				
	Nancy	16				
	Sam WRIGHT	22				
147	Rich. DEARMOND	51	Farmer	2,500	1,100	
	Cynthia	51				Va.
	Elias	23				Tenn.
	Susan	20				
	Cynthia	18				
	Granville	16				
148	James VON	24	Tenant		75	
	Rebecca	21				
	Alexander	3				
149	John HARPER	39	Waggon maker	1,000	350	
	Sarah	39				
	Mary	12				

Page 22   9 June 1860

	Name	Age	Occupation	Real	Pers.	Birthplace
	Margaret	9				Tenn.
	John	7				
	Thomas	4				
	Charles	1				
	Julia GIBSON	14				
150	Rebecca MORTON	48	Farmer	1,000	200	
	John	17				

	Name	Age	Occupation	Real	Pers.	Birthplace
	Sarah	14				
	Dorcas	12				
	Fielding	9				
	James	5				
151	Harrey ROAN	37	Farmer	3,000	1,000	
	Mary ROAN	40				Va.
	Isabella ROAN	27				Tenn.
	Preston ROAN	22	Student at law			
	Hetty ROAN	19				Tenn.
	Tennessee	18				
	Rebecca	5				
	Mary	2				
	Sam THOMPSON	28	Labourer		125	
152	Robt. JOHNSON	44			50	
	Sarah JOHNSON	42				N. Car.
	Richard JOHNSON	23				Tenn.
	Eagleton (m)	14				
	Silvester	9				
	Isabel	3				
153	Milton GILLISPEY	30	Farmer	7,000	8,000	
	Narcissa	26				
	Samuel	8				
	Narcissa	6				
	James	4				
	Philander	2				
	John	6/12				
	William GILLISPEY	16	Boarder		7,000	
154	Sam RAY	69	Tenant		600	
	John RAY	36				
	Sarah	24				
	William	4				
	James	1				
	Nancy J. RAY	26				

Page 23   11 June 1860

	Name	Age	Occupation	Real	Pers.	Birthplace
155	John BEAL	37	Farmer	6,000	1,200	Tenn.
	Ann	25				Va.
	William	8				Tenn.
	James	4				
	Hetty	1				
	James A. FULKNER	17	Indentured			
156	Davon POPLIN (f)	51	Spinster			
	William	18	Labourer			N. Car.
	Anson	15				
	Geo. POPLIN	21	(convict)			

District 12   P. O.: Rockford

	Name	Age	Occupation	Real	Pers.	Birthplace
157	Houstin SHEFFER	22	Tenant		125	Tenn.
	Harriet	21				
	Meryde (m)	2				
	Sarah Jane	9/12				
158	William SHEFFER	50	Farmer	1,500	600	
	Betsy	50				
	Neil SHEFFER	19			100	
	Magran (f)	23				
	William	1				
159	Wash HAFELY	49	Farmer	800	450	
	Elizabeth	25				
	Winston	20				
	Jane	15				
	Samuel	12				
	Betsey	11				
	Nancy	8				
	Thomas	7				
	William	3				
	Martha	1				
160	Kenneth SHARP	30	Farmer	700	300	
159	Minerva	27				
	Joan	5				
	William	4				
	Elias	2				
	Columbus	2/12				
161	Henry FINGER	29	Tenant		300	
	Eliza	32				
	Susan	27				
	John	19				
	Marion (m)	15				

Page 24   11 June 1860

	Name	Age	Occupation	Real	Pers.	Birthplace
	Frank	13				
162	Sally K. MARTIN	69	Farmer	5,000	7,500	Tenn.
	John MARTIN	16	Student			Miss.
	Henry MARTIN	14				"
	Eliz Martin	33	Lady	3,000		Tenn.
163	Sam McKAMY	34	Farmer	4,500	6,000	
	Martha	39				
	James	3				
	Sarah	4/12				
164	John MARTIN	38	Farmer	7,500	8,550	
	Isabella	22				Va.
	Florence	5				Tenn.
	Adda	3				

	Name	Age	Occupation	Real	Pers.	Birthplace
165	William KIDD	55	Tenant		3,500	
	Susan KIDD	44				
	Sarah KIDD	25				
	Margaret KIDD	2	Tenant			
	Jas. M. KIDD	21	Labourer		200	
	Martha	17				
	Nancy	10				
	Adeline	3				
	Charles	6/12				
166	John HUNT	51	Farmer	6,000	3,000	
	Lucindy	41				
	Henson	18				
	Calaway	14				
	John	12				
	George	8				
	Sarah	7				
	James Buchannan	4				
	Baby (f)	1/12				
167	Mary DEADNEY	81	Farmer	600	800	
	Alexander ROSE	22	Labourer			
168	Fanny CALDWELL	48	Spinster		50	
	Catherine	23				
	Mary	20				
	James	19				
	Nancy	18				
	Martha	16				
	Gardner	13				

Page 25   11 June 1860

	Name	Age	Occupation	Real	Pers.	Birthplace
	Sarah	8				Tenn.
	James	4				
	Joseph	1				
169	James MAYS	38	Farmer	1,000	750	
	Susan	35				
	Virena	14				
	George Washington	12				
	Martha	11				
	Sirepta (?) (f)	10				
	Ann	6				
	Mary	4				
	Sarah	10/12				
170	Benj. TOOPS	40	Cabinet maker	100	230	
	Susan	32				N. Car.
	James	14				Tenn.
	George	9				
	Oliver	4				
	Peter	2				

	Name	Age	Occupation	Real	Pers	Birthplace
171	Jonathan TOOPS	41	Tenant		300	
	Mary	41				N. Car.
	Susannah	18				Tenn.
172	Vance SIMMS	60			100	
	Mary	25				
	Ellen	16				
	William	20				
173	Jacob TOOPS	50	Smith & farmer	600	1,000	
	Eliza	38				
	Mary	12				
	George	7				
	Thomas	2				
	Henry CRUSE	13	Apprentice			
174	Camel ADNEY	30	Tenant		500	
	Betsey	25				
	Mary	3				
	Sarah	1				
175	Sarah HENDERSON	38	Farmer	6,000	7,000	
	George	7				
	Samuel	5				
	Benj. JENNINGS	57	Tenant		500	Va.
175	Ann Eliza	51				

Page 26   12 June 1860

	Name	Age	Occupation	Real	Pers	Birthplace
	Mary JENNINGS	26				
	John JENNINGS	23	Preparing for M. M.			
176	Benj. DUNCAN	52	Farmer	5,500	6,000	Tenn.
	Jas. DUNCAN	30	Blacksmith		700	
	Boar FORD	21	Apprentice			
177	P. F. DUNCAN	28	Tenant		700	
	Margarett	22				
	James	2				
	Ben	6/12				
	Ellen McCOLLOUGH	11	Home			
178	James KENNEDY	26	Tenant		600	
	Sarah	24				
	Hetty	2				
	Rachel	11/12				
	Elvira SIMMS	15	Help			
179	William FINLY	26	Miller		800	
	Dorcus	28				
	Albert	2				
	Rebecca FINLY	14	Help			

District 12   P. O.: Rockford

	Name	Age	Occupation	Real	Pers.	Birthplace
180	Jesse DELOZIER	36	Tenant	800	800	
	Susan	30				
	George	9				
	Campbell	7				
	Diane	4				
	Joseph	2				
181	Nicholas VINEYARD	70	Farmer	6,000	11,000	Va.
	Martha VINEYARD	25				Tenn.
182	Jas. WOLF	71	Farmer	600	400	Va.
	Margaret	48				Tenn.
183	Majors WOLF	26	Labourer			
	Jo WOLF (m)	22			100	
	Betsey	19				
	Alexander	11/12				
184	And. LONG	27	Tenant			
	Nancy	26				
	Sarah	5				
185	George CALDWELL	39	Farmer	4,000	3,500	
	Mary	36				
	Nancy	13				
	Susannah	11				

Page 27   12 June 1860

	Name	Age	Occupation	Real	Pers.	Birthplace
186	Althea SHERREL	40	Spinster			Tenn.
	Sarah	20				
	John	17				
	Wilson	14				
	Matilda	8				
187	Nancy GILLESPEY	59	Farmer	5,000	8,500	
188	Addison RORIX	43	Farmer	25,000	21,500	
	Rebecca RORIX	28				
	Ann Eliza	7				
	Burrel	5				
	John	2				
	James	6/12				
	Peggy RORIX	54	Lady		3,000	
189	Housten GHORELY	39	Tenant		200	
	Dicey	30				N. Car.
	Henry	18				Tenn.
	Margarett	13				
	Mary	10				
	Mary Ann	8				
	Rebecca	6				

	Name	Age	Occupation	Real	Pers.	Birthplace
	Naomi	3				
	Cassander	1				
	D. BADGETT	21	Labourer			
	John SHARP	21	Labourer			
190	Will NELSON	31	Tenant		200	
	Harriet	28				
191	Mitchel DAVIS	26	Farmer	2,000	1,200	Va.
	James PALMER	25	Tenant		500	Tenn.
	Caroline	20				
	John	1				
192	Dr. Jeff STONE	53	Farmer & M.D.	5,000	25,000	Conn.
	Isana STONE	30				Tenn.
	Oliver	14				
	Henrietta	11				
	Samuel	5				
193	Thomas OGLE	23	Labourer			
	Elizabeth	25				
	Philip	2				
	Andrew	1/2				
194	Polly WOLF	35	Spinster			Va.

Page 28   12 June 1860

	Name	Age	Occupation	Real	Pers.	Birthplace
	Sophronia	7				Tenn.
195	William DAVIS	63	Farmer	1,000	8,000	Va.
	James DAVIS	38	Labourer			
	Mary DAVIS	36				
	Robt. DAVIS	25				
	Mary	14				Tenn.
	Cornelia	11				
196	Peter FRENCH	27	Farmer	2,000	1,000	
	Malindy	22				
	Minervy	4				
	James	1				
197	George NEIGHMON	69	Farmer	8,000	1,700	
	Ann	70				Va.
	Margarett	30				Tenn.
	Harrey NEIGHMON	25			500	
	Matilda MOORE	14				
198	Lewis HOUSER	24	Tenant			
	Julia	22				
	Nancy CRUSE	32				

District 12   P. O.: Rockford

	Name	Age	Occupation	Real	Pers.	Birthplace
199	Barchley HAFELY	37	Farmer	500	300	
	Betsey	31				
	Susan	13				
	Washington	10				
	Margarett	8				
	William	3				
200	Nicholas VINEYARD, Jun.	36	Farmer	2,000	700	
	Martha	37				
	Catherine	13				
	Nancy	12				
	Mary	10				
	Robert	8				
	Joseph	6				
	Boy not named yet	3				
201	Philip HOUSER	45	Tenant		200	N. Car.
	Mary	48				Va.
	Alexander HOUSER	23	Labourer			Tenn.
	Sarah HOUSER	21				
	Henry	20				
	William	16				
	Amanda	15				

Page 29   1 June 1860

	Name	Age	Occupation	Real	Pers.	Birthplace
	Enoch	9				Tenn.
	Jacob	7				
202	James W. FRENCH	30	Farmer	6,000	1,000	
	Elizabeth	30				
	Thomas	9				
	Jacob	8				
	William	7				
	Duff	5				
	Stephen	3				
	John	1				
203	Prior CRUSE	30	Tenant		75	
	Caroline	30				
	Elizabeth	5				
	John	3				
	James	1				
	Rufus CRUSE	12	Help			
	Hetty CRUSE	74	Miller			Va.
204	Arnold CHAMBERS	39	Farmer	1,200	800	Tenn.
	Malinda	42				
	William	20				
	Sarah	18				
	James	12				
	Margaret	8				
	Nancy	5				

District 12   P. O.: Rockford

	Name	Age	Occupation	Real	Pers.	Birthplace
205	James HUMPHREY	25	Tenant		100	
	Dolly	24				
	Ann	5				
	Lewis	1				
206	James KIDD	25	Tenant		125	
	Mary	20				Ga.
	Tennessee (f)	4/12				Tenn.
207	Robt. KIDD	61	Farmer	1,000	800	Va.
	Esther	56				Tenn.
	Elizabeth	16				
	Jane	14				
208	Charles OTT	33	Vine dresser		400	Baden, Germany
	Mary	31				Tenn.
	Marcus	3				
	Jos.	1				
	Simon	5/12				

Page 30   13 June 1860

	Name	Age	Occupation	Real	Pers.	Birthplace
	Katy HOLLIS	90	Witch			Unknown
209	John McKINNEY	45	Tenant		500	Ky.
	Paulina	43				Va.
210	Neil Wolf	42	Tenant	500	300	Tenn.
	Elizabeth	36				
	Laura	8				
	Nancy	6				
	Peter	5				
	Franklin	2				
211	Alexander BROOKS	24		500	150	
	Margarett	35				
	William	1				
	Ann WOLF	30			44	
	Frank WOLF	25	Labourer			
212	Alex KENNEDY	58	Manft. & farmer	56,000	30,000	
	Mary Ann	30				
	Alex KENNEDY	21				
	William	18				
	Jane (m)	16				
	Gustavus	14				
	Houston	11				
	Rufus	9				
	John	7				
	Wexler	3				
	Brownlow	4/12				
	William SIMMS	19	Labourer			

District 12   P. O.: Rockford

	Name	Age	Occupation	Real	Pers.	Birthplace
213	John KINNAMON	49	Farmer	2,000	1,000	N. Car.
	Rachel	39				Tenn.
	Arthur	14				
	Samuel	13				
	Dorcus	11				
	Esther	6				
214	Campbell GILLESPEY	56	Farmer	8,000	2,000	
	Ann	25				England
	Mathew	20				Tenn.
	Ellen	18				
	John	14				
	Mary	12				
	Sarah	2				
215	Stephen S. PORTER	34	Farmer	25,300	16,750	Va.

Page 31   13 June 1860

	Name	Age	Occupation	Real	Pers.	Birthplace
	Catherine PORTER	32				
	James	9				
	Isabella	7				
	Louise	5				
	Amelia	1				
216	Capt. Jas. PORTER	57	Farmer	20,000	15,600	Va.
	Rebecca	50				Tenn.
	Robert	19				
	Rebecca PARKS	13				
217	Maj. Alex McNUTT	70	Farmer	15,000	10,000	Va.
	Mary McNUTT	65				Tenn.
	Margaret TIPTON	70	Lady		5,000	
218	Robert McNutt	38			8,500	
	Lucretia McNUTT	35				
	Lucretia	3				
	Mary	1				
	Jo MANN (m)	23	Labourer			
	Jim TOSH	38			100	Va.
	Elias HITCH	33	Labourer	300	400	Tenn.
219	James WEAR	47	Farmer	2,600	2,500	
	Margaret WEAR	43	Housekeeper	500	2,850	
	Mary WEAR	38		500	2,850	
	Jane WEAR	36		500	2,850	
220	Moses AYLETT	38	Farmer			Va.
	Isabella AYLETT	28	Housekeeper			Tenn.

District 12   P. O.: Rockford

	Name	Age	Occupation	Real	Pers.	Birthplace
221	John WEAR	71	Farmer	5,000	4,100	(Born in Indian fort) Tenn.
	Dorcus WEAR	64				
	Margaret WEAR	27				
	Lavina WEAR	25				
	Mary WEAR	23				
	John WEAR	22				
222	Margaret WEAR	62	Farmer	1,000	5,000	Va.
	Robert WEAR	33				Tenn.
	Amandy WEAR	29				
	Malvina WEAR	26				
	Barbary WEAR	21				
	David	19				
	Isabella	16				
	Sarah	2/12				
223	Preston WEAR	63	Farmer	5,000	4,500	

Page 32   District 9   P. O.: Maryville   14 June 1860

	Name	Age	Occupation	Real	Pers.	Birthplace
	Elizabeth WEAR	64				Tenn.
	Martha WEAR	62				
	Lucina WEAR	50				
	Franklin BOWLS	22	Labourer			
224	Lacome KELLY	60			50	Va.
	Francis KELLY (f)	50				
	Parker KELLY	18				Tenn.
	Alexander	13				
	Ellen	12				
	Eliza	9				
225	Ross YOUNG	30	Labourer			
	Sarah	28				
	Robina (m)	8				
	Toby (m)	3				
	Laura	1				
226	Phebe TEDFORD	59	Farmer	9,000	1,700	
	Mary TEDFORD	30				
	Robt. TEDFORD	25				
	Darius TEDFORD	23				
227	John CAMPBELL	23	Tenant			
	Mary	22				
	Hester	5/12				
228	Daniel FULKNER	32				Va.
	Elizabeth	23				Tenn.
	Susan	11				
	Sarah	8				
	John	1				

	Name	Age	Occupation	Real	Pers.	Birthplace
229	Esther IRVIN	53	Tenant			
	Ann IRVIN	50				
	Betsy IRVIN	42				
	Ann	17				
	James	15				
230	Jas. H. TEDFORD	28			500	
	Isabella	25				
	Hugh	5/12				
231	Hu L. McNutt	26	Farmer	5,000	4,000	
232	John KELLY	26	Tenant			
	Mosthena	24				
	Mary	5				
	Sarah	3				

Page 33   14 June 1860

	Name	Age	Occupation	Real	Pers.	Birthplace
	Joseph	2				Tenn.
	Baby (f)	1/2				
233	Samuel WEAR	36		10,000	4,000	
	Sarah	38				
	Eliza	10				
	James	8				
	Mary	6				
	William	2				
234	Sam STINNET	38	Tenant		75	
	Martha	37				
	John	11				
	William	4				
	Margarett	1				
235	Morgan SMITH	40	Tenant		100	
	Margerett	45				
	Saml	16				
	James	14				
	Isabella	12				
	John	7				
	Calvin	4				
236	Martin BROWN	51	Tenant	1,800	500	
	Nancy	52				
	Jane	25				
	James BROWN	22	Labourer		125	
	Margarett	19				
	Riley	17				
	Lozinda	15				
	Ann	13				

	Name	Age	Occupation	Real	Pers.	Birthplace
	District 9					P. O.: Maryville
237	David LEMON	50	Farmer	3,000	800	
	Ruth LEMON	52				Va.
	John LEMON	23	Labourer		100	Tenn.
	Joseph LEMON	21			100	
	David	18				
	Sarah	17				
	James	15				
	Isabella	12				
238	William Martin	36	Farmer	1,500	1,200	
	Jane	23				
	Laura	2				
239	John Hermin	31	Tenant		60	

Page 34 — 14 June 1860

	Name	Age	Occupation	Real	Pers.	Birthplace
	Mary Ann	30				Tenn.
240	Edmond KIDD	32	Farmer	2,500	1,400	
	Margarett	32				
	Elbert	8				
	James	6				
	Mary	5				
	Mike	2				
	Jacob	6/12				
	Riley KIDD	23	Labourer		350	
241	Thomas BAKER	21			50	
	Margarett	24				
	John	1				
242	Jos. Kelly	29	Labour			
	Mary	29				
	William	6				
	Francis (f)	4				
	Susy	2				
	Rachel JAMES	24				
	Mary	3				
243	Mary C. FURGESON	67	Lady	1,200	350	Va.
	Martha GOODLIN	24		600	150	Tenn.
244	William CASHEN	32	Farmer	500	850	
	Nancy	30				
	Mary	15				
	John	14				
245	John DYER	31	Farmer	5,000	2,500	
	Margarett	26				
	Cynthia DYER	60				Va.
	Elizabeth DYER	26				Tenn.

1860 U. S. CENSUS OF BLOUNT COUNTY, TENNESSEE

District 9   P. O.: Maryville

	Name	Age	Occupation	Real	Pers.	Birthplace
246	Taf HUNTER (mul)	45	Labourer		100	
	Eliza (bl)	30				
	Juliet (mul)	19				
	James (mul)	17				
	Robert (mul)	14				
	Michel (mul)	12				
	Samuel (mul)	10				
	Hannah (mul)	7				
	William (mul)	5				
	George (mul)	3				
	Baby (f) (mul)	1/2				

Page 35   15 June 1860

	Name	Age	Occupation	Real	Pers.	Birthplace
	Lebanna (?) (f) (bl)	3				Tenn.
	Alabama (m) (bl)	1				
247	William ORR	34	Farmer	1,250	600	
	Mary	36				
	Robert	13				
	Nancy	11				
	Sarah	9				
	Martha	6				
	Mary	4				
248	Mary ALLPHIN	48		1,800	1,500	
	Jane ALLPHIN	23				
	John ALLPHIN	27				
	Charles	18				
249	Nathan M. YOUNG	26	Labourer			
	Mary	28				
250	John FROW	59	Farmer	5,000	7,500	
	Jane FROW	61				
	Thomas FROW	30		5,000	3,000	
	Nelson FROW	19				
	Marshall	17				
	Sarah BIRD	6	Indentured			
	David STRANG	60	Seceder minister		200	Scotland
251	Newton YEAROUT	38	Farmer	3,000	3,000	Tenn.
	Isabella	23				
	Sarah	4				
	Dau (?) (f)	1				
	John McCLURE	6	Indentured			
	Mike HEISKELL	65	Labourer			N. Car.
	Lucindy CANUE (?) (m)	33				Tenn.
252	Hamilton THOMPSON	34	Farmer	4,000	2,500	
	Lucindy	30				
	Alailan (f)	8				

-33-

	Name	Age	Occupation	Real	Pers.	Birthplace
	Robert	6				
	William	4				
	Samuel	2				
	Baby (m)	3/4				
253	James RAWLSTON	23	Labour			
	Matilda	22				So. Car.
	John	4				Tenn.
	Tebeth RAWLSTON (f)	60				Va.

<u>Page 36</u>   <u>15 June 1860</u>

	Name	Age	Occupation	Real	Pers.	Birthplace
254	Nancy AIKEN	40	Spinster			Va.
	Henry Clay	18				Tenn.
	James Polk	16				
	Robert	11				
	Ida	2				
255	Andrew EARLY	75	Retired farmer	1,000	1,000	Pa.
	Winefed EARLY	72				Va.
	Sarah EARLY	27				Tenn.
	Howard EARLY	32			1,400	
	Isabella	23				Va.
	Mary	5				
	Baby (f)	10/12				Tenn.
256	William VON	49	Tenant		200	N. Car.
	Judy VON	45				
	Martha VON	21	Spinster			Tenn.
	Polly	14				
	William	10				
	Addison	8				
	Lena	3				
	Adam CLEMENS (mwy)	19	Labourer			
	Ethlinda (f)	19				
257	Sinvill GIBBS	45	Tenant		150	
	Mahala	45				N. Car.
	Geo. Washington	21				Tenn.
	Sarah	18				
	Catherine	13				
	Robert	14				
	Susannah	11				
	Clementine	10				
	William	9				
	Sinville (m)	3				
	Martha	2				
	Baby (f)	10/12				
258	Henry CLEMINGS	56	Barker			Va.
	Margaret	50				
	Eliza CLEMINGS	30				
	Catherine	22				
	Margarett	3				Tenn.
	Nancy	1				

	Name	Age	Occupation	Real	Pers.	Birthplace
259	Loucan (?) Hicks (m)	32	Tenant		60	N. Car.

Page 37   15 June 1860

	Name	Age	Occupation	Real	Pers.	Birthplace
	Rose	32				N. Car.
	William	2				Tenn.
	Baby (m)	1/12				
	Russle PASS	21	Tenant			
	Margary	17				
	Margarett	1				
260	James JOHNSON	79	(High constable waiten on the court)		75	N. Car.
	Nancy	68				
	Pebe (f)	18				Tenn.
	Martha	14				
	William ROLLEN	50	Labourer			N. Car.
	Holly	39				Tenn.
261	Reuben KEITH	49	Labourer		75	N. Car.
	Lucy	53				
	Margaret	18				
	Polly	14				
	Nathan	10				Ky.
	Gabriel KEITH	22	Labourer			N. Car.
	Eliza	22				Tenn.
	John	1				
262	Sarah TEDFORD	35	Farmer	5,000	2,000	
	Martha	15				
	Charles	13				
	Edward	12				
	Lyman	8				
	Malindy	5				
263	John OGLE	27	Tenant			
	Mary	33				
	James	1				
264	John TEDFORD	58	Farmer	4,800	1,200	
	Howard TEDFORD	33	Overseer		1,500	
	Catherine	28				
	Robert	3				
	John	1				
	Nancy McCARTY	44				
	William OGLE	18	Labourer			
265	Alexander DUNCAN	49	Farmer	5,000	3,000	
	Fidelia	43				
	John	11				
	Calvin	7				

District 9   P. O.: Maryville

	Name	Age	Occupation	Real	Pers.	Birthplace
Page 38						15 June 1860
	Margaret	4				Tenn.
	Jane DUNCAN	70	Lady		1,200	
	Andrew DUNCAN	59	Farmer	1,500	500	
266	Isaack MINS	36	Tenant		500	
	Catherine	29				
	Esther	11				
	William	10				
	John	7				
	Martin	5				
	Alexander	3				
	Sarah Ann HENDRICK	20	Help			
267	Rachel TEAFETELLER	70	Old lady			N. Car.
268	Will TEAFETELLER	37	Farmer	780	1,140	Tenn.
	Sarah	30				
	Cornelia	11				
	John	8				
	Margaret	4				
	Theressa	2				
	Perdilla (f)	2/12				
269	Sophia THOMPSON	51	Farmer	1,500	1,000	So. Car.
	Robert THOMPSON	23	Labourer			Tenn.
	Abigail THOMPSON	21				
	Mary	19				
	Caroline	17				
	Ellen	15				
	Jane	12				
270	Elizabeth STEPHENS	48	Tenant		500	
	Henrietta	19				
	Calvin	18				
	Polly	17				
	Fransina	15				
	Richard	14				
	Margarett	12				
	Russel	11				
	Samuel	10				
	David	8				
	Matildy	7				
	Pebe	4				
	Andrew	1				
271	Jane BRIGHT	45	Tenant			
Page 39						15 June 1860
	William	19				Tenn.
	Mary	16				
	Peter	12				
	Hannah	9				

District 9   P. O.: Maryville

	Name	Age	Occupation	Real	Pers.	Birthplace
272	Jordan TEMPLE	50	Tenant		350	N. Car.
	Matildy	43				Tenn.
	James	20				
	Elizabeth TEMPLE	22				
	Willie	16				
	David	13				
	George	11				
	Jane	9				
	Isaack	5				
273	John E. TOOLE	36	_____ & farmer	12,000	18,000	
	June	34				Ky.
	Edward	14				Tenn.
	Charlie	9				
	Eliza	11				
	Theressa	8				
	Lizzy	3				
	Ruth	4/12				
	Amelia BRABSON	10	Pupil			
	Robert RHEA	23	Student			
	Daniel MEEK	20	"			
	J. A. MARTIN	18	"			
	Gid S. WHITE	16	"			
274	Will PLEMENS	57	Tenant		500	N. Car.
	Susan	57				Tenn.
	Margaret	23				
	James PLEMENS	20				
	Martha	19				
	Ellen	17				
	Carolina	14				
275	Dan TRUNDLE	37	Tenant		500	
	Martha	28				
	Elizabeth	15				
	Margarett	14				
	Mary	6				
	Lethe (f)	5				
	Opelia	3				

Page 40   16 June 1860

	Name	Age	Occupation	Real	Pers.	Birthplace
	Ainsey McCLURE (m)	21	Labourer		100	Tenn.
	Margaret DEARMOND	40	Help			
	Christiana DEARMOND	30	"			
	Libby	26	"			
276	Charles McCLURE	28	Tenant		300	
	William	5				
	Houston	8/12				
	Theressa McCLURE	16	Help			
	Sam	8				
	Robert	6				
	Eli McCLURE	55	Labourer			

-37-

District 9   P. O.: Maryville

	Name	Age	Occupation	Real	Pers.	Birthplace
277	Martha SMITH	52	Tenant			
	John	28	Tenant		800	
	Martha SMITH	27	Help			
	William PAGE	28	Tenant		800	
	Sarah PAGE	24				
	James	4				
	Martha	2/12				
278	Alexander CARNES	29	Tenant		125	
	Nancy	25				
	John	5				
	Joseph	4				
279	Geo MINGLES	28	Tenant		100	Va.
	Malvina	26				Tenn.
	Rebecca	4				
	Fanny	2				
280	James MARTIN	68	Farmer	2,000	700	Va.
	Ignatious MARTIN	35	Assistant	1,500	300	Tenn.
	Mary	21				
	John	12				
	James	9				
	Samuel	7				
	Robert	3				
	Charlie	1				
	Robert MARTIN	29	Labourer		200	
281	Housten McKEALLY	47	Tenant		700	
	Mary	46				
	Samuel	15				
	Margarett	12				
	Barbary	10				

Page 41   16 June 1860

	Name	Age	Occupation	Real	Pers.	Birthplace
282	Margaret LUSTER	76	Farmer			
	Eliza Jane	35				
283	Elija NELSON (mwy)	20	Farmer	1,200	200	
	Amanda	19				
284	Elija NELSON	41	Farmer	1,800	2,500	N. Car.
	Martha	41				Tenn.
	Wesley	15				
	Sarah	12				
	David	9				
	Mary	7				
	Tennessee	4				
	Richard	3				
	William	5/12				
	Elija JAMES	21	Labourer			
285	Jacob SMITH	60				
	Angelina	33				
	Charles	19				Va.

	Name	Age	Occupation	Real	Pers.	Birthplace
	Frelinghyson (m)	15				
	Phebe	14				
	William	12				
	Andrew	11				
	Belsora (f)	6				
286	Mary EVERETT	44	Tenant		250	Va.
	William EVERETT	21	Labourer			Tenn.
	John	20				
	Calvin	17				
287	Jacob FULKNER	66	Shoemaker			Va.
	Polly	63				Tenn.
	Sarah	23				
	Susan	16				
	Henry	13				
	Elija	4				
	Mary	2				
	James	5/12				
288	James LAWRENCE	28	Tenant		1,500	
	Louisa	26				
	Ella	6/12				
289	William KELLER	33	Saddler		250	Va.
	Nancy	31				Tenn.
	James	7				

Page 42   16 June 1860

	Name	Age	Occupation	Real	Pers.	Birthplace
	Sarah Jane (twins)	6				Tenn.
	Martha Ann	6				
	Mary	4				
	Malinda	1				
290	Nimrod BYERS	25	Tenant		75	So. Car.
	Susan	20				Tenn.
	Mary	3				
	John	2				
291	Joseph HODGON	48	Carder & spinner	1,200	1,500	England
	Dinah	46				
292	William LAURENCE	33	Tanner	5,000	9,250	Tenn.
	Margarett	30				
	John	7				
	Mary	6				
	Ellen	4				
	Enold	4/12				
	Malindy SEIBNER	27	Domestic			
	J. B. MORRIS	31	Saddler		500	
	Will McCLURE	23	Labourer			
	Daniel TIMSON	22	Journman Tanner			

District 9   P. O.: Maryville

	Name	Age	Occupation	Real	Pers.	Birthplace
293	William TIMSON	29	Tanner		800	
	Lydy Ann	24				
	Sary Jane	2				
	William	6/12				
	Jesse CASHEN	70				Va.
294	And C MONTGOMERY	58	Farmer	22,500	33,600	
	Rebecca	37				Tenn.
	Minerva	21				
	Juliet	19				
	Green	17				
	Clementine	13				
	William	12				
	Lizzy	9				
	Colville	3				
295	David MITCHEL	86	Farmer	1,500	1300	Va.
	Dolly	76				
	James MITCHEL	36				Tenn.
	Fanny	27				
	Susan	9				
	Martha	8				

Page 43   16 June 1860

	Name	Age	Occupation	Real	Pers.	Birthplace
	Sarah	6				Tenn.
	Lucy	3				
	David	5/12				
	Sarah MITCHEL	16				
296	Jos CLEMENS	26	Tenant		50	Va.
	Nancy	31				Tenn.
	Columbus	5				
	Spencer	3				
	Samuel	4/12				
297	Columbus COWAN	48	Farmer	5,000	7,000	
	Mary Jane	29				
	Phebe	9				
	Samuel	2				
	Martha COWAN	44				
	Eliza COWAN	35				
	Lucy	30				
	John RODDY	11				
298	Frank COWAN	43	Carpenter			
	Elizabeth	40				
	Samuel	17				
	Thomas	15				
299	Thomas CLARK	32	Farmer	4,000	4,000	
	Mary	28				
	Josephine	8				
	Philander (m)	4				
	John MOON	25	Labourer		700	

-40-

District 9					P. O.: Maryville	
	Name	Age	Occupation	Real	Pers.	Birthplace
300	Philander CLARK	31	Farmer	4,000	1,200	
	Margaret	19				
	James	2				
301	Sinclair DEARMOND	36	Tenant		1,000	
	Elizabeth	34				
	Mary	7				
	Elizabeth	4				
	Ellen	1				
302	John Hart	37	Farmer	2,000	900	
	Sarah	33				
	James	8				
	Martha	6				
	Ellen	3				
	Joseph	6/12				

Page 44   18 June 1860

303	Willie REVEL*	54	Labourer			N. Car.
	Dicey	57				
	James REVEL	24				
	Abel REVEL	22				
	Emily	18				
304	Mary DUNCAN	52	Farmer	4,000	4,200	Tenn.
	Richard DUNCAN	29	Overseer			
	Ann	19				
	George	17				
	Mary	15				
	Margarett	12				
305	Thomas Hart	33	Farmer	2,500	2,000	
	Melissa	23				
	George PEARSON	12	Indentured			
306	William HENDERSON	50	Carpenter		125	
	Rebecca	45				
	Mary	20				
	William	16				
	Francis (f)	12				
	Thomas	9				
307	Alexander EAGLETON	27	Farmer	1,500	1,750	
	Leona	26				
	James	7				
	William	3				
	Sarah	1				
308	John CLEMANS	23	Tenant		50	
	Elizabeth	24				
	David	2				
	Mary	5/12				

*The enumerator listed this entire family as "color uncertain".

District 9   P. O.: Maryville

	Name	Age	Occupation	Real	Pers.	Birthplace
309	Elizabeth GIBSON	50				
	David	18				
	Minerva	14				
	Marion GIBSON (m)	22	Labourer			
	Mary	22				Va.
	William	1				Tenn.
310	Robert EAGLETON	62	Farmer	1,200	3,000	
	Elizabeth	64				
	John EAGLETON	25				
	David EAGLETON	24				
	Libby	18				

Page 45   18 June 1860

	Name	Age	Occupation	Real	Pers.	Birthplace
311	John EAGLETON	74	Gentleman	500	5,000	Tenn.
	Lavina	68				
	Barbary McCOY	44	Help			N. Car.
312	Jos. ARMBRISTER	43	Farmer	6,000	1,500	Tenn.
	Margarett	32				
	Catherine	16				
	Charles	10				
	Samuel	7				
313	James OGLE	23	Tenant			
	Ruth OGLE	23				
314	Chas STONE	27	Farmer	12,000	20,000	
315	Rufus PATE	43	Tenant		600	
	Eliza	44				
	Barckley	19				
	John	16				
	Dorcas	15				
	Betsey	13				
	Isaack	11				
	George	8				
	Maddison	3				
316	Jas HOWARD	50	Tenant			So. Car.
	Thelath	56				
	Rebecca	35				
	Harriet	16				
	Nancy	15				
	William	6				
317	Jno. M. PRIDE	30	M. D. & Farmer	9,500	5,000	
	Sally E.	23				
	Samuel	5				
	Augusta	4				
	Oliver	2				
	Anna	1				

	Name	Age	Occupation	Real	Pers.	Birthplace
318	Jas W. HANUM	26	Farmer	6,600	6,500	Va.
	Laura A.	23				Ala.
	William H.	4				Tenn.
	Isla (f)	1				
319	Sam BLAIR	36	Tenant		100	
	Mary	22				
	Mary	2				
	Agnes	5/12				

Page 46   18 June 1860

	Name	Age	Occupation	Real	Pers.	Birthplace
320	Fielding POPE	59	Pres. m. & farmer	58,000	32,000	Va.
	Ann E.	50				
	Fielding	17	Student			Tenn.
	Return (m)	15				
	W. A. GEORGE	31	Labourer			
	John LANE	21	"			
321	Saml BICKNELL	75	Gentleman		500	Va.
	Margarett	73				Tenn.
322	S. T. BICKNELL	42	Lawyer & farmer	8,000	8,000	
	Mary	40				
	Muggy (f)	18				
	Laura	16				
	John	14				
	Sam	12				
	Willie	8				
	Jessie (m)	2				
	Mary ROBINSON	4				
323	Robert TEMPLE	25	Labourer		50	
	Mary	23				
324	Will WALKER	37	Clk & farmer	4,500	2,500	
	Mary	25				
	Ellen	9				
	Alice	3				
	Joseph	1				
	Robert J. ALLEN	21	Student			
	Will BROWN	20				
	W. E. SLOAN	18				
325	William WALLACE	65	Gentleman	16,000	38,300	
	Mary S. T. WALLACE	36				Mass.
326	Reuben L. CATES	64	Saddler	3,000	1,000	N. Car.
	Amanda	60				Tenn.
	John CATES	27	M. D.		2,000	
	Charles CATES	20				
	John CARDWELL	15				

	Name	Age	Occupation	Real	Pers.	Birthplace
327	Daniel BROYLES	28	Saddler	400	300	
	Martha	26				
	Elizabeth	5				
	Mary	3				
	James	8/12				
	Mary HARE	23				

Page 47 - TOWN OF MARYVILLE   19 June 1860

	Name	Age	Occupation	Real	Pers.	Birthplace
328	John L. CRAIG	46	(Prof. of ancient language)	2,500	2,000	Tenn.
	Sidney	42				
	Mary	16				
	Nancy	14				
	Samuel	11				
	Hester	9				
	John	5				
	William	3				
	Jas. McCAMPBELL	23	Student			
	William HENRY	19	"			
	Wade RUTLEDGE	18	"			
	James JOHNSON	18	"			
329	Jas. F. BLOUNT	55	Jailer	400	1,000	N. Car.
	Caroline	46				Tenn.
	Sarah HEADRICK	18				
	Ann	1				
	Martha DEVINEY	15				
	Jason BARNES	35	Brickmason (convict)			
	David OGLE	24	Labourer (insane)			
330	William McGINLY	37	Lawyer	1,700	450	
	Elizabeth	23				
	Mary	6				
	James	4				
331	Jacob EASTERLY	31	Waggoner	600	400	Kentucky
	Nancy	27				Tenn.
	Jacob	6				
	Sarah	3				
	Barbary	1				
	Addie SMITH	12	Help			
332	Jas. M. TOOLE	40	Merchant	15,000	60,000	
	Hannah	25				
	Elizabeth	14				
	George	12				
	Robert	6				
	Adalaide	2				
333	Jesse G. WALLACE	34	Lawyer	1,000	2,500	
	Margarett	29				
	Eliza	8				
	Ann	4				
	Hugh	3				

District 9   P. O.: Maryville

	Name	Age	Occupation	Real	Pers.	Birthplace
Page 48						19 June 1860
	Susan	8/12				Tenn.
334	Frank HOOD	42	Tailor		150	
	Eliza	38				
	Robert	16				
	Mary	14				
	Joseph	11				
	William	9				
	Francis (m)	3				
	John	10/12				
	Hannah HARRIS	17				
	Minervy McTEER	40	Lady	1,000	150	
	Ransome BOWERMAN	40	Tax collector			
	Isaack TAYLOR	35	M. D.	150	5,000	
335	Henry SESLER	55	Stage contractor	800	4,500	Va.
	Elizabeth	53				
	Elizabeth	10				
336	Jacob SESLER	34	Blacksmith	1,600	2,000	
	Virginia	36				Tenn.
	Mary	6				
	Rachel JACOBS	17	Help			
337	Riley McGHEE	59	Clerk		100	N. Car.
	Rebecca	57				
	Sam McGHEE	31	Labourer		50	
338	Jas M. GREENWAY	60	Bookkeeper		200	Va.
	Penelope	49				Tenn.
	Catherine	22				
	John	17				
	David	14				
	Sarah	11				
	Margarett	9				
	Eliza	6				
339	J. G. SMITH	60	Clerk		600	England
	Sarah	20				
340	Wash TEOFETELLER	47		700	400	Tenn.
	Margarett	43				
	Phebe	16				
	John	14				
	Margaret	12				
	Texana (f)	8				
	George	5				
Page 49						19 June 1860
341	W. T. DOWEL	39	Meth. M. & merchant	5,500	12,000	Ala.
	Sarah	31				N. Car.
	John	14	(Insane)			Tenn.

1860 U. S. CENSUS OF BLOUNT COUNTY, TENNESSEE

District 9   P. O.: Maryville

	Name	Age	Occupation	Real	Pers.	Birthplace
	Richard	12				
	Sarah	10				
	William	8				
	Brownlow	5				
	Mary	2				
	John SMITH	22	Clerk		300	N. Car.
	W. B. JOHNSON	23				Tenn.
	J. D. FRENCH	24			600	"
342	Thos. J. LAMAR	33	P. M. & Prof An. Lau.	1,250	2,400	
	M. E. LAMAR	29				Mo.
	Kate	3				"
	Martha	3/12				Tenn.
343	William C. WALLACE	31	Merchant	1,000	2,500	
	Florida	22				Ala.
	Martha	5				Tenn.
	Ida	4				
	Robinson	4/12				
	J. L. ROBINSON (m)	38	P. M. & Prof. of Theo.	500	1,000	Ga.
	W. B. HEARTSELL (m)	19	Clerk		500	Tenn.
	J. M. HEARTSELL (m)	17				
344	Joseph A. FAGG	26	Merchant	13,200		
	Jane	27				
	Julius	5				
345	Henry MILLER	27	Merchant		6,100	
	Mildred	27				
	Julius	4				
	Lizzy	2				
	Susan	6/12				
	Sarah A. MILLER	24	Lady			
346	Henry R. HAYS	40	Shoemaker	1,000	500	N. Car.
	Eliza	40				
	John	20				
	Rebecca	19				
	Haywood	15				
	Cadwalder	12				
	Thomas	10				
	Carolyn	8				Tenn.

Page 50   19 June 1860

	Name	Age	Occupation	Real	Pers.	Birthplace
	Malvina	5				Tenn.
347	Ann E. BLACKBURN	28		1,500	250	
	Mary	11				
	Elizabeth	9				
	James	7				
	Nelly	2				
	Samuel GILLESPEY	26	Student medicine	500	100	

-46-

	Name	Age	Occupation	Real	Pers.	Birthplace
348	Jane McCAMPBELL	58			300	
	Samuel	18	Student			
349	Jas. S. COBB	49	Waggon maker		150	
	Matilda	40				
	Eveline	19				
	Thomas COBB	6				
	Harry COBB	4				
350	James CARNES	26	Carriage maker	600	1,300	
	Caroline	23				
	William	5				
	Charlie	1				
	·Robert EVERETT	43	Labourer			
351	William WILBERN	22	Blacksmith		150	
	Lucretia	18				
352	John CARNES	22	Carriage painter	350	800	Va.
	Mary	21				Tenn.
	Allen SMITH	21	Labourer			Ky.
353	John ALLEN (mwy)	25	Apprentice		100	Tenn.
	Ellen	16				Ga.
354	A. H. HICKS	31	Carpenter	1,200	600	Tenn.
	Mary	23				
	Martha	6				
	John	4				
	Marcellis (m)	1				
	Marcus L. HICKS	17				
	F. H. LIGON	25	Carpenter			So. Car.
355	W B. KING	23		600	450	Tenn.
	Rebecca	22				
356	Joseph CURTIS	38	Carpenter		200	
	Mary	38				
	James	18				
	William (f)	15				
	Samuel	11				

Page 51   19 June 1860

	Name	Age	Occupation	Real	Pers.	Birthplace
	Mary	5				Tenn.
	Nancy	1				
357	John E. HUDSON	56	Keeper of Boarders		500	Va.
	Joanna	53				N. Car.
	Jane	12	Indentured			Tenn.
	Jane SMITH	15				
	J. M. HARRIS	24	Student			
	J. M. CROSBY	20	"			
	Sam DIKE	22	"			

District 9   P. O.: Maryville

	Name	Age	Occupation	Real	Pers.	Birthplace
	(John E. HUDSON, cont'd)					
	Jno. WEBB	20	"			
	W. H. TILE	21	"			
	Sam INMAN	17				
	Barckley THOMPSON	35	Constable		400	
	H. A. RICE	20	Student			
358	Maj W. McTEER	43	Balt. Drummer		300	
	Margaret	42				
	Priscilla McTEER	22	Teacher			
	Theodore	16				
	Charles	13				
	Richard	11				
	George	7				
	Polly HENRY (bl)	75				
359	Will BROWN	66	Saddler		300	Va.
	Peggy	70				
	James BROWN	33	Carpenter			Tenn.
	Peggy	9				
360	Jas. WILSON	79	Gentleman	15,000	22,600	Va.
	Jane	69	Lady	2,000	9,000	N. Car.
361	Roderic McKENSIE	46	Hotel keeper	4,000	1,500	Scotland
	Mary	42				Tenn.
	Ann	19				
	Margarett	17				
	Isabella	15				
	John	12				
	Joseph	10				
	William	8				
	James	4				
	Frank	1				
	John CLARK	25	Stage driver			Va.
	A. R. NEIL	20				Miss.

Page 52   19 June 1860

	Name	Age	Occupation	Real	Pers.	Birthplace
	J. G. GILLIAM	20	Student			Ala.
	John ALEXANDER	18	"			Tenn.
	George CURRY	17	"			Ga.
	Mark KNIGHT	17	"			
	F. A. G. HANDY	19	"			Va.
	Peter McLARIN	33	"			Scotland
362	Pleasant ALLEY	27	Stagedriver			Tenn.
	Elizabeth	27				N. Car.
	Daniel	5				
	Leler (f)	1				

District 9

P. O.: Maryville

	Name	Age	Occupation	Real	Pers.	Birthplace
363	Johatt DAVIS	23	Stone mason			Va.
	Nancy	21				Tenn.
	Flora	10/12				
364	Eli NUN	30	Saddler		500	
	Nancy	31				
	Martha	3				
	John	1				Florida
	Caleb THOMAS	15	Student			N. Car.
	James DAVIS	37	Constable		1,200	Tenn.
	Polly VANCE (mul)	35	Domestic			
366	Ezekiel GRINDSTAFF	25	Striker		300	
	Temperance	30				
366	Martha RHEA	64			750	N. Car.
	Will RHEA	27	Labourer			Tenn.
	Martha RHEA	33				
	Margarett RHEA	26				
	Samuel	20				
	Mary	17				
367	John BOGLE	30	Surveyor	6,000	8,100	
	Elizabeth	20				
	Hugh	1				
	Sarah SAFFELL	22	Lady	6,000	6,500	
368	Jane OWENS	85	Lady	200	18,000	Va.
369	Thomas JOHNSON	44	Labourer			N. Car.
	Louisa	37				Tenn.
	Milburn	18				
	Wesley	12				
	Sam	11				
	Mathew	4				
	Robert	7/12				

Page 53

19 June 1860

	Name	Age	Occupation	Real	Pers.	Birthplace
370	Silas RHEA	32	Miller		600	Tenn.
	Martha	23				
	John	1				
371	John CURTIS	70	(Boss fiddler & carpenter)	1,000	500	N. Car.
	Fanny	68				
372	Nancy STERLING (bl)	29	Washerwoman		50	
	Eliza (mu)	8				
	Mary (mu)	6				
	Cordelia (bl)	1				
373	Sally TOOLE (bl)	24	Washerwoman		50	
	Lucindy (bl)	8				
	Martha (bl)	8/12				

District 9   P. O.: Maryville

	Name	Age	Occupation	Real	Pers.	Birthplace
374	Jas. C. DODD	39	Shoemaker	200		N. Car.
	Harriet E.	29				
	William	3				
375	Asa PRESLEY	40	Blacksmith	500		N. Car.
	Barbary	53				
	James	19	Labourer			So. Car.
	Dazdemonia	16				
376	William PRESLEY	39	Labourer			Tenn.
	Mary	27				
	James	16				
	Nancy	12				
	Clarissa	10				
	Sarah	4				
	Margarett	2/12				
	Hannah JOHNSON	22				
377	C. C. WILDER	33	Grocery keeper			Vermont
378	Milly JOHNSON	59	Lady	600	125	S. Car.
	A. B. JOHNSON	31	Tailor			
379	Dr. Sam PRIDE	60	M. D. & Farmer	10,500	16,000	Tenn.
	Martha	54				
380	Thomas POPE	33	Merchant	1,300	6,000	
	Mary Ann	29				
	Samuel	5				
	Fielding	3				
	John	11/12				
381	Decatur MORRIS	26	Labourer			N. Car.
	Penelope	27				
	Sarah	5				Ga.

Page 54   19 June 1860

	Name	Age	Occupation	Real	Pers.	Birthplace
	James	3/12				Tenn.
382	Elizabeth TOOLE	60	Lady	7,000	3,000	
	Samuel TOOLE	20	Student at law	5,000	1,000	
	Ellen BRABSON	14	At school			
383	Nathaniel WILLIAMS	27	Labourer	600	150	
	Malindy	24				
	Marcellus	7				
	Leone (f)	5				
	John	1				
	Nancy HENDICKSON	50			30	Va.
	Jerome HENDICKSON	21	Grocery keeper			Tenn.

	Name	Age	Occupation	Real	Pers.	Birthplace
384	John MOOK	41	Carpenter	1,200	7,500	Austria
	Theressa	29				
	Cathelen	5				
	Mary	3				
	Leman (m)	1				
	Leman FRICK (m)	30	Carpenter			Austria
385	Will INGRAM	33	Waggoner		50	Va.
	Mary	29				Tenn.
	Elizabeth	6				
	John	4				
386	Samuel LEA (bl)	45	Tinner	2,000	600	
	Cynthia (mu)	45				
387	Melissa CATES	22	Seamstress	850		N. Car.
	David	6				
	Robert	2				
388	James J. BLOUNT	25	Labourer	300	400	
	Elizabeth	27				
	Mary	5				
	Hester	4				
	James	1				
389	Martin SHEAY	42	Rail Roader	400	1,000	Ireland
	Bridgett	40				
	Timothy	11				
	Patrick	8				Montreal
	Sally	6				Va.
	Bridgett	4				Tenn.
	Martin	1				
Page 55						19 June 1860
391	Will WOLFORD	35	Waggon maker			
391	Will WOLFORD	35	Waggon maker	1,000	600	Va.
	Mary	26				Tenn.
	Fannie	2				
	Jesse (m)	11/12				
392	Mary WILSON (mu)	20	Washer woman			
	Henry (mu)	5				
	Richard (mu)	3				
	Samuel (mu)	6/12				
393	Frank ASBERRY (bl)	55	Shoemaker			
394	James WELLS	50	S. mith & farmer	4,000	3,000	N. Car.
	Clarissa	40				Tenn.
	Benjamin	19	Student			
	Mary	16				
	Henry	14				
	John	12				
	Adalaide	6				

District 9   Town of Maryville   P. O.: Maryville

	Name	Age	Occupation	Real	Pers.	Birthplace
	Clarissa	2				
	William HUTTON	30	Sheriff	1,000	3,000	
	Nancy	21				
	Joseph	9/12				
395	Andrew McCLAIN	53	Tanner	6,200	8,000	
	Elizabeth	43				N. Ham.
	John	20	Clk.			
	Opelia	16				
	George	11				
	Eliza	7				
	Maldy (f)	4				
396	Charles COBB (bl)	53	Tanner		300	
	Hannah (bl)	50				Va.
	Mary PRITCHET	31	Hooker			Tenn.
	Baby (f)	6/12				
397	Jas. H. GILLESPEY	61	M. D.	8,000	3,000	
398	J. C. FAGG	50	Stage Contractor	1,500	41,000	
	Elizabeth	48				
399	Stephen McREYNOLDS	50	Judge	4,600	25,000	
	Joseph McREYNOLDS	21	Law student			
	J. A. HOUSTEN	29	Lawyer		10,000	
	Mary	23				
	A. YOUNG (?)	30	Student			N. Car.
	Will ASHLEY	30	Clk.			England

Page 56   20 June 1860

	Name	Age	Occupation	Real	Pers.	Birthplace
400	James W. EVERETT (mwy)	34	Farmer	1,000	5,500	Tenn.
	Rosalie	20				
	Will KERR	22	Clk.			
401	Jacob McGINLEY	29	Tenant		75	
	Libby	26				
	Martha	6				
	Joana	8/12				
402	Devereux WRIGHT	40	Farmer	6,000	6,000	Tenn.
	Nancy	32				
	Nelson WRIGHT	70	Gentleman		500	Va.
	John GRAY	24	Student			Tenn.
	Franklin MOONEY	24	"			
403	James PORTER, Jr.	29	Farmer	4,080	2,200	
	Sophronia	24				
	Margaret	2				
	Mary MOORE	26	Help			

District 9   P. O.: Maryville

	Name	Age	Occupation	Real	Pers.	Birthplace
404	Elizabeth HICKS	52	Tenant		150	N. Car.
	Kesiah (f)	31	(deaf)			
	Rose Ann	29	(deaf)			Tenn.
	Sarah	20				
	John	18	(deaf)			
	Elizabeth	14				
	Nancy	12				
405	James D. HICKS	26	Tenant		300	Tenn.
	Sarah	20				
	Susanna	5				
	Nancy	2				
406	S. M. HICKS	23	Tenant		300	
	Martha	23				
	Mary*	1				
	Eliza	3/12				
407	James WOLF	32	Tenant		300	
	Ibby	23				
	J. Vincent	5				
	John	2				
408	Nick RUSSEL	25	Tenant		200	
	Thomas	14				
409	I. K. ANDERSON	39	Farmer	3,000	1,500	
	Rebecca	32				
	William	11				

Page 57 - District 8   P. O.: Maryville   21 June 1860

	Name	Age	Occupation	Real	Pers.	Birthplace
	Eliza	9				Tenn.
	Sophronie RUSSEL	20				
	Calvin RUSSEL	18				
410	M. M. ANDERSON	35	Farmer	2,000	1,000	
	(twins)					
411	Isaack ANDERSON	35		2,500	1,500	
	Mary	30				
	John	5				
	Joseph	4				
	Laura	2				
	Thomas	1				
412	Erskin TEDFORD	32	Pres. Minister		700	
	Martha	18				
	Joseph	14				
413	John MURR (mwy)	21	Tenant		50	
	Emeline	19				

*The enumerator apparently omitted Mary Hicks from the family of S. M. Hicks, and went back and added her on the same line with Eliza and then listed her again on the last line of the page.

District 8   P. O.: Maryville

	Name	Age	Occupation	Real	Pers.	Birthplace
414	Thomas ROSS	55	Farmer	300	275	
	Elizabeth	53				
	Narcissa	17				
415	John DEARMOND	65	Farmer	7,000	2,100	
	John DEARMOND, Jr.	27				
	Margarett D.	23				
	Mary D.	21				
	Susan	20				
	Cynthia	16				
	James PRIVET	12	Indentured			
416	Guilford McNEDDY	42	Farmer			
	Mary	37				
	Ferdinand	20				
	Aaron	19				
	William	17				
	Nancy	15				
	Sidney (f)	13				
	Robt. Philander (twins)	11				
	John Alexander (twins)	11				
	Mildred	8				
	Stephen	7				
	Martha	2				
417	Col. BOYD	57	Farmer	1,200	1,150	
	Eliza	45				
	James BOYD	21			100	

Page 58   21 June 1860

	Name	Age	Occupation	Real	Pers.	Birthplace
	Campbell	20				Tenn.
	John	17				
	Mary	14				
	Miriam	12				
	Nancy BOYD	38			125	
418	And. F. HANNAH	54	Farmer	2,500	8,000	
	Letha	53				Va.
	John	17				Tenn.
	William	15				
	Martha	13				
	Archibald	10				
	Mary Jane	1				
419	James HAMEL	24	Tenant		500	
	Margarett	21				
	Mary	5				
	William	3				
	Hetty	8/12				
	Margarett HAMEL	60			500	

District 8   P. O.: Rockford

	Name	Age	Occupation	Real	Pers.	Birthplace
420	James MARTIN	45	Tenant		75	
	Rosan (f)	40				
	Jacob	15				
	William	13				
	Vincent	11				
	Jane	8				
	Isaack	5				
	Mary	2				
421	Jeremiah MARTIN	20	Tenant		75	
	Mary	18				
	Nancy	6/12				
422	Joseph GODA RD	22	Tenant		650	
	Margarett	20				
	John	1				
423	J. P. RAWLSTON	39	Farmer	3,000	1,100	
	Mary	37				
	Margarett	15				
	William	13				
	Julia	10				
	Ellen	4				
	George	2				
	Amanda HANNAH	50	(insane)			

Page 59   21 June 1860

	Name	Age	Occupation	Real	Pers.	Birthplace
424	Will RAWLSTON	29	Tenant		400	Tenn.
	Susan	20				
	James	2/12				
	Thomas MILLER	8				
425	Philip RAWLSTON	32	Farmer	150	100	
	Telitha	35				
	Mary	5				
	Millard Fillmore	3				
	Julia	4/12				
426	James SCOTT	31	Farmer	7,000	1,600	
	Lotty Jane	25				
	Sarah	6				
	Joseph	4				
	Hester	3				
	Lotty	3/12				
	Eliza RODDY	19				
427	John McCOLLOUGH	44	Farmer	6,000	2,000	
	Emily	37				Indiana
	Isabella	19				
	Leander	15				
	John	11				Tenn.
	Margarett	5				

	Name	Age	Occupation	Real	Pers.	Birthplace
428	David LUSK	38	Tenant		600	
	Mary	20				
	John	16				
	William	14				
	Elizabeth	12				
	Julia	11				
	Martha	7				
	Samuel	6				
	Robert	3				
429	William SCOTT	60	Farmer	5,000	700	Va.
	Ann	58				N. Car.
	Martha	25				Tenn.
	Albert	3				
430	James MARTIN	38	Tenant		75	
	Sarah	28				
	Mary	10				
	John	4				
	Milo	3				

Page 60

	Name	Age	Occupation	Real	Pers.	Birthplace
	Lilah	10/12				Tenn.
431	George SNIDER	36	Tenant		150	
	Elizabeth	32				
	James	13				
	Ibby	12				
	Jacob	10				
	Joseph	9				
	Hetty	2				
432	Joseph HOLLIDAY	24	Tenant		125	England
	Nancy	19				Tenn.
433	John BRADBURN	59	Tenant	500	100	N. Car.
	Rachel	54				Tenn.
	William BRADBURN	22			30	
	Jerry	13				
	Sarah	9				
434	Philander PARKER	68	Farmer	1,500	500	Conn.
	Will S. PARKER	50	Tenant			N. York
	Clara	9				Tenn.
435	Thomas CARPENTER	35	Farmer	3,700	2,150	N. Car.
	Martha	34				Tenn.
	Pleasant HILL (mwy)	22				
	Matilda	22				

	Name	Age	Occupation	Real	Pers.	Birthplace
436	Abel CARPENTER	37	Farmer	2,000	1,500	N. Car.
	Susan	36				Va.
	Martin	17				Tenn.
	John	14				
	Caleb	13				
	Betsy	12				
	Lorinda	11				
	Andrew	9				
	Pope	6				
	William	5				
437	John Everett	49	Farmer	1,500	5,500	N. Car.
	Malinda	46				Tenn.
	Basheba	16				
	William	13				
	John	10				
438	Geo. P. RUTLEDGE	47	Gentleman	600	1,500	
	Delia	47				Ala.
	Robert RUTLEDGE	21	M. D.			

Page 61   21 June 1860

	Name	Age	Occupation	Real	Pers.	Birthplace
	George	19				Tenn.
	Ophelia	15				
	William	10				
	Laura	7				
439	John DAVIS	45	(Christ Ch. Min. & Farmer)	2,000	925	
	Martha	43				
	Hetty	20				
	Mary	18				
	Rosa	16				
	Melisse	15				
	John	14				
	William	12				
	Lutetia	10				
	Emeline	8				
	Andrew DAVIS	25	Carpenter		250	
	Geo. DAVIS	22				
440	Sterling LANIER	66	(Proper. Montvale Springs)	88,400	52,525	N. Car.
	Sarah D.	58				Ga.
	William B. LANIER	38	Farmer			So. Car.
	Lucy	24				Ga.
	Sally	13				Cal.
	Clark	5				Ala.
	Jane	2				Tenn.
	Sidney	1				"
	Julien MYNIER	30	Gardner			Switzerland
441	Lue ENCREDE	32				France
	Jennet	28				"
	Marie	10				"
	Henry	3				"

District 8   P. O.: Maryville

	Name	Age	Occupation	Real	Pers.	Birthplace
442	Jefferson NEIGHMON	35	Tenant		600	Tenn.
	Elizabeth	33				
	Jacob	12				
	James	10				
	Sarah	9				
	Nancy	7				
	John	6				
	Margary	3				
	Andrew	1/12				
443	David GRINDSTAFF	49	Blacksmith	500	400	
	Elizabeth	45				

Page 62   District 8   P. O.: Montvale   21 June 1860

	Name	Age	Occupation	Real	Pers.	Birthplace
						Tenn.
	George	16				
	John	14				
	William	12				
	Caroline	11				
	Esther	7				
	Eliza	5				
444	Ann E. GLASS	39	Potter			
	Sarah	32				Ga.
	John	11				Tenn.
	Cordelia	10				
	Benjamin	7				
	Theressa	6				
	Millard	5				
	James	1				
445	John WHITEHEAD	68	Farmer	2,500	600	N. Car.
	Hannah	64				Tenn.
446	Samuel WHITEHEAD	24	Tenant		150	
	Margaret	25				
	Sarah	4				
	William	2				
	John	3/12				
447	James WHITEHEAD	42	Farmer	1,000	700	
	Lucindy	40				N. Car.
	Eliza	19				
	William	16				
	Rebecca	14				
	Lucretia	11				
	Isaac	6				
	John	4				
	Hannah	2				
	Sally ELLIOTT	78	(Pauper)			
448	Peter STONE	26	Tenant			
	Melvina	24				
	Tennessee (f)	9/12				

	Name	Age	Occupation	Real	Pers.	Birthplace
449	Julia RAWLSTON	64	Farmer	400	300	N. Car.
	Margaret	26				"
	Martha RAWLSTON	22				"
	Prudence	17				"
	David MILLER	30	Labourer		400	England
	Sarah	24				Tenn.

Page 63   22 June 1860

	Name	Age	Occupation	Real	Pers.	Birthplace
	Allison	6				Tenn.
	Joseph	4				
	Benjamin	6				
450	Joseph KELLER	33	Farmer	400	350	
	Elizabeth	25				
	Martha	7				
	Cressy	6				
	William	4				
	George Washington	2				
	John	1				
451	John POTTER	53	Farmer		500	
	Davis POTTER	27	Labourer			
	Hannah POTTER	33				
	Polly POTTER	31				
	Thomas POTTER	24	Labourer			
	Sarah	20				
	Alfred	19				
	Richard	17				
	James	15				
	John	13				
	Allsop	12				
	Henry	11				
	Isaack	11				
	Martha	10				
452	John HOLLIDAY	59	Tenant		250	England
	Mary	51				
	Elizabeth	27				
	Sarah	20				
	Isabella	19				
	Mary	13				
	John	11				
	Eleanor	9				Tenn.
	Lydia	7				
453	J. W. MORTON	37	Farmer	600	650	
	Eliza	35				
	Hetty	11				
	Adam	9				
	John	7				
	Harmon	6				
	Hannah	4				

Page 64   21 June 1860

	Name	Age	Occupation	Real	Pers.	Birthplace
	Isaack	1				Tenn.

	Name	Age	Occupation	Real	Pers.	Birthplace
454	Esq WHITEHEAD	48	Farmer	800	800	
	Mary	28				
	Elizabeth	11				
	Henry	9				
	William	5				
	Isaack	1				
455	Sarah WHITEHEAD	70				
456	George KELLER	65	Farmer	1,000	4,000	Va.
	Eve	60				
	William	18				Tenn.
	Thomas	13				
457	John KELLER	23	Tenant		150	
	Sarah	22				
	Hetty	2				
	William	1				
458	Alfred WHITEHEAD	45	Farmer Blksmith	300	600	
	Jincy	35				
	Mary	19				
	Margarett	16				
	Betsey	14				
	William	11				
	Martha	8				
	Hannah	2				
459	David WHITEHEAD	34	Farmer	250	300	
	Elizabeth	32				
	William	11				
	James	3				
460	William WHITEHEAD	38	Farmer	200	200	
	Rebecca	35				
	David	15				
	Jane	12	(Weak Minded)			
	John	10				
	James	8				
	Daniel	6				
	Mary	5				
	Thomas	4				
	Alfred	2				
	Baby (f)	2/12				
461	Betsey HALL	37			50	
Page 65						22 June 1860
	Polly	13				Tenn.
	Elija	8				
	Andrew Jackson	6				
462	Andrew WHITEHEAD	30			500	
	Mary	26				

	Name	Age	Occupation	Real	Pers.	Birthplace
	Asa (m)	8				
	Malvina	7				
	Pinckney	6				
	Jim Buster	5				
	Sarah	1				
463	Samuel GIBSON	57	Farmer	600	300	N. Car.
	Ruth	44				
	Andrew GIBSON	19				
	Mary	18				Tenn.
	David	17				
	Joseph	13				
	William (twins)	11				
	Jane	11				
	James	8				
	Nancy	6				
464	Samuel KELLER	39	Gunsmith	600	600	Va.
	Elizabeth	35				Tenn.
	Nancy	15				
	Joseph	14				
	George Washington	13				
	Susan	12				
	John	10				
	Ethelindy	8				
	Isaack	6				
	Mary	4				
	Sarah	2				
465	Henry SIMERLY	32	Farmer	400	200	
	Margarett	30				
	William	4				
	James	2				
466	Mary RUSSELL	56	Weaver		150	So. Car.
	Edward	23	Labourer			Ga.
	George	17				So. Car.
467	John SIMERLY	39	Farmer	1,000	600	Tenn.
	Sarah	32				

Page 66   P. O.: Maryville   22 June 1860

	Name	Age	Occupation	Real	Pers.	Birthplace
	Caroline	16				Tenn.
	Jacob Jefferson V.Buren	10				
	Mary	7				
	James	6				
	Martha	3				
	Susan	4/12				
468	William SIMERLY (f)	70			50	So. Car.
469	James BRADBURN	30	Farmer	125	100	Tenn.
	Katy	28				
	Charlie	10				

Name	Age	Occupation	Real	Pers.	Birthplace
Lydia	8				
John	6				
Adam	4				
Baby (m)	1				
470 Thomas RUSSLE	22	Tenant		100	
Sophronia	22				
Martha	4				
Mary	5/12				
471 Peter CLEMENS	66	Farmer	2,000	500	Va.
Samuel CLEMENS	26	Labourer	1,200	300	Tenn.
Minercy C.	30				
Margaret	16				
472 John KENNEDY	58	Farmer	1,500	600	
Stephen KENNEDY	30	Overseer			
Mary	23				
Andrew	2				
Alley	10/12				
473 Jesse WHITEHEAD	49	Farmer	1,500	1,000	Va.
Theressa	44				
James	18				Tenn.
Franklin	16				
William	14				
Sarah	12				
Mary	9				
John	6				
Isaack	2				
474 Martha CLEMENS	44	Tenant		250	
Perdilla	20				
Phebe	18				
Dorcas	16				

Page 67   25 June 1860

Name	Age	Occupation	Real	Pers.	Birthplace
Margaret	14				Tenn.
Lithe	11				
Martha	9				
Elizabeth (twins)	7				
Rachel	7				
Tennessee (f)	5				
475 Saml. WILBURN	47	Tenant		200	N. Car.
Margarett	28				Tenn.
John	20				
Margaret	19				
Nancy	17				
Barnett	15				
Taylor	12				
Sarah	9				

	Name	Age	Occupation	Real	Pers.	Birthplace
476	John HUTSELL	73	Farmer	750	200	Va.
	Mary	70				
	Margaret	20				Tenn.
477	George HUTSELL	51	Tenant		500	Va.
	Martha	44				
	Elizabeth	23				Tenn.
	William	20				
	John	17				
	Jefferson	12				
	Samuel	9				
	Isabel	8				
	Margarett	6				
	Stephen	1				
478	Jacob HUTSELL	47	Tenant		300	Va.
	Rebecca	47				N. Car.
	Eveline	18				Tenn.
479	Edward WILKERSON	38	Farmer	2,500	4,500	
480	Jacob MURR	60		200	250	
	Fanny	53				N. Car.
	Alexander MURR	25			250	Tenn.
	Margarett	20				
	Jacob	10				
481	Newton McConnel	51	Farmer	1,500	1,200	Va.
	Nancy	51				Tenn.
	John McCONNEL	26				
	Moses M.	20				

Page 68   P. O.: Maryville   25 June 1860

	Name	Age	Occupation	Real	Pers.	Birthplace
	Merdilla (f)	17				Tenn.
	Nancy	9				
	Isaack	8				
	Joseph	4				
482	George CUPP	59	Farmer	500	550	
	Lucy	42				
	James CUPP	26			200	
	John	17				
	Sarah	8				
	Mary	4				
483	Jacob LONG	55	Farmer	4,000	1,100	N. Car.
	Mary	58				Tenn.
	Nancy	34			100	
	Andrew LONG	21				
	Riley	17				
	James	13				
	Mary	4				
	Robert	1				

District 8   P. O.: Montvale

	Name	Age	Occupation	Real	Pers.	Birthplace
484	James LONG	24	Tenant		350	
	Mary	24				
	Lerona	8				
	George	7/12				
485	Green CUPP	35	Farmer	600	950	
	Susan	38				
	Mary	12				
	Margarett	8				
	Malvina	6				
	Harriet	4				
	Darius	1				
	Paulina SIMERLY	18	Help			
	Nancy	4/12				
486	John GODDARD	55	Farmer	1,000	1,200	
	Martha	40				
	Eliza	19				
	William	18				
	Nathaniel	15				
	Andrew	14				
	John	11				
	Harriet	9				
	Margarett	7				

Page 69   P. O. Maryville   25 June 1860

	Name	Age	Occupation	Real	Pers.	Birthplace
	James	11/12				Tenn.
487	James CUPP	34	Farmer	400	100	
	Margarett	39				
	Mary	15				
	William	14				
	Henry Clay	10				
	Riley	8				
	Francis (f)	6				
	Betsey	4				
	Martha	1				
	Baby (m)	1/12				
488	Will TEOFETELLER	58	Tenant		100	N. Car.
	Ann	53				
	Mahala	22				
	Catherina	20				
	Jane	19				
	Samuel	14				
	William	9				
489	Nancy McDANIEL	32	Farmer	1,200	250	
	Lucy	10				
	James	8				
	Henry	6				
	Riley	3				
	Clarissa	1				

District 8   P. O.: Maryville

	Name	Age	Occupation	Real	Pers	
490	John YEAROUT	32	Farmer		800	
	Joana	28				
	Jacob	9				
	Catharine	7				
	Martha	3				
	Nathaniel	5/12				
491	Lewis RUSSELL	33	Farmer	1,500	650	
	Mary	33				
	Mary	7				
492	John SCRUGGS	31	Tenant		500	
	Mary	28				N. Car.
	Eliza	5				Tenn.
	Thomas	1				
493	Geo. W. HUTSELL	32	Farmer	1,000	4,000	
	Mary	29				
	George	6				Ga.

Page 70   25 June 1860

	Name	Age	Occupation	Real	Pers	
	Martha	4				Tenn.
	Sarah	1				
494	Parsons WALLER	34	Tenant		900	
	Julia	32				
	James	12				
	Adaline	9				
	Jacob	6				
	Susan	1				
495	Susan SMITH	73	Farmer	3,500	100	Va.
	Elizabeth	41				
496	Geo. HUTSEL Sr.	67	Farmer	1,500	800	
	Betsey	51				N. Car.
	Matilda	20				Tenn.
	Ephraim	6				
497	And. THOMPSON	43	Tenant		500	
	Catharine	41				Va.
	John	19				Tenn.
	Mary	18				
	Betsey	14				
	Bogle	11				
	William	9				
	Nancy	6				
	George	4				
	Andrew	1				
498	Samuel BELL	38	Farmer	3,000	1,700	
	Martha	33				
	Mary	10				
	Alexander	2				

	Name	Age	Occupation	Real	Pers.	Birthplace
	Margaret	9/12				
	Eliza BELL	17				
499	Milas SCROGGS	60	Farmer	2,500	900	N. Car.
	Elizabeth	63				Va.
	Martha	27				Tenn.
500	Elkana JOHNSON	35	Farmer	1,500	1,500	
	Mary	33				
	William	11				
	Calvin	9				
	Mary	7				
	Feridinand	6				
	Martha	4				
Page 71						26 June 1860
	Margaret JOHNSON	24				Tenn.
501	Rosanna WALLACE	44	Farmer	3,000	2,000	
	Aaron WALLACE	23	Labourer			
	Abram	20				
	Fletcher	18				
	William	17				
	Nancy	16				
	Malindy	14				
	Andrew	10				
	John	7				
	Benjamin	2				
502	Joseph BRAWDY	56	Farmer	3,000	1,600	
	Nancy	61				Va.
	Andrew BRAWDY	29				Tenn.
	Isaack	26				
	Perdilla McCONNEL	16	Help			
	Nancy McGINLEY	8				
503	William CLEMENS (mwy)	32	Farmer	2,200	900	
	Mary	21				
504	James SIMERLY	27	Tenant		200	
	Polly	23				
	William	7				
505	Abraham SIMERLY	24	Tenant		100	
	Lucindy	25				
	Mary	6				
	Nancy	3				
	Louisa	9/12				
506	Henry RUSSLE	45	Farmer	750	1,000	
	Margarett	46				
	Isaack	19				
	Nancy	17				
	Richard	14				

District 8   P. O.: Maryville

	Name	Age	Occupation	Real	Pers.	Birthplace
	Jane	8				
	Miriam HOOKER	75				
507	Allsop WHITE	33	Farmer	2,500	1,500	
	Nancy	30				
	James	8				
	Sally	6				
	Nancy	3				
	William	5/12				

Page 72   26 June 1860

	Name	Age	Occupation	Real	Pers.	Birthplace
508	Will JOHNSON	18				Tenn.
	Isaack RUSSLE	23	Tenant		400	
	Mary	20				
	James	1				
509	Isaack RUSSLE Sen.	43	Tenant		200	
	Lena	45				
	Riley	20				
	Jane	18				
	Thomas	16				
	Polly	14				
	Houston	12				
	James	3				
510	Mary GAINS	48	Tenant			
	Martha GAINS	23				
	Mary	16				
	Thomas	14				
	Lucy	10				
	Margarett	7				
	Sarah	2				
511	Barbary GIBSON	39	Tenant			
	Mathew	13				
	Crawford (Dumb)	8				
	Samuel (Dumb)	6				
	James	2				
512	Richard NICHOLS	39	Farmer	2,500	1,200	
	Rebecca	42				
	Isaack	19				
	James	15				
	Sarah	6				
513	James GRINDSTAFF	45	2,	2,000	450	
	Matilda	44				
	William GRINDSTAFF	23			200	
	Mary	17				
	James	15				
	John	12				
	Andrew Jackson	3				

	Name	Age	Occupation	Real	Pers.	Birthplace
514	Crawford HALL	53	Tenant		250	N. Car.
	Elizabeth	50				Tenn.
	Amandy	19				
	Esther	16				

Page 73   26 June 1860

	William	1				Tenn.
515	James HALL	34	Farmer	800	500	
	Barbary	34				
	Elizabeth	12				
	Margarett	10				
	Lafayette	7				
	Mary	5				
	Eliza	3				
	Rebecca	1				
516	John FAGG	46	Tenant			
	Jane	46				
	Nancy FAGG	25				
	James FAGG	23				
	Isaack	19				
	Nancy	18				
	Martha	15				
	Allsop	12				
	John	8				
	James	6				
	Mary	2				
517	Joseph RUSSELL	25	Tenant		250	
	Sophronia	24				
	Mary	5				
	Sarah	2				
518	Isaack RUSSELL	27	Farmer	1,400	300	
	Permilia	25				
	Eliza	6				
	Darthula	5				
	Louisa	9/12				
	James McDANIEL	10				
519	Abram RUSSELL	59	Tenant		150	
	Mary	53				N. Car.
	Caroline	20				Tenn.
	William	19				
	Thomas	12				
	Marandy	13				
	Polly	10				
	Sarah	3				
520	Peter HOUSER	36	Farmer	1,200	700	Tenn.
	Elizabeth	25				

District 8   P. O.: Maryville

	Name	Age	Occupation	Real	Pers.	Birthplace
Page 74						26 June 1860
						Tenn.
	John	10				
	James	7				
	Catharine	5				
	Mary	4				
	Margarett	2				
	Sarah	1				
521	John HOUSER	69	Farmer	60	50	Penn.
	Sarah	52				Tenn.
522	John RUSSELL	60	Farmer	1,800	1,000	
	Rebecca	45				
	Jacob	20				
	Polly	15				
	Elizabeth	14				
	Sarah	13				
	Barckley	11				
	Morgan (m)	9				
	James	5				
523	Jacob SIMERLY	62	Farmer	6,000	1,900	Tenn.
	Mary	34				
	Jacob	5				
	Phebe	4				
	James	2				
	John	6/12				
524	Jerry SIMERLY	37	Farmer	3,000	500	
	Anna	35				
	Mary	13				
	Henry	12				
	Betsey	11				
	Solomon	10				
	Sarah	8				
	James	5				
	Happy Anna	2				
525	Polly HARRIS (m)	36	Tenant		50	
	Elizabeth	14				
	Peter	12				
	Lucy	8				
526	N. B. McCLAIN	35	Farmer	1,500	1,000	
	Dorthula	36				
	John E.	15				
Page 75						27 June 1860
						Tenn.
	Elizabeth	14				
	Laura	10				
	James	3				
	Nancy	2/12				

District 8   P. O.: Maryville

	Name	Age	Occupation	Real	Pers.	Birthplace
527	Isaack BOREN	43			500	
	Rebecca	37				
	William	11				
	Jane	9				
	Sarah	7				
	Mary	5				
	Isaack	3				
	Temple (f)	6/12				
528	Cyrus CURTIS	62		500	100	N. Car.
	Polly	88				
529	Martha CURTIS	44				
	Josiah	10				Tenn.
530	Martha SWAGGERTY	23			200	
	Phebe	16				
	Martha	12				
	William	11				
	Margaret	10				
	Sarah	6				
	Cynthia	5				
531	Jerry WOLF	36			100	
	Elizabeth	38				
	Mary	16				
	Cyrus	15				
	Monroe	12				
	Maryaan	10				
	Dialthea	8				
	Albert	6/12				
532	Sarah BRITT	70			100	N. Car.
	Jackson	26				
	Elbert	24				
	Jane	22				
	Elizabeth	3				
	Sophronia	1/12				
533	Jas. B. RUSSELL	27	Farmer	300	300	
	Margaret	30				
	Elizabeth	11				

Pzge 76   27 June 1860

	Name	Age	Occupation	Real	Pers.	Birthplace
	William	8				Tenn.
	Isaack	4				
	Mary	2				
534	Lorenzo EVERETT	34	Tenant		200	Indiana
	Lucindy	34				
	John	11				
	William	9				
	James	7				
	Phebe	4				
	Mary	1				

District 8   P. O.: Maryville

	Name	Age	Occupation	Real	Pers.	Birthplace
535	Jo TEOFETELLER	25	Tenant		25	
	Nancy	20				
	Betsey	2				
536	Moses McCONNEL	47	Farmer	5,000	8,500	Va.
	Jane	59				Tenn.
	John	19				
	Polly WILLIAMS	63		1,000	2,800	Va.
	James DAVIS	11				Tenn.
537	Henry LONG	30	Carpenter	200	150	
	Christiana	30				
	David	11				
	John	9				
	Mary	7				
	Boy not named	3				
538	Jacob RUSSELL	22	Tenant		150	
	Patiance	22				
	William	5/12				
539	James PAUL	27	Farmer	400	225	
	Susan	24				
	John	5				
	William	3				
	George	6/12				
540	William KENT	28	Farmer	300	250	Ga.
	Nancy	22				Tenn.
	Gilbert	1				
	Baby (f)	8/12				
541	James RUSSELL	46	Farmer	2,500	1,400	
	Sarah	47				
	Mary	18				
	Edward	16				

Page 77   27 June 1860

	Name	Age	Occupation	Real	Pers.	Birthplace
	James B.	14				
	Sarah	13				
	Rhoda	12				
	Henry	11				
	Elizabeth	6				
	John	4				
	Andrew	9				
	Esther LONG	70				N. Car.
542	John SNEED	50	Farmer	200	350	Ala.
	Mary	42				Tenn.
	James	20				
	Mary	18				
	John	15				
	Esther	13				
	Sarah	9				

District 8   P. O.: Maryville

	Name	Age	Occupation	Real	Pers.	Birthplace
543	Isaack RUSSELL	50	Farmer	800	700	
	Jane	38				
	Alfred	6				
	Samuel	5				
	John	3				
	Isaack	1				
544	William EVERETT	68	Farmer	1,200	600	Va.
	Mary	67				Tenn.
545	Christiain LONG	66	Cabinet maker	400	600	Penn.
	Elizabeth	56				Tenn.
	Glendi	21				
	Nancy	19				
	Martha	13				
	William	10				
546	Robert LONG	29	Tenant		200	
	Lelah	28				
	Christian	5				
	Jesse (m)	3				
547	Tewalt MITCHEL	38	Tenant			
	Fanny	34				
	Rebecca	12				
	John	9				
	Mary	8				
	James	7				
	Martha	6				

Page 78   27 June 1860

	Name	Age	Occupation	Real	Pers.	Birthplace
	Patiance	5				Tenn.
	Thomas	2				
	William	4/12				
548	John McGINLEY	35	Farmer	2,000	3,000	
	Mary	37				
	William	17				
	Joseph	14				
	Hardin	12				
	Nancy	2				
	Baby	4/12				
	James McDANIEL	13	Labourer			
549	Alfred McCONNEL	33	Farmer	8,000	4,600	
	Lusana	29				
	Fidella	9				
	William	7				
	Mary	3				
	Laura	7/12				
	Elizabeth McCONNEL	75				Va.

District 8   P. O.: Maryville

	Name	Age	Occupation	Real	Pers.	Birthplace
550	John McCAULEY	74	Tenant		500	Tenn.
	Mary	76				
	Margarett	48				
551	James McCONNEL	39	Farmer	3,500	5,500	
	Martha	37				
	Margarett	10				
	Mary	9				
	James	5				
	Moses	5/12				
552	Mary McDANEL	42	Hooker		50	
	Elizabeth	35				
	Louisa Jane	18				
	James	15				
553	David GREER	40	Tenant		150	
	Rachel	30				
	Eliza	14				
554	Jos Steel	29	Carpenter	300	200	
	Sarah	21				
	Benjamin	5				
	Baby (f)	3/12				
	Sarah CANNON	34	Lady		1,000	
	Robert	10				

Page 79   District 14   P. O.: Gambles Store   28 June 1860

	Name	Age	Occupation	Real	Pers.	Birthplace
555	M. WILLIAMS	37	Farmer	3,500	2,000	Tenn.
	Rachel	30				
	Elizabeth	14				
	Jane	12				
	William	10				
	Sarah	7				
	Moses	5				
	Mary	1				
	William ROGERS	7				
556	Cyrus GRAHAM	25	School Teacher		250	Va.
	Martha	20				Tenn.
	Sally	6/12				
557	John McCAULEY	25	Blacksmith		150	
	Rachel	24				Ga.
	William	4				
	Velante (f)	1				
558	Ezekiel JOHNSON	60	Miller		100	So. Car.
	Sarah	54				Tenn.
	Mary JOHNSON	33	Spinster			
	Margarett	23				
	George	20				
	Hetty	10				

	Name	Age	Occupation	Real	Pers.	Birthplace
559	William LONG	22	Tenant		200	
	Sarah	20				
	John	3/12				
560	John M. LOWRY	37	Farmer	4,000	1,200	
	Mary	41				
	John	4/12				
	Thomas RIDDLE	13	Indentured			
561	John GIBSON	Tena	Tenant		50	
	Brittania	21				
562	Robert COULTER	25	Tenant		1,000	
	Sarah	26				
	Samuel	7				
	John	4				
	Martha WILLIAMS	50				
563	William WHITE	35	Farmer	40	150	
	Nancy	25				
	Betsey	12				
	Margarett	10				

Page 80   28 June 1860
Tenn.

	Name	Age	Occupation	Real	Pers.	Birthplace
	Isaack	8				
	Rebecca	6				
	John	4				
	Sarah	2				
564	James EVERETT	54	Tenant		1,200	
	Happy	52				
	Serena EVERETT	29				
	Robt.	20				
	Aaron	17				
	Amantha	14				
	Selithe	13				
	James	10				
	John	8				
565	William BRYANT	26	Tenant		50	
	Mary	24				
	Madison	5				
	Tennessee (f)	2				
566	Moses KEYS	42	Farmer	6,000	600	Va.
	Charlotte KEYS	50				
	Nancy KEYS	54				
	Margaret KEYS	46				
	Martha KEYS	35				
	Newton PRIVET	14	Home			Tenn.
567	Blount LOVE	20	Tenant		1,200	
	Mary	18				

District 14   P. O.: Gambles Store

	Name	Age	Occupation	Real	Pers.	Birthplace
568	Daniel HEADRICK	40	Farmer	3,000	1,200	
	Clarissa	40				N. Car.
	William HEADRICK	21		1,000	200	
	Caroline	20				
	Jane	17				
	Lebo (m)	15				
	John	13				
	Clementine	12				
	Susan	11				
	Leander	10				
	Mary	7				
	James	5				
	Texanna (f)	4				
	Jake	3				
	Neil	1				

Page 81   District 14   P. O.: Maryville   28 June 1860

	Name	Age	Occupation	Real	Pers.	Birthplace
569	Perry HEADRICK	43	Farmer	560	250	Tenn.
	Selithe	43				
	John	20				
	Sarah	17				
	Brackson	14				
	Phebe	11				
	Martha	10				
	Ellen	6				
	Margarett	3				
570	Jane ROWAN	48	Farmer	1,000	700	
	Sarah ROWAN	43				
571	Josiah DULANY	36	Tenant		350	
	Ellen	22				
	Eliza	8/12				
	John MALLONEE	50	Waggon maker		150	
	Caroline	18				
	Thomas	16				
	Elbert	11				
	John	6				
572	Thomas BRAWDY	33	Farmer	1,000	700	
	Martha	27				
	Mary	6				
	Joseph	5				
	Nancy	2				
573	Jos MARTIN (mwy)	20	Tenant		175	
	Matildy					
574	Wallace CALDWELL	52	Farmer	1,000	500	
	Nancy	42				Ky.
	Susannah	15				Tenn.
	Mary	14				
	Sarah	12				

	Name	Age	Occupation	Real	Pers.	Birthplace
	Nancy	10				
	John	7				
	Malinda	5				
	Ellen	1				
575	John CLEMENS	67	Farmer (Weak Minded)	1,000	300	Va.
	Viney	40				
	Eve	38				
	Eliza	36				
	Matilda	32				

Page 82   28 July 1860

	Name	Age	Occupation	Real	Pers.	Birthplace
576	William HEADRICK	25	Tenant		110	Tenn.
	Martha	27				
	Ahart (m)	8				
	William	6				
	Ann	3				
	Mary	1				
577	William DAVIS	65	Farmer	1,400	900	N. Car.
	Rachel	63				So. Car.
	John DAVIS	25				Tenn.
	Mary DAVIS	20				
578	Isaack WELLS	56	Farmer	6,000	1,550	N. Car.
	Patsy	42				Tenn.
	Robert WELLS	35	(Weak Minded - Dumb)			
	John WELLS	21				
	Texana	18				
	Leonidas	16				
	Ferdinand	12	(Weak Minded - Dumb)			
579	Stephen WELLS	29	Tenant		700	
	Nancy	23				
	Mary	3				
	Isaack	1				
580	Larender BIRD	33	Tenant	1,200	200	
	Milly	26				
	Anna	9				
	Rebecca	7				
	William	5				
	David	3				
	Milly	5/12				
581	James WEAR (mul)	75	Tenant			N. Car.
	Ruficy (f) (mul)	34				Tenn.
	Adnerson (mul)	16				
	Jane (mul)	15				
	Ann (mul)	13				
	James (mul)	12				
	Moses (mul)	7				
	Stephen (mul)	3				
	Martha (mul)	1				

District 14   P. O.: Maryville

	Name	Age	Occupation	Real	Pers.	Birthplace
582	Will EVERETT	32	Farmer	1,800	900	
	Pauline	25				
	Mary	2				

Page 83   28 June 1860

	Name	Age	Occupation	Real	Pers.	Birthplace
583	Robt. EVERETT	26	Farmer	800	350	Tenn.
	Margarett	24				
	Sarah	13				
584	J S M EVERETT	34	Farmer	1,000	750	Ky.
	Jane	33				Tenn.
	Nancy	12				
	James	8				
	Margarett	6				
	Robert	2				
585	Sarah HEADRICK	74			700	
586	John EVERETT	50	Farmer	1,000	400	
	Susan	52				N. Car.
	Solomon	20				Tenn.
	Elizabeth	16				
	James	14				
587	William BRANNOM	50	Tenant		225	N. Car.
	Lavina	40				
	Green	20				Tenn.
	Noah	19				
	Mary	16				
	Wade	13				
	Jonathan	10				
	Josiah	9				
	Winta (f)	6				
	William	3				
	Samuel	1				
588	John BOLEN	26	Tenant		50	
	Martha	22				
	John	3/12				
589	Rufus McCAULEY	43	Farmer	150	100	
	Catharine	41				
	Nancy	16				
	Esther	9				
	James	7				
590	Henry CLEMENS	47	Farmer	200	300	Va.
	Margarett	36				Tenn.
	Joseph	16				
	Henry	14				
	James Madison	12				
	Matildy	8				Ga.

Page 84   28 June 1860

	Name	Age	Occupation	Real	Pers.	Birthplace
	Samuel	5				Tenn.
	David	6/12				

District 14   P. O.: Maryville

	Name	Age	Occupation	Real	Pers.	Birthplace
591	Thomas LONG	30	Farmer	600	450	
	Mary	25				
	John	9				
	Polly	4				
	Emily	3				
	William	1				
592	Mary CARNEY	45				Ireland
	Cornelius	6				
	Jacob RIDDLE	30				Tenn.
	Isabella TUCKER	20				
593	James HANEY	53	Labourer		25	N. Car.
	Catharine	35				
594	John FISHER	48	Tenant		50	
	Sally	38				
	Thomas	14				
	Peter	13				
	James	11				
595	John COULTER	33	Farmer	8,000	4,000	Tenn.
	Catharine	49				
	William	18				
	Calvin	13				
	Nancy	9				
	Catharine	5				
	Nancy PRIVET	49				
596	John WHITE	34	Miller & Farmer	8,000	1,600	
	Leah	34				
	Nancy	12				
	James	10				
	William	8				
	Robert	4				
	John	1				
	John RIDDLE	17	Indentured			
597	John LONG	26	Miller		150	
	Semanthy (m)	27				
	Jacob	5				
	Happy Ann	4				
	Mary	3				
	James	1				

Page 85   29 June 1860

	Name	Age	Occupation	Real	Pers.	Birthplace
598	Isaack WHITE Jun.	27	Farmer	800	350	Tenn.
	Isaack WHITE Sen.	71				Va.
599	John STEEL	39	Farmer	1,500	800	N. Car.
	Elizabeth	30				Tenn.
	William	12				
	James	10				
	Calvin	8				
	Artesy June	6				
	Nancy Ann	6				
	Franklin	4				

District 14   P. O.: Maryville

	Name	Age	Occupation	Real	Pers.	Birthplace
	Mary	1				
	Baby (f)	2/12				
600	William WATERS	23	Tenant		150	
	Sophronia	23				
	John	2				
	Naomi	6/12				
601	Caswell GIBSON	43	Tenant	500	150	
	Matildy	37				
	William	17				
	John	13				
	Nancy	11				
602	Mary WATERS	70	Farmer	1,200	350	N. Car.
	Benj. STEEL	37	Manager			
	Malindy	35				Tenn.
	Enoch	3				
	James	1				
	Sally TUCKER	50	(Pauper & insane)			
	Oley CATON (f)	45	(Pauper & insane)			
	Frasey CATON (f)	25	(Pauper & insane)			
603	James WATERS	32	Farmer	3,000	1,200	
	Mary	34				
	Jane	9				
	Enoch	4				
	Moses	2				
	Margarett CROSS	17	Help			
	Enoch MORRISON	13				
	Geo HISE	40	Labourer			
604	James KINNAMON	33	Tenant		50	
	Mary	28				
	Wesley	5				
	James	4				

Page 86   District 14   P. O.: Gamble's Store   29 June 1860

	Name	Age	Occupation	Real	Pers.	Birthplace
	Rachel	9/12				Tenn.
605	Will L. EVERETT	29	Tenant		50	
	Mary	30				
	Hetty	6				
	Margarett	4				
	James	1				
606	Thos NICHOLS	65	Farmer	4,500	1,000	N. Car.
	Mary	42				Ky.
	James	6				Tenn.
	Andrew Jackson	3				
607	Lewis EVERETT	30	Tenant		250	
	Martha	29				
	Sarah	1				
	Sally KINNAMON	50	Home		25	
	Lucy KINNAMON	18	"			

	Name	Age	Occupation	Real	Pers.	Birthplace
608	William NICHOLS	35	Farmer	800	760	
	Catharine	35				N. Car.
	Elija	13				Tenn.
	Sarah	8				
	Thomas	5				
	Richard	3				
	John ELDERS	73	(Pauper)			N. Car.
	Nancy	84				Va.
609	Elija NELSON	78	Farmer	1,000	1,000	N. Car.
	Nancy	52				
	Luther NELSON	22				Tenn.
	Hetty	18				
	Martha	15				
	Jacob	14				
	David	12				
610	David NICHOLS	23	Tenant		350	
	Elizabeth	23				
	William	2				
611	John BAKER	53	Cooper	500	200	Va.
	Sally	52				
	Samuel	18				Tenn.
	Anderson	14				
	Sarah	9				
612	Vincent EVERETT	31	Farmer	1,200	1,000	

	Name	Age	Occupation	Real	Pers.	Birthplace
	James	3				Tenn.
	Ann EVERETT	62				Va.
	Sarah ROGERS	82	(Pauper)			
613	James STEEL	28	Tenant		50	N. Car.
	Naomi	26				Tenn.
	William	6				
	James	4				
	Saphrona	3				
	Ann	9/12				
614	Mary McGINLY (m)	51	Tenant		250	
	Martha	17				
	Mary	16				
	Sarah	12				
	Nancy	9				
	William	5				
615	Barchley IRVIN	48	Carpenter		350	
	Rachel	26				
	Murat (m) 19					
	George	15				
	Martha	12				
	Hester	7				
	John	2				
	James	10/12				
616	John MORRISON	46	Tenant			
	Melissa	48				
	Sarah	20				

District 14   P.O.: Maryville

	Name	Age	Occupation	Real	Pers.	Birthplace
	Eliza	17				
	James	16				
	Jerry	10				
	Martha	8				
	Matildy	5				
617	John McDANIEL	27	Tenant		175	
	Esther	26				
	William	6				
	Sarah	4				
	James	3				
	Permelia (f)	11/12				
618	Jas McCAULY (mwy)	35	Tenant			
	Elizabeth	18				
619	Moses GAMBLE	30	Farmer	700	850	Tenn.

Page 88   District 14   P.O.: Gamble's Store   29 June 1860

	Name	Age	Occupation	Real	Pers.	Birthplace
						Tenn.
	Ann	29				
	Mary	8				
	Hugh	5				
	Jane	2				
	Phebe I. SWAGGERTY	15	Help			
620	William CHRISTOPHER	22	Tenant		40	
	Mary	21				
	Margaret	9/12				
621	John E. GAMBLE	32	Farmer	5,000	3,000	
	Malvina	37				
	William	11				
	Elizabeth	5				
	Laura	1				
	Michael DAMERON	1	Home			
	Will WILLIAMS	25	Trader	20	1,000	
622	Moses GAMBLE	65	Farmer	1,000	2,425	
	Jane	58				
	Ann CALDWELL	13				
	Margaret JOHNSON	21				
623	Geo. CROSS	53	Tenant		40	
	Hester	34				
	John	14				
	William	8				
	Joseph CROSS	20	Labourer			
624	Rachel GAMBLE	73	Lady	4,000	1,200	Va.
	Mary A. GAMBLE	20				Tenn.
	Rachel CALDWELL	15				
625	Joseph CALDWELL	22	Tenant		150	
	Polly	24				
	Moses	4/12				
626	John REAGAN	72	Tenant		600	
	Jane	71				
	Margarett	37				
	Jane	33				
	Hester	15				
	Margarett	10				

District 14   P. O.: Gamble's Store

627	John GAMBLE	47	Farmer	5,500	1,000	
	Elizabeth	30				
	Alexander	5				
	James	3				

Page 89   29 June 1860

	John	1				Tenn.
628	Augusta CUMMINGS (m)	25			40	
	Martha	24				
	Emily	5				
	Mary	2				
	Baby (f)	2/12				
629	Jasper Henry	27	Farmer	2,000	700	
	Eliza	28				Penn.
	Sarah	5				Tenn.
	Samuel	3				
	Margarett	2				
	Gray (m)	3/12				
630	Samuel HENRY	25	Farmer	2,000	600	
	Rebecca	23				
	Jasper	2				
631	William KIBBLE	33	Tenant		600	
	Polly	34				So. Car.
	James	12				Tenn.
	John	10				
	William	6				
	Sally BOLEN	11	Home			
632	David McCLANAHAN	34	Tenant		300	
	Milly	38				
	Saml	5				
	Elizabeth HUBBARD	12	Home			
	Isaack McCLANAHAN	25				
633	Alexander McCLAIN	44	Farmer	15,000	8,000	
	Matilda	43				N. Car.
	Joseph McCLAIN	31				Tenn.
	George	19				
	John	18				
	Andrew	16				
	Rebecca	14				
	James	12				
	Nancy	9				
	Alexander	7				
	Mary	4				
	Lucy	2				
634	Allen GARMER (mul)	69	Farmer	3,000	1,250	N. Car.
	Silphy (mul)	49				

Page 90   30 June 1860

	John GARMER (mul)	25	Labourer		200	Tenn.
	Dolly (mul)	22			60	
	Mary (mul)	1				
	Allen GARMER (mul)	23	Labourer			

-82-

District 14   P. O.: Gamble's Store

	Name	Age	Occupation	Real	Pers.	Birthplace
635	William GARNER (mul)	28			3,000	
	Susan (mul)	24				
	Allen (mul)	7				
	John (mul)	5				
	Sis (mul)	4				
	Thomas (mul)	1				
636	Sam CLEMENS	26	Tenant		300	Va.
	Mary	29				Tenn.
	Merridy (m)	10				
	Ann	7				
	Elizabeth	6				
	James	4				
	Willis	1				
637	John McGILL (mwy)	24	Tenant		75	
	Elizabeth					
638	Alfred SEATON	39	Farmer	4,000	1,500	
	Mary	24				
	Granville	14				
	Philip	12				
	Bruce	10				
	Amandy	9				
	Mary	6				
	Margarett	3				
	Jo CRESWELL	75	(Pauper)			N. Car.
	Nancy WILLEX (?)	20	Help			Tenn.
639	Samuel WILLIAMS	30	Farmer	3,000	1,400	
	Sarah	24				Va.
	William	2				Tenn.
	Eliza	9/12				
	Judson ROGERS	12	Home			
640	Moses GAMBLE	27	Farmer	3,000	2,000	
	Angeline	24				
	James CUMMINGS	32	Labourer		60	
641	A. B. GAMBLE	72	Farmer	4,000	1,000	Va.
	Elizabeth	66				
	Esther	45				Tenn.

Page 91   30 June 1860

	Rachel	30				Tenn.
	Alexander	22				
	Sarah ELIDGE	18				
	James RIDDLE	16	Labourer			
642	John HEADRICK	40	Farmer	6,000	3,500	
	Catharina	35				
	William	14				
	James	12				
	Nancy	10				
	John	8				
	Anna	6				
	Caroline	4				

-83-

	Name	Age	Occupation	Real	Pers.	Birthplace
	Rachel	1				
	Betsey HUBBARD	40				
	Tennessee (f)	7				
643	Joseph LARMER (?)	59	Tenant		100	N. Car.
	Betsey	44				
	Eli	16				
	Elisha	12				
	Arche	10				
	Dicey	8				
	Anderson	5				
644	Benjamin MORTON	29	M. D.	600	5,000	
	Martha	23				
	Martha McCOLLOUGH	10	Home			
	Houstin SHERREL	26	Student M. D.			
645	Lindsay VINEYARD	47	Tenant		400	Va.
	Aggrassina(?)	50				
	Dorcas	24				
	Martha	20				
	Samuel	18				
	Josephine	15				
	Thomas	13				
	Harriett	11				
	Fielding	9				
	Sarah	7				
646	John McKAMY	60	Farmer	1,000	500	Tenn.
	Elizabeth	52				
	Martha	20				
	Margarett	18				

	Name	Age	Occupation	Real	Pers.	Birthplace
	James	15				
	Elizabeth	12				
	William	9				
	Thomas SHAVER	41	Tenant		1,000	
647	Philip DAVIS	60		600	300	N. Car.
	Jane	45				Tenn.
	Rhoda	20				
	Mary	18				
	Calvin	16				
	Arnold	8				
	Alexand (m)	5				
648	Granville DAVIS	30		500	50	
	Barbary	20				
649	Jacob NEIGHMON	39	Farmer	2,000	1,500	
	Elizabeth	40				Va.
	Isabella	11				Tenn.
	Margarett	10				
	Mary	5				
	Martha	3				

District 14   P. O.: Maryville

	Name	Age	Occupation	Real	Pers.	Birthplace
650	William GODARD	48	Farmer	4,000	1,800	
	Margarett	41				
	Lucinda	21				
	Elias	19				
	Euphrasia (f)	17				
	William	16				
	Mary	14				
	James	10				
	Caroline	7				
	Johnson	7	Indentured			
651	Enoch COPLEY	25	Mechanic		1,000	N. York
	Ellen	25				Penn.
	B. F. WILLARD	32	Cabinet Maker			N. York
	Jonas HOATS	30	Blacksmith			Penn.
652	Josiah GAMBLE	27	Farmer	5,000	1,000	
	Mary	24				
	Rebecca	6				
	Jane	2				
	James HENRY	58				
	Sarah	54				
653	James W CARVER	56	Farmer	1,000	580	So. Car.

Page 93   District 14   Gamble's Store   2 July 1860

	Name	Age	Occupation	Real	Pers.	Birthplace
	Elizabeth	57				Tenn.
	James	18				
654	Geo COWAN	46	Farmer	1,000	1,500	
	Margarett	30				
	Nancy	19				
	James	15				
	Mary	4				
655	And PERRY	55	Farmer	4,500	2,500	Va.
	Rosanna	57				
	Jane	20				Tenn.
	Malindy	18				
	Andrew	15				
656	Jesse DONELSON	23	Farmer	1,500	1,800	
	Rebecca	23				
	Margarett	1				
657	James DONELSON	34	Farmer	2,000	4,060	
	Jane	18				
	Sarah	4/12				
	Elizabeth DONELSON	22				
	Dryden	15				
658	Solom FARMER	54	Farmer	3,000	700	
	Rebecca	52				
	William FARMER	26			150	
	Joseph FARMER	24			150	
	James	20				
	Mary	18				
	John	16				
	Elizabeth	12				

	Name	Age	Occupation	Real	Pers.	Birthplace
659	Samuel HENRY	83	Farmer	12,000	31,000	
	Deborah	62				
	Arthur HENRY (mwy)	23			700	
	Angeline	20				
	Mary	20				
660	Lorenzo PERKINS	58	Tenant		200	
	Serepta	34				
	George	12				
	Phebe	10				
	John	9				
	Nancy	2				
661	Vance WALKER	58	Farmer	2,000	2,500	

Page 94   2 July 1860

	Name	Age	Occupation	Real	Pers.	Birthplace
	Catharine	59				
	Sarah	11				
	James WALKER	30				
662	William B. PARRISH	25	Tenant		200	So. Car.
	Polly	25				Tenn.
	Richard	6/12				
663	William PERRY (mwy)	24	Farmer		500	
	Elizabeth	20				
664	Philip DONELSON	63	Tenant		1,000	Va.
	Sally	52				
	Polly DONELSON	34				Tenn.
	Nancy	20				
	Philip Jun.	18				
	Lorenzo	13				
665	Nancy HENRY	56	Farmer	3,000	2,050	
	Saml HENRY	24				
	Julia	18				
	James	7/12				
	Pleasant HENRY	22				
666	James COULTER	29	Farmer	300	1,050	
	Margarett	27				
	Richard	7				
	William	5				
	Elizabeth	2				
667	Isaack GOODEN	41			75	
	Susan	42				
	James	12				
	Samuel	10				
	Nancy	8				
	Ake	6				
668	Sally BOLEN	63	Tenant		50	N. Car.
	Nancy BOLEN	23				Tenn.
	James	15				
	Jenny	5				
	Sarah	2				

District 14   P. O.: Gamble's Store

	Name	Age	Occupation	Real	Pers.	Birthplace
669	Betsy CLAMPET	44	Tenant		20	
	Jane	18				
	Sarah	15				
	Rachel	13				
	Mary	10				

Page 95   2 July 1860

	Name	Age	Occupation	Real	Pers.	Birthplace
670	Sarah CLAMPET	86				Delaware
	Henry CLAMPET	61				N. Car.
	Sally CLAMPET	26				Tenn.
	Margarett CLAMPET	15				
	Samuel	10				
	Mythenia (f)	5				
	Elizabeth	6/12				
671	Silas GRAVES	49	Broom Maker		20	
	Nancy	49				
	Barbary	13				
	Jane	11				
	Martha	8				
	Cassy	2				
672	Thomas KIBBLE	60	Farmer	600	100	
	Nancy	39				
	Eliza	12				
	Robert	10				
	John	6				
	Alfred	5				
	Nancy CANNON	78				
673	Peter SUMMER	37	Tenant		125	N. Car.
	Emeline	35				
	Dorcas	16				
	George	14				
	William	12				
674	Jane KIBBLE	34	Tenant		30	Tenn.
	Stephen DAVIS	42				
	Polly	42				
	Charlotte	20				
	Eliza	17				
	Jane	14				
	Mary	12				
	Sarah	10				
	William	6				
	Rebecca	4				
	Walter	5/12				
675	Sam HENRY	34		1,500	500	
	Catharine	37				
	Sarah	10				
	Rebecca	8				

Page 96   3 July 1860

	Name	Age	Occupation	Real	Pers.	Birthplace
	Mary	6				Tenn.
	Joseph	3				
	Elizabeth	6/12				

	Name	Age	Occupation	Real	Pers.	Birthplace
676	William CUMMINGS	32	Tenant		60	
	Delila	24				So. Car.
	James	3				Tenn.
	Sarah	1				
	Susan	2/12				
677	William ELLISS	36	Farmer	500	600	
	Lucy	36				N. Car.
	Emily	17				Tenn.
	Andy	15				
	Jacob	12				
	John	9				
	James	4				
	Margastte (f)	2				
678	John FARMER	18	Tenant		100	
	Emily	18				
	Baby (f)	6/12				
679	John WILSON	50	Blacksmith		200	
	Polly	34				
	Rebecca	16				
	Adam	15				
	William	13				
	Joseph	11				
	John	8				
	Samuel	5				
	James	1				
680	Manly KIBBLE	53	Farmer	15,000	400	
	Rebecca	52				
	Mary KIBBLE	24	Spinster			
	Catharine	21				
	John	20				
	Sam	17				
	Pleasat	15				
	Anderson	12				
	Richard	8				
681	Jacob SUMMER	50	Tenant		75	
	Margaret	50				
	Rebecca SUMMER	26	Hooker			

Page 97   3 July 1860

	Name	Age	Occupation	Real	Pers.	Birthplace
						Tenn.
	James	19				
	Margarett	13				
	Jasper	10				
	Lodzy (f)	8				
	Mary	4				
	James	1/365				
682	Geo LATHAM	45	Farmer	150	150	
	Marena	32				
	William	14				
	Harvey	13				
	Nancy	10				
	Margarett	8				

District 14   P. O.: Gamble's Store

	Name	Age	Occupation	Real	Pers.	Birthplace
	Mary	6				
	Eliza	3				
	John	7/12				
683	Mike SUMMERS	28	Tenant			
	Elizabeth	27				
	Elvira	10				
	George	8				
	Levi	4				
	Peter	2				
684	Adam GARNER	40			150	
	Telitha	40	Labourer			
685	Abija SIMMONS	55	Farmer	300	250	
	Mary	35				
	Mary	13				
	Thomas	11				
	Elizabeth	9				
	John	7				
	Martha	6				
	Neil	3				
	Catharine	10/12				
686	John CLARK	45	Farmer & Sheriff	6,000	3,500	
	Priscilla	26				
	James	20				
	Benjamin	19				
	Adaline	17				
	Jane	15				
	John	14				
	Elizabeth	12				

Page 98   District 13   P. O.: Gamble's Store   4 July 1860

	Name	Age	Occupation	Real	Pers.	Birthplace
						Tenn.
	Thomas	11				
	Theodore	9				
	Edward	6				
	Priscilla	3				
687	William DUNLAPP	50	Tenant		100	
	Susan	45				
	Rebecca	17				
	John	15				
	Rachel	13				
	James	10				
688	Matilda DUNLAPP	33	Farmer	4,000	3,300	N. Car.
	Isabel	14				Tenn.
	Adam	12				
	James	10				
	Elija	8				
	William	6				
	Matildy	4				
	Nancy	2				
	Hayne DUNLAPP	32	Labourer			
689	Hannah GARNER	59				N. Car.
	James DUNLAPP	33	Tenant		500	

	Name	Age	Occupation	Real	Pers.	Birthplace
	Rusha (f)	30				Tenn.
	Margarett	6				
	Mary	3				
	Joseph	1				
	Mary BOLEN	14	Help			
	James BOLEN	6				
690	John NORTON	39	Farmer	3,500	1,800	
	Nancy	38				
	Nicholas	14				
	Polly	13				
	Jane	10				
	Joseph	9				
	George	7				
	Nancy	5				
	Nathan	4				
	John	1				
691	George STONE	37	Labourer		50	S. Car.
	Rebecca	30				
	William	10				Tenn.

Page 99   4 July 1860

	Name	Age	Occupation	Real	Pers.	Birthplace
	Andrew Johnson	8				Tenn.
	Alfred	5				
	Parthena (f)	3				
	Angelina	1/12				
692	Rachel CUMMINGS	74	Farmer	2,000	650	Va.
	Frank CUMMINGS	36				Tenn.
	Elizabeth	27				
	Andrew	12				
	John	9				
	Ann	8				
	William	5				
	Vance	2				
	Baby (m)	3/12				
693	Noah EVERETT	41	Farmer		500	Indiana
	Anna	41				Tenn.
	James	18				
	Thomas	13				
	Libby	12				
	Ellen	9				
	George	6				
	Isabella	2				
694	Rhoda PARMER	53	Spinster		400	Tenn.
	Peggy FINLY	51				
	Jane PARMER	49				
	Perdena	45				
	Martha	9				
	James	7				
695	James MILLSAPP	30	Tenant		300	
	Aletissa	37				
	Mary	4				
	Jesse (m)	2				

District 13   P. O.: Gamble's Store

	Name	Age	Occupation	Real	Pers.	Birthplace
696	Saml McHENRY	42	Farmer	2,000	1,500	
	Catharine	30				
	Thomas	8				
	Fanny	4				
	Elizabeth	1				
	Nancy McHENRY	37				
697	Peggy REAGAN	60	Tenant		150	
	Jasper SUIT	35				
	Jane	28				

Page 100   District 13   P. O.: Ellajoy   4 July 1860

	Name	Age	Occupation	Real	Pers.	Birthplace
698	John BOLEN	26				Tenn.
	Polly	25				
	Robert	6				
	Margaret	3				
	Andrew (twins)	4/12				
	Jackson	4/12				
699	Michael KOONTZ	55	Farmer	10,000	2,300	
	Mary	51				Va.
	Samuel KOONTZ	24				Tenn.
	Columbus	17				
	Joseph	15				
	Nancy	12				
	Lucy	10				
700	George DAVIS (mwy)	21	Tenant		700	
	Mary	19				
701	Robert MURREN	61	Farmer	800	1,050	Va.
	Catharine	59				
	Matilda MURREN	37	Spinster			Tenn.
	Rachel (twins)	35				
	Catharine	35				
	Mary	23				
	Robert MURREN Jun.	30				
	Lydia	28				
	Nancy	26				
	Margarett	23				
	Augustine	19				
	William	17				
702	Samuel MURREN	42	Tenant		500	
	Mary	19				
	Margarett	9				
	William	7				
	Ann	4				
703	Adam GRAVES	67	Farmer	6,000	2,400	
	Mahala	43				
	Mary	15				
	Stephen	11				
	Jane	9				
	Martha	8				
	William	5				
	John	3				

District 13   P. O.: Ellajoy

	Name	Age	Occupation	Real	Pers.	Birthplace
Page 101		District 13		P. O.: Ellajoy		4 July 1860
	Mahala	1				Tenn.
704	Joseph ELENBERG	30	Tenant		100	So. Car.
	Elizabeth	24				N. Car.
	Sarah	3				Tenn.
	Julia	1				
705	Elizabeth HUBBARD	60	Tenant		25	
	Sarah	38				
	Francis (f)	13				
	Nancy	9				
	Lydia	2				
706	Elizabeth GRAVES	38	Tenant		50	
	Hugh	17				
	John	10				
	Patsey	10/12				
707	Lydia GRAVES	75				N. Car.
	David DIXON	44	Tenant		175	
	Betsey	42				
	David	18				Tenn.
	Thomas	14				
	Ellen	10				
	David CUTSHAW	8	Home			
	William CUTSHAW	6				
708	Charles HUBBARD	35	Tenant		50	
	Sarah	27				N. Car.
	Marian (f)	13				Tenn.
	Polly	11				
	Elizabeth	8				
	James	4				
709	Thomas TOWNSEND	23	Tenant		25	
	Kitty	20				
	John Adams	4				
	James	1				
710	Marion ROGERS (m)	30	Farmer	800	550	
	Margarett	36				
	William	10				
	John	8				
	Landon	6				
	Jacob	5				
	Martha	2				
	Joseph	1				
Page 102						4 July 1860
711	Jacob TIPTON	44	Farmer	600	1,000	Tenn.
	Dorcas	45				
	John TIPTON	22				
	Sarah	21				
	Martha	19				
	Marena (f)	17				
	Peter	15				
	Newton	14				

District 13   P. O.: Ellajoy

	Name	Age	Occupation	Real	Pers.	Birthplace
	Benjamin	13				
	Bradford	11				
	Houston	9				
	Dorcas	4				
712	John TIPTON	71	Farmer	2,500	900	
	Martha	70				
713	Calvin DAVIS	38	Farmer	600	750	
	Sereldy	36				
	Jane	18				
	William	16				
	Julius	14				
	Marcus	11				
	Mary	9				
	Sarah	7				
	Archey	5				
	Nancy	3				
	Campbell	1				
714	Geo DAVIS	24	Farmer	600	500	
	Martha	22				
	Jane	2				
	Charity	1				
715	William DRAKE (mwy)	25			250	N. Car.
	Elizabeth	28				Tenn.
716	Wiley DAVIS	34	Farmer	600	400	
	Caroline	33				
	William	10				
	John	6				
	Guilford	4				
	Jane	2				
	Samuel Willing (twins)	3/12				
	James Anderson	3/12				
	Martha McMURRY	32				

Page 103   4 July 1860

	Name	Age	Occupation	Real	Pers.	Birthplace
717	Sally BOLEN	40	Spinster		50	Tenn.
	William	18				
	Mitchel	16				
	John	14				
	Andy	4				
	Henry	3				
718	John McMURRY	70	Tenant		350	N. Car.
	Margarett	58				Tenn.
	Tennessee (f)	28				
	Sarah	26				
	Isabel	20				
719	James DAVIS	23	Farmer	500	350	
	Jane	21				
	Rebecca	1				
720	William DAVIS	22	Tenant		150	
	Hannah	22				
	Wain	3				

District 13   P. O.: Ellajoy

	Name	Age	Occupation	Real	Pers.	Birthplace
721	Shade ROGERS	58	Farmer	450	200	N. Car.
	Sally	60				
	Rebecca	30				
	Mary	27				
	Harry	19				
	Viney	18				
	William	4				
722	George ROGERS	27	Farmer	100	125	
	Feriby	25				
	Rebecca	3				
	Baby (m)	1/12				
723	Sampson GARNER	23	Tenant		200	
	Martha	24				
	Rebecca	1				
724	Amos GARNER (mwy)	20	Tenant		75	
	Virena	17				
725	John FLANNEGAN	55	Tenant			
	Nancy	53				
	Caroline	25				
	Susan	21				
	Thomas	15				
	John	13				
	Billy	4				

Page 104   4 July 1860

	Name	Age	Occupation	Real	Pers.	Birthplace
	Mary	8/12				Tenn.
726	ELi GARNER	45	Farmer	500	1,000	N. Car.
	Elizabeth	38				Tenn.
	Mathew	18				
	Nancy	16				
	Elizabeth	14				
	Jane	13				
	Eli	11				
	Francis (m)	10				
	Ransome	8				
	Mansel	7				
	Alexander	5				
	Levi	2				
	Eveline	8/12				
727	Nelson ROGERS	29	Farmer	300	600	
	Emily	32				
	Jesse (m)	12				
	Charity	11				
	Selah	9				
	Sarah	7				
	William (Twins)	6				
	John	6				
	Polly	4				
	Irvin	3				
	George	1				

-94-

	Name	Occupation		Real	Pers.	Birthplace
728	Selah ROGERS (f)	55				N. Car.
	Elizabeth CARTER	75	Tenant		50	
	James CARTER	25				Tenn.
729	Wilson ROGERS	34		300	300	
	Ellen	26				
	Sally	3				
730	James BLACK	54	Farmer	7,000	1,400	
	Betsey	48				
	Ellen	21				
	Elizabeth	17				
731	Martha BOLEN	31	Tenant		100	
	Matildy	20				
	Addie	11/12				
	Polly BOLEN	70	Spinster		25	N. Car.
	Jane BOLEN	35				Tenn.

	Name	Occupation		Real	Pers.	Birthplace
	Harrison	12				Tenn.
	Polly	10				
	Rachel	6				
	William	2				
732	Hugh BOGLE	37	Farmer	4,000	14,800	
	Jane	22				
	Andrew	6				
	Jane HAYDEN	60				
	Nathan JEFFRIES	64		200	100	Va.
733	Saml McANALLY	37	Farmer	700	350	Tenn.
	Mary	36				
	William	10				
	Caroline	8				
	Joseph	6				
	Sarah	4				
	Samuel	1				
734	Marian TOWNSEND (m)	60	Tenant			So. Car.
	John TOWNSEND	29				
	James TOWNSEND	20				
	Nancy	23				
	Martha	19				
	Cass (f)	6				
	Tom	3				
	Marian (f)	2				
	Harry	10/12				
735	Isaack LEFOLLET	47	Shoemaker		25	N. Car.
	Sophia	35				
	John	20				Tenn.
	Caroline	18				
	Ephraim	16				
	Jerry	13				
	William	8				
	Lucy	5				

District 18   P. O.: Ellajoy

	Name	Age	Occupation	Real	Pers.	Birthplace
736	George DAVIS	63	Farmer	3,000	1,500	
	Cathrine	35				N. Car.
	James	15				
	William	14				
	Jane	8				
	George	6				
	Sarah	2				

Page 106   5 July 1860

	Name	Age	Occupation	Real	Pers.	Birthplace
737	James W. DAVIS	39		1,000	650	Tenn.
	Polly	35				
	Hannah	14				
	Andrew	11				
738	Jackson MURREN	44	Farmer	1,000	800	
	Mary	15				
	Ann MURREN	50	Help			
739	William DAVIS	32	Farmer	2,500	800	
	Sarah	30				
	William	10				
	James	8				
	Lavina	5				
	Andrew Jackson	3				
740	Hugh GAMBLE	31	Farmer	1,500	550	
	Emeline	35				
	Mary	8				
	Sarah	7				
	Josiah	5				
	Eveline	4				
	Telitha	2				
	Susy	1				
741	Peter DAVIS	65	Farmer	100	300	
	Hannah	57				N. Car.
	Catharine DOLOZIER	40		800	50	Tenn.
	James	16				
	Hudson	14				
	Diana	11				
	Hannah	9				
	Peter	4				
	Jesse (f)	2				
742	Telford ROGERS	34	Farmer	100	300	
	Martha	27				
	Lavina	14				
	Selina	8				
	William	6				
	Addison	4				
	Sarah	2				
743	Caleb DAVIS	27	Tenant		450	
	Susan	24				
	Martha	5				

Page 107   5 July 1860

	Name	Age	Occupation	Real	Pers.	Birthplace
	Elizabeth	3				Tenn.

District 13   P.O.: Ellajoy

	Name	Age	Occupation	Real	Pers.	Birthplace
744	Henry BOLEN	50	Tenant	100	75	
	Terry (f)	45				
	Alvira	18				
	Louisa	16				
	Pleasant	14				
	John	12				
	Emeline	10				
	Hetty	8				
	Elija	6				
	Larkin	4				
	Susan	3				
	Baby (m)	1				
745	Vincent ROGERS	73	Farmer	600	1,775	N. Car.
	Abigail	65				Tenn.
	Elizabeth ROGERS	35				
	Mary ROGERS	23				
	Willoby ROGERS (m)	31				
	Andrew	11				
746	Jas R. DAVIS	24	Farmer	200	450	
	Mareny	29				
	Abigail	4				
	John	2				
747	John ROGERS	35	Farmer	150	400	
	Hetty	38				
	Isabel	12				
	Jesse (m)	11				
	Sarah	9				
	Selah	8				
	Nancy	7				
	Hetty	6				
	Elizabeth	3				
748	Shedrack BOLEN	50	Farmer	500	500	
	Selah	25				
	Bede (f)	15				
	John	13				
	Margarett	9				
749	Reben REAGAN	38	Farmer	400	300	Va.
	Elizabeth	38				Tenn.
	Harrison	12				

Page 108   5 July 1860

	Mary	10				Tenn.
	Nancy	8				
	Cyrus	6				
	William	5				
	John	4				
	George	3				
	Elizabeth	3/12				

	Name	Age	Occupation	Real	Pers.	Birthplace
750	Elija GARNER	30	Labourer		100	
	Elizabeth	33				
	John	5				
	Marcus	3				
	Andrew	1				
751	Asa ROGERS	35	Farmer	1,500	550	
	Eliza	44				
	Elizabeth M. McCfee (?)	21	Help			
	Dorcas	16				
	Hannah	10				
	James	8				
	Jesse (m)	4				
	Eliza	1				
752	John HENLY (?)	36	Farmer	600	500	
	Mary	38				
	Pinckney	10				
	John	8				
	Saml	4				
	Ruthy	1				
753	William DAVIS	50	Farmer	2,500	1,200	
	Nancy	35				
	Nancy DAVIS	29				
	John	18				
	Margarett	16				
	William	12				
	Anderson	9				
	Anthony	3/12				
754	James DAVIS	40	Farmer	3,000	4,800	
	Rachel	39				
	Alfred	17				
	John	16				
	William	14				
	Sarah (twin)	12				

Page 109   5 July 1860

                                                                    Tenn.

	Name	Age	Occupation	Real	Pers.	Birthplace
	James (twin)	12				
	Isaack	9				
	Saml	7				
	Andrew	5				
	Huldah	3				
755	Valentine DAVIS	52	Farmer	1,000	600	
	Betsey DAVIS	22				
	John	20				
	Peggy	18				
	Rebecca	16				
	Nancy	12				
	Rachel	10				
756	John JEFFRES	48	Farmer	600	900	
	Margarett	36				
	Caroline	15				
	James	11				

District 13   P. O.: Ellajoy

	Name	Age	Occupation	Real	Pers.	Birthplace
	Malissy	9				
	John	8				
	Nancy	2				
757	James JEFFRES	50	400	700		
	Betsy	60				
	Joana JEFFRES	28				
	Hugh JEFFRES	21				
758	William McTEER	80	Farmer	8,000	1,000	Penn.
	Mary	75				Tenn.
759	William MURREN	56	Farmer & Miller	1,000	250	
	Ann McTEER	85		2,500	1,500	
	Eliza PRIOR	16	Help			
760	James McTEER	37		300	1,000	
	Lavicey	40				
	Mary	16				
	Jane	14				
	Martha	12				
	Margarett	10				
	William	7				
	Eliza	5				
	John	2				
	Andrew	5/12				
761	James KINNAMOND	60	Tenant		300	N. Car.
	Utally	55				Va.

Page 110   5 July 1860

	Name	Age	Occupation	Real	Pers.	Birthplace
						Tenn.
	Elizabeth	25				
	John KINNAMOND	21				
	Sarah	18				
	Martha Ellen (twins)	16				
	Eliza Ann	16				
	Wilson	11				
762	Maj McTEER	39		500	1,500	
	Nancy	37				
	William	16				
	Elizabeth	15				
	Hetty	12				
	Mary	7				
	Alexander	3				
763	Jesse MILSAPS	55	Tenant		500	
	Jane	32				
	Elizabeth	17				
	Jesse Wallace (m)	15				
	Blackburn	12				
	Margarett	7				
	William	1				
764	Daniel NICHOLSON	50	Tenant		40	
	Polly	45				
	John	17				
	Betsy	16				

Name	Age	Occupation	Real	Pers.	Birthplace
Emeline	13				
James	11				
Robert	5				
Sarah Angeline **Elvira**	38				
765 Isaack BURNETT	38	Tenant		50	
Fanny	40				
Nancy	13				
Jefferson	12				
Samuel	10				
William	5				
Isaack	1				
766 Hannah DUNLAPP	55	Tenant		100	
Polly	25				
Samuel	23				
Hiram	16				
Marian (f) (Twins)	16				

Page 111   6 July 1860

Name	Age	Occupation	Real	Pers.	Birthplace
Rhoda	15				Tenn.
Jefferson	12				
767 Henry NORTON	30		1,600	400	
Sarah	30				
William	7				
Nancy	3				
Sarah	1				
768 Preston HOPKINS	32	Tenant			N. Car.
Nancy	32				
Benjamin	10				
Esther	9				**Tenn..**
William	7				
Sarah	5				
Alfred	3				
769 William ARMBRISTER	57	Saddler	400	500	
Jane	40				
Isabella	19				
John	17				
James	11				
Asa (m)	7				
Margarett BLANG	65	Help			Va.
770 William SARTEN	70	Cooper		50	N. Car.
Sarah	59				Va.
Thomas SARTEN	23	(Deaf & Dumb)			N. Car.
Lewis SARTEN	18	Labourer			Va.
Sarah	16				
771 Robert HOUSTEN	57	Farmer	2,000	1,100	Tenn.
Dorothy	53				
Saml	20	Student			
Robert	16				
Dorothy	12				
James HOUSTEN	66				

	Name	Age	Occupation	Real	Pers.	Birthplace
772	Mary STAFFORD	74	Spinner			Va.
	Anna STAFFORD	45				N. Car.
	Saml	13				
	Joseph	11				
	Matildy	9				
	Benjamin	7				
	Alice Rowena May	2				Tenn.
	William TAYLOR	10				

Page 112   6 July 1860

	Name	Age	Occupation	Real	Pers.	Birthplace
773	Robert McKAMY	26	Farmer	3,000	3,800	Tenn.
	Louisa	19				
	Sarah	2				
	James	6/12				
774	William CRUSE	25	Farmer	500	600	
	Mary	21				
	Sam Wallace	1				
	Jerry THOMAS	11	Help			
775	Kezziah CRUSE (f)	60	Spinster			
	Rachel CRUSE	58				
	Frank CRUSE	25		100	400	
776	John McCULLOCH	30	Farmer	6,000	2,100	
	Martha	33				
	Elizabeth	10				
	Samuel	8				
	Russel	4				
	Robert	2				
	Baby (f)	1/12				
	Martha HOUSEHOLDER	19	Help			
777	Milas HOOPER	40	Farmer	1,000	1,000	N. Car.
	Margarett	36				Tenn.
	Moses	8				
	Ellen	6				
	Elizabeth	4				
	Saml	2				
	Caroline	1				
	Elizabeth HOOPER	70				N. Car.
	Jane ROGERS	16	Home			
	William HOUSER	17	Help			
778	William MALCOM	32		800	450	Tenn.
	Elizabeth	31				
	James	7				
	Saml	5				
	Phebe Elzena (Twins)	4				
	Nancy Parthena	4				
779	Hugh HOLLAND	60	Farmer	5,000	11,200	
	Martha	59				N. Car.
	William HOLLAND	22	Student			Tenn.

District 13   P. O.: Ellajoy

	Name	Age	Occupation	Real	Pers.	Birthplace
780	Andrew BOGLE	50	Farmer	3,500	1,700	
	Elizabeth	56				

Page 113   6 July 1860

	Name	Age	Occupation	Real	Pers.	Birthplace
	Nancy	18				Tenn.
	Robert	12				
781	Hugh M. BOGLE	29			1,000	
	Mary	29				
	Mary	5				
	James	3				
	Andrew	1				
	Will T. McGILL	23	Labourer			
	Jane ELLEDGE	13				
782	Elisha GARNER	35	Labourer			
	Elizabeth	30				
	Caloway	13				
	James	11				
	Udora	7				
	John	6				
783	Barton JOHNSON	64	Farmer		100	So. Car.
	Mary	66				Penn.
784	William JOHNSON	42		2,000	1,800	Tenn.
	Martha	36				
	James	12				
	Mary	10				
	David	8				
	Michael	6				
	Benjamin	3				
	David JOHNSON	25				
785	Benjamin BROWN	50	Farmer	1,500	900	Va.
	Elizabeth	36				Tenn.
	Saml BROWN	22				
	Elizabeth	18				
	Rebecca	16				
	Joseph	14				
	Sarah	12				
	Margarett	10				
	Malindy	2				
	John	1				
786	Jesse PATTY	52	Blacksmith		300	So. Car.
	Elizabeth	45				Tenn.
	John	18				
	Joshua	17				
	Delilah	14				

Page 114   6 July 1860

	Name	Age	Occupation	Real	Pers.	Birthplace
	Martha	9				Tenn.
	Jesse (m)	7				
	David	5				
	Josephine	3				

District 13   P. O.: Ellajoy

	Name	Age	Occupation	Real	Pers.	Birthplace
787	Samuel KELLER	56	Tenant		25	
	Catharine	57				
	Jane	19				
	Tabithy	17				
	Narcissa	10				
788	James W. PATTY	19	Chair Maker		50	
	Elizabeth	19				
	Baby (m)	1/12				
789	Thomas KELLER	20	Chair Maker		50	
	Mary	24				
	Margarett	3/12				
790	Robert FLANNEGAN	20	Chair Maker		50	
	Sarah	22				
	Matildy	4/12				
791	Hiram BOGLE	41	Farmer	11,000	12,000	
	Martha	30				
	Mary	14				
	Joseph	13				
	Harriet	11				
	Sidney	9				
	Robert	5				
	Caroline	3				
	William	1				
	Lavina BOGLE	30				
	Saml DUNLAPP	23				
792	Malindy BOGLE	45	Farmer	1,500	600	
	Charlotte ROSE	22	Help			
	Benjamin CUNNINGHAM	19	Help			
	Anderson TAYLOR	31	M. D.	2,300	2,000	Tenn.
	Andrew TAYLOR	27	M. D.		1,000	
	Martha BRAKEBILL	23	House Keeper			
	Nancy	10	Home			
	Jordan	5				
793	Isaack MANTHY	41	Gun Smith	500	500	
	Elizabeth	39				
	John	20				

Page 115   6 July 1860

	Name	Age	Occupation	Real	Pers.	Birthplace
	Diana	17				
	Tabithy	14				
	Edward	12				
	Mary	7				
794	James McCLANAHAN	33	Tenant		150	
	Polly	25				
	Mary	8				
	John	7				
	Catharine	3				
	William	1				
795	William THOMAS	32	Tenant		1,500	
	Nancy	29				
	Antipie (m)	4				

District 13   P. O.: Ellajoy

	Name	Age	Occupation	Real	Pers.	Birthplace
	Jesse (m)	3				
	George	1				
	Lucy DELOZIER	32				
796	Ed PORTER	78	Tenant			Maryland
	Montgomery LANGLY	24				Tenn.
	Virginia	30				
	Polly	6				
	Elizabeth	2				
	Lucy PORTER	30	Hooker			
	Joseph	3				
797	James DAVIS	69	Farmer	4,000	1,000	N. Car.
	Elizabeth	74				
	Polly McCLANAHAN	73				
798	John HALEY	59	Tenant		400	S. Car.
	Abigail	59				
	John	17				Tenn.
799	Mary HOOPER (m)	40	Tenant		400	N. Car.
	Harvey HOOPER	22				Tenn.
	Wilson	8				
	Elvira HOOPER	38				N. Car.
800	Vance EVANS	28	Tenant		75	Tenn.
	Mahala	32				
	Nancy	3				
	Margarett	4/12				
801	Joseph SHADDEN	78	Farmer	1,000	1,350	Va.
	Jane SHADDEN	47				Tenn.
	Margarett	45				

Page 116   7 July 1860

	Name	Age	Occupation	Real	Pers.	Birthplace
	Elizabeth SHADDEN	42				Tenn.
	Amos T. SHADDEN	37				
802	John CUNNINGHAM	55	Tenant		200	
	Sarah	25				
	Dardes (m)	9				
	Wiley	7				
	Thomas	6				
	James	2				
803	Alexander SHAVER	25	Tenant		150	
	Nancy	44				
804	William McMURRY	69	Farmer	3,000	1,750	N. Car.
	Margarett	54				Tenn.
	Alexander	33				
	Mary McMURRY	27				
	Margarett McMURRY	25				
	Caroline McMURRY	23				
	John McMURRY	27				
	Joseph	19				
	William	17				
	Marcus	14				
	Sarah	11				

	Name	Age	Occupation	Real	Pers.	Birthplace
805	Isaack HINDS	45	Farmer	2,500	1,400	
	Cynthia	40				
	Robt HINDS	21				
	Joshua	20				
	William	17				
	Joseph	15				
	Margarett	13				
	Sarah	11				
	Elizabeth	6				
	Eveline	2				
806	Andrew CRESWELL	45	Farmer	1,500	500	
	Ann	39				
	Elizabeth	16				
	Mary	15				
	Margarett	13				
	Alexander	9				
	Nancy	6				
	William	3				
807	William HUNTER	30	Waggon Maker	400	400	

Page 117   7 July 1860   Tenn.

	Name	Age	Occupation	Real	Pers.	Birthplace
	Jane	22				
	Mary	5				
	Martha	3				
	Joseph	1				
	Mary LANGLY	26	Help			
808	Samuel FLANNEGAN	30	Chair Maker	600	500	
	Lucy	28				
	Louisa	5				
	Catharine	4				
	Marshall	3				
	Sarah	1				
	Harriet HUNTER	25	Help			
809	John HOUKE	37	Farmer	5,000	2,300	Tenn.
	Nancy	28				
	William	12				
	Hulda	9				
	Sarah	5				
	Nancy	1				
	Ben CHANDLER	19	Labourer			
810	Thomas PICKENS	48	Farmer	4,000	2,500	Tenn.
	Jane	16				
	Susan HEADRICK	12				
811	Andrew EVANS	25	Tenant		50	
	Rebecca	21				
	Elizabeth	3				
	Mary	2				
	Baby (f)	2/12				
812	Cynthia PICKENS	49	Tenant		850	
	Samuel PICKENS	23				

District 13   P.O.: Ellajoy

	Name	Age	Occupation	Real	Pers.	Birthplace
	Harrison	19				
	Isabella	17				
813	Robert PICKENS	50	Farmer	3,500	3,700	
	Elizabeth	32				
	Isabella	11				
	Robert	10				
	John	8				
	Saml	6				
814	Ellen McMURRA	60	Farmer	1,000	850	
	Barckly	28				
	Sarah	24				

Page 118   7 July 1860

	Name	Age	Occupation	Real	Pers.	Birthplace
	Sarah HUBBARD	10				Tenn.
815	George LANGLY	54	Blacksmith		250	N. Car.
	Elizabeth	55				Tenn.
	Jane LANGLY	28				
	Susan	26				
	Elizabeth	22				
	Mary	12				
	David LYON	78	(Pauper)			Unknown
816	Campbell SHADDEN	44	Farmer	1,200	3,700	Tenn.
	Ruticia	47				
	Jane	10				
	Malindy	7				
	James	5				
817	William McCLERGE	52	Farmer	3,000	1,400	
	Matildy	51				N. Car.
	Eliza	28				
	John	23				Tenn.
	Jane	22				
	Joseph	20				
	Sarah	18				
	Ellen	16				
	William	12				
	Isabella	10				
	Mary	8				
	Elizabeth McCLERGE	90				Va.
818	James BOYD	44	Farmer	2,000	1,400	Tenn.
	Abigail	40				
	Nathaniel	14				
	Mary	12				
	Ann	10				
	William	8				
	Sarah	5				
819	Anderson BOYD	43	Farmer	2,500	1,500	
	Elizabeth	40				
	James	13				
	Eliza	9				
	Hannah BOYD	81				So. Car.
	Sarah BOYD	52				Tenn.

	Name	Age	Occupation	Real	Pers.	Birthplace
820	Wiley CUNNINGHAM	32	Tenant		650	
	Sarah	31				

Page 119   7 July 1860

	Name	Age	Occupation	Real	Pers.	Birthplace
						Tenn.
	Ben	10				
	James	9				
	Oliver	8				
	John	5				
	Lavina	3				
	Ann	10/12				
821	Lewis FORESTER	45	Tenant		400	N. Car.
	Ann	47				Tenn.
	William	19				
	James	18				
	Mary	16				
	Marquies (m)	8				
	Joseph	5				
822	Polly HEADRICK	60	Tenant		100	
	Elizabeth HEADRICK	35	Help			
	Daniel HEADRICK (twins)	30	Labourer			
	Rebecca HEADRICK	30	Spinster			
823	Abram LAW	50	Tenant		50	N. Car.
	Sally	22				So. Car.
	Henry	6				Tenn.
	Jane	3				
824	John VINEYARD	71	Farmer	1,000	250	Va.
	Jane	67				
	Sarah VINEYARD	40				Tenn.
825	Thomas VINEYARD	36	Tenant		800	
	Ann	37				
	Eveline	13				
	Henry	11				
	John	10				
	Elizabeth	6				
	Nancy	4				
	Margarett	3				
	Sophronia	6/12				
826	George CUPP	55	Blacksmith	800	800	
	Elizabeth	49				
	Catharine	32				
	Elizabeth	23				
	Jacob CUPP	21	Labourer			
	Clarindy	19				
	Andrew	12				

Page 120   Not Dated

	Name	Age	Occupation	Real	Pers.	Birthplace
						Tenn.
	Lowsy (f)	10				
	William	9				
	Rachel	4				

District 13   P. O.: Ellajoy

	Name	Age	Occupation	Real	Pers.	Birthplace
827	Ann BRAKEBILL	58	Farmer	5,000	1,700	
	John BRAKEBILL	23			150	
	Sereptha	18				
	Selona	15				
828	David HOUSER	65	Tenant		75	N. Car.
	Catherine	65				Tenn.
829	Polly FRENCH	50	Farmer	400	300	
	Jane THOMAS	38				
	Rufus FRENCH	16				
830	Henry BRAKEBILL	42	Farmer	2,300	1,200	
	Anna	42				
	Washington	12				
	William	7				
	Andrew	2				
	Elvira DONELSON	23	Help			
831	James TOOPS	25	Tenant		300	
	Martha	24				
	Benjamin	7				
	Nancy	5				
832	George TOOPS	60	Farmer	1,000	1,200	
	Sarah TOOPS	60				Va.
	Lucindy TOOPS	22				Tenn.
	Campbell	20				
	Andrew	19				
	Harrey	7				
833	Jacob GORMON	47	Distiller		700	N. Car.
	Margarett	37				
	Gene (?) (m)	18				
	Martha	15----	(Deaf & dumb at school in Knoxville)			
	Patterson	13				
	Adaline	12				Tenn.
	Laura	11				
	Rachel	6				
	William	4				
	Florence	2				
	John	2/12				
834	Philip CUMINGS	55	Tenant		400	

Page 121   9 July 1860

	Elizabeth	52				Tenn.
	Susan Langlet	18				
	Jacob	16				
	Jackson	14				
	Philip CUMINGS Jr.	27	Tenant		75	
	Eliza	24				
	Susan	6				
	Philip	4				
	Mary	2				
	Jerry	3/12				

District 13   P. O.: Ellajoy
_____

	Name	Age	Occupation	Real	Pers.	Birthplace
835	Elizabeth HAFELY	54	Farmer	2,000	600	
	Andrew HAFELY	21				
	Charles	18				
836	Col A KIRKPATRICK	57	Farmer	13,800	11,200	
	John KIRKPATRICK	34				
	Malindy VANCE (mul)	43			400	
	William SISEMORE (mul)	19				
837	Saml PRIOR	50	Labourer		100	
	Anna	54				
	Margarett	13				
	Howard	11				
838	Henry RUSEY	38	Miller		600	N. Car.
	Polly	37				
	Margarett	14				
	James	12				Tenn.
	Elizabeth	10				
	Mary	8				
	William	6				N. Car.
	Haseltine (f)	1				Tenn.
839	Hugh L. HENRY	23	Farmer	2,500	2,400	
	Mary	35				
	Francisco	11				
	Margarett	10				
	Saml	8				
	Rebecca	6				
	Rachel	2				
	Arthur	6/12				
840	Nancy COULTER	52	Farmer	3,000	1,150	
	John COULTER	28				
	Ann	28				

Page 122   District 15   P. O.: Ellajoy   10 July 1860

	William	7				Tenn.
	Andrew	5				
	Susana	10/12				
	Andrew COULTER	16			1,200	
841	Mary HENRY (mul)	27				
	Mary (mul)	6				
	Ann (mul)	4				
	John (mul)	2				
842	William HENRY	27	Farmer	2,000	650	
	Catharine	27				
	James	5				
	Saml	3				
	Nancy	1				
	Martha	18				
843	Saml COWDEN	64	Wheel Right		50	N. Car.
	Nancy	50				Tenn.
	Nancy	20				

District 15   P. O.: Ellajoy

	Name	Age	Occupation	Real	Pers.	Birthplace
	Saml	18				
	Rebecca	14				
	George	12				
844	Marcus CHANDLER	25	Tenant		325	N. Car.
	Elizabeth	23				Tenn.
	Jane	2				
	Nancy	10/12				
845	Mary WATERS	78	Farmer	1,000	850	Penn.
	Adam WATERS	38				Tenn.
	Eliza LOWE	18				
846	Silas McGILL	32	Labourer		25	
	Temprance LOWE	35			175	
	John	19				
	Nancy	14				
	Richard	12				
	Lavater	10				
	Jefferson	4				
	Mary	1				
847	George WATERS	49	Tenant		700	
	Polly	48				
	Andrew Jackson	15				
	Susan	13				
	Jane	12				

Page 123   10 July 1860

	Name	Age	Occupation	Real	Pers.	Birthplace
	Francis (m)	10				Tenn.
	Newton	9				
	Lindy	8				
	Margarett	7				
	Pleasant	6				
848	Leo DAVIS (f)	70	Hooker		50	N. Car.
	Viney DAVIS	40				Tenn.
	Betsy OGLE	18				
	William	16				
	Tillman	12				
	Richard	10				
	John	3				
	Thomas	1				
849	James McFARLAN	25	Tenant		125	
	Margarett	25				
	William	6				
	Sarah	4				
	Calvin	1				
850	John TERENTON	66	Tenant		400	
	Elizabeth	44				
	John TAYLOR	24			300	
	John WATERS	11				
	Caley TERENTON	11				
	Burney (f)	8				

District 15   P. O.: Ellajoy

	Name	Age	Occupation	Real	Pers.	Birthplace
851	Isaack HUSKEY	34	Farmer	500	500	
	Delila	32				
	Mary	9				
	Louis	2				
	Stephen	5/12				
852	Abram HICKS	46	Tenant		100	
	Rachel	30				
	John	13				
	Rebecca	12				
	Elizabeth	10				
	Barckley	8				
	Houston (Twins)	7				
	Henry	7				
853	James WALKER	67	Farmer	10,000	2,800	
	Phebe	64				
	Ellen TAYLOR	24	Help			

Page 124   District 15   P. O.: Gamble's Store   10 July 1860

	Name	Age	Occupation	Real	Pers.	Birthplace
						Tenn.
	Houston WALKER	20				
	Phebe	13				
	John	10/12				
854	John WALKER	32	Tenant		1,000	
	Sally	33				
	Alexander	11				
	James	10				
	William	7				
	Phebe	4				
	Joseph	1				
855	Aaron BURNS	35	Tenant		800	
	Susan	34				
	Phebe	12				
	James	10				
	Elizabeth	8				
	John	6				
	Thomas	4				
	Martha	10/12				
856	Joseph WALKER	37	Tenant		500	
	Elizabeth	37				
	Phebe	17				
	Jane	16				
	Mary	14				
	James	10				
	Nancy	8				
	Sally	6				
	Betty	2				
	John	1/52				
857	Robt McGILL	73	Tenant (Pauper)		50	
	Betsey	50				
	Catharine	25				
	Tom	20				
	Ann	6				

	Name	Age	Occupation	Real	Pers.	Birthplace
	Pleasant	4				
	Isaack	2				
	Mary	1				
858	Taraton WEAR	38	Farmer	400	300	
	Richard KIBBLE	49	Farmer	5,000	.10,000	
	Elizabeth	47				
859	Spencer WALKER	27	Tenant		225	
Page 125						10 July 1860
	Vance	7				Tenn.
	William	5				
860	Sam WALKER	40	Farmer	1,000	300	
	Polly	37				
	Vance	14				
	Thomas	11				
	Rebecca	9				
861	Pleasant WALKER	20	Tenant			
	Fanny	21			210	
	Andrew Jackson	9/12				
	Sally FARR	7	Home			
862	William WALKER	33	Tenant		460	
	Nancy	25				
	Catharine	7				
	James	5				
	Betsy	3				
	Spencer	11/12				
863	Elija HATCHER	67	Farmer	2,500	1,500	
	Rebecca	58				
	Joseph	16				
	Manoah	14				
	Reuben HATCHER (mwy)	18	Tenant			
	Rebecca	22				
864	William HATCHER	35	Tenant		75	
	Lodicea	34				
	Jasper	13				
	Elija	12				
	Mary	10				
	John	8				
	Anderson	4				
	Thomas	1				
865	Richard HATCHER	27	Tenant		200	
	Lodicea	22				
866	James HATCHER	27	Tenant		200	
	Hannah	32				
	Elija	5				
	Rebecca	3				
	Saml	1				
867	Elija HATCHER	30	Tenant		350	
	Hannah	28				

District 15   P. O.: Gamble's Store

	Name	Age	Occupation	Real	Pers.	Birthplace
	Page 126					10 July 1860
	Thomas	8				Tenn.
	Mary	6				
868	Saml COWHORN	45	Farmer	10,000	1,750	
	Milly	35				
	William	15				
	Levi	13				
	Martha	12				
	John	11				
	Alexander	10				
	Daniel	7				
	Lydia	5				
	Robert	3				
	Rhoda	1				
869	Thomas RUSSELL	34	Farmer	300	300	
	Jane	30				
	Caroline	12				
	Catharine	9				
	Johnson	7				
	Sarah	5				
	William	2				
870	Wilson DAVIS	30	Tenant		225	
	Delila	25				
	Harrey	3				
	Catherine DAVIS	60				N. Car.
	Delila LAW	74				
871	George TAYLOR	19	Tenant		125	Tenn.
	Hannah	15				
872	Calvin McCONNEL	21	Tenant		50	
	Elizabeth	17				
	Jasper	2				
	Samuel	1				
	Jane McCONNEL	60	Help			
873	Elizabeth BLAIR	75	Farmer	2,500	300	Va.
	George BLAIR	45				Tenn.
	Anna	40				
	John	20				
	William	18				
	Elizabeth	15				
	Samuel	13				
	Abe Houston	10				
	Page 127					10 July 1860
	Alexander	6				Tenn.
	Adam	5				
	Elijer	2				
874	John BLAIR	50	Farmer	1,000	550	
	Isabel	50				
	Rebecca	13				
	Sally	9				

	Name	Age	Occupation	Real	Pers.	Birthplace
875	Sam LANE	46	Farmer	400	225	
	Isabel	40				
	Calvin LANE	21				
	Rebecca	18				
	Abram	17				
	James	14				
	Mary	11				
	Rachel	8				
	Richard	7				
	Marian (f)	5				
	Betty	4				
	Sabina	1				
876	Silvester LAW	53	Farmer	700	250	N. Car.
	Nancy	45				Tenn.
	Sarah LAW	19				
	Nancy	18				
	Abram	15				
	Selina	13				
	James	12				
	Rachel	10				
	Lena	5				
877	Benjamin DAVIS	54	Farmer	1,000	1,000	So. Car.
	Mahala	46				
	Philip	18				Tenn.
	Elizabeth	17				
	Malisser	13				
	James	10				
	Benjamin	8				
	Mahala	5				
878	George AMERINE	77	Farmer	20,000	12,500	Penn.
	Huldah	59				Tenn.
	John AMARINE	30			1,000	
	Hutsel AMERINE	22			200	

Page 128		District 15		P. O.: Tuckqualeechee		11 July 1860
						Tenn.
	Jonathan	13				
	Moses	10				
879	John ELLIS	25	Tenant		600	
	Paulina	23				
880	John CHRISTOPHER	45	Tenant		400	
	Peggy	45				
	Thomas	19				
	Sally	15				
	Alsop	13				
	Isaack	11				
	Irvin	8				
	Decatur	6				
	Abscence (Twins)	5				
	Milsence	5				

	Name	Age	Occupation	Real	Pers.	Birthplace
881	William LONG	45	Tenant		100	
	Malindy	46				
	William	9				
	Malindy	8				
	Martha	7				
	Mary	6				
882	Andrew McKINLY	30	Tenant		50	
	Betsy	35				
	Clementine	10				
	Parthenia (f)	8				
	John	6				
	Francis (f)	4				
883	John BASS	40	Tenant		250	N. Car.
	Betsy	40				
	Sarah	15				Ga.
	Pedrick (f)	13				
	Nancy	12				
	Jane	10				
	Cooney (m)	8				
	Eliza	6				Tenn.
	Alexand McClain	4				
884	Nicholas BREWER	54	Farmer	2,000	850	N. Car.
	Isabel	48				
	Andrew BREWER	25		1,000	125	
	William BREWER	22				
	John	19				

Page 129   11 July 1860

	Name	Age	Occupation	Real	Pers.	Birthplace
	George	17				Tenn.
	Doctor	14				
	Elizabeth	12				
	Catherine	10				
	Robert	8				
	Stephen	6				
	Joseph	4				
885	James BREWER	28	Tenant		150	
	Hetty	20				
	Elizabeth	7				
	Elija	6				
	Rebecca	5				
	Catherine	4				
	Nicholas	1				
886	Levi BREWER	30	Tenant		200	
	Elizabeth	30				
	William	10				
	Thomas	8				
	Nicholas	6				
887	Anderson WALKER	40	Tenant	150	50	
	Elizabeth	14				
	Tina	12				
	Jane	10				

	Name	Age	Occupation	Real	Pers.	Birthplace
888	Sam LANE Jr.	23	Tenant		25	
	Catherine	22				
	Elizabeth	3				
889	Reuben ROBISON	43	Tenant		75	N. Car.
	Malindy	25				
	Berter (m)	13				
	Young	12				Tenn.
	Elizabeth	9				
	Harriet	6				
	John	3				
890	Moses BOSS	80	Tenant		150	N. Car.
	Sally	81				
	Thomas BARKER	50	Tenant		100	
	Eliza	50				
	Henry	18				
	James	14				
	Sarah	12				

Page 130   11 July 1860

	Name	Age	Occupation	Real	Pers.	Birthplace
	Mary	8				Tenn.
	Margarett	5				
891	John WILBERN	50	Farmer	800	800	N. Car.
	Elizabeth	21				Tenn.
	Angeline	19				
	William	18				
	Housten	16				
	Andy	14				
	James	10				
892	Samuel ROWAN	40	Tenant		100	
	Catherine	40				
	Marcellas	15				
	Jane	14				
	Saml	12				
	George	10				
	James	8				
	Susan	6				
	Mary	4				
	Mandy	2				
	William	3/4				
893	Sam DAVIS	45	Tenant		600	N. Car.
	Fanny	48				Tenn.
	William DAVIS	23			100	
	Elizabeth	20				
	David	19				
	Martha	11				
	Sally	8				
894	Anna DAVIS	63	Tenant		600	N. Car.
	Margarett D.	60			150	
	Adam FURGESON	47	Tanner		75	
	Mary	40				Tenn.
	William	11				

	Name	Age	Occupation	Real	Pers.	Birthplace
	Richard	9				
	Edward	5				
	Mary	3				
	Caroline	6/12				
895	William DAVIS	30	Tenant			
	Catherine	25				
	James	3				
	Milly	6/12				

Page 131   11 July 1860

	Name	Age	Occupation	Real	Pers.	Birthplace
	Martin DAVIS	25	Tenant		50	Tenn.
	Eliza	20				
896	Martin TIPTON	30	Tenant	200	200	
	Margarett	25				
	George	4				
	Jonathan	6/12				
	Absolom HENLY	27			75	
897	John McCLAHAHAN	50	Farmer	800	400	
	Mary	47				
	Martha	15				
	Peter	12				
	Susan	10				
	John	8				
	Phebe	6				
	George	4				
898	Wash SNIDER	30	Tenant		600	
	Elizabeth	26				
	James	8				
	Mary	6				
	Lafayette	5				
	Martha	3				
	Baby (m)	6/12				
899	William FAN	62	Basket Maker		25	
	Mandy	37				
	Thomas	11				
	Powel	7				
	Patsy	1				
900	Pegg FRY (f)	65	Tenant		100	
	Margarett FRY	30				
	George FRY	29	(Pauper)			
	Alfred FRY	21				
	Lena	20				
	Tilum (m)	6				
	Buck	3				
901	Patterson DUNN	31	Farmer	1,000	950	
	Sarah	30				
	Levi	8				
	Elizabeth	5				
	Mary	3				
	Martha LAMBERT	15	Help			

District 15   P. O.: Tuckqualeechee

	Name	Age	Occupation	Real	Pers.	Birthplace
	Patrick SULIVAN	35			25	Ireland
	Lucy	28				Tenn.
	Jerry	6				
	John	4				
	Katy	11/12				
902	John HANLY	30	Tenant		500	
	Jane	25				
	Susan	3				
	George	2				
	Green FAN	20	Labourer			
903	Lewis DAVIS	40	Tenant		500	
	Rebecca	35				
	Eliza	18				
	Martha	16				
	Sarah	13				
	Mahala	11				
	Malindy	9				
	Matildy	7				
	William	5				
	Baby (f)	1				
904	Henry T. MITCHEL	55	Farmer	300	200	
	Mary	50				
	Prudence MITCHEL	21				
	Charlotte	18	(Weak mind & dumb)			
905	Peter SNIDER	84	Farmer			Va.
	Mary	84				Penn.
	George SNIDER	55	Farmer & Merchant	10,000	9,500	Tenn.
	Susan	45				
	Ellen	13				
	William	11				
	Dolly	9				
	Ann	6				
	John	3				
	Thomas HICKS	25	Labourer			
	Viney PORTER (bl)	55			150	
906	Daniel EMMITT	46	Farmer		1,500	
	Mary	44				
	James EMMITT (mwy)	21				
	Eliza	20				
	Louisa	19				

Page 133   11 July 1860

	Name	Age	Occupation	Real	Pers.	Birthplace
	Elizabeth	12				Tenn.
	Fredrick	10				
	Daniel	8				
	Gilbert	6				
907	Rhoda LAW	34	Tenant		800	
	John	13				
	Martha	11				
	Delila	9				
	Rufus	3				
	Nancy SMITH	30	Help			

	Name	Age	Occupation	Real	Pers.	Birthplace
908	William DAVIS	55	Farmer	3,000	1,650	N. Car.
	Sally	49				Tenn.
	Nancy DAVIS	28				
	Elizabeth DAVIS	26				
	Rebecca DAVIS	22				
	Thomas DAVIS	21				
	Philip	19				
	Anna	14				
	Eliza	12				
909	John BRICKEY	55	Farmer	500	500	
	Nancy	45				
	Elizabeth BRICKEY	24				
	Martha BRICKEY	20				
	Jane	18				
	Peter	16				
	Jackson	14				
	George	12				
	Wiley	10				
	Leander	8				
	Sophier	6				
910	Margaret BATEY	60				
	Elizabeth BRICKEY	52	Tenant	1,000	300	
911	William PETERSON	60	Blacksmith			
	Betsey	60				
	Emeline PETERSON	40				
	James PETERSON	33				
	Susan PETERSON	22				
	Rebecca	20				
	Margarett	4				
	William	1				

Page 134   11 July 1860

	Name	Age	Occupation	Real	Pers.	Birthplace
912	Reuben ALLEN	66	School teacher		50	Tenn.
	Polly	40				
913	Edward PEARCE	30	Labourer		50	
	Elizabeth	20				
	Martin	1				
914	David FOX	50	Tenant		50	So. Car.
	Mary	40				N. Car.
	James	16				Tenn.
	Melvin	13				
	Sarah	11				
	Daniel	9				
	Elizabeth	3				
	Caroline	1				
915	Amandy DUNN	40	Tenant		200	
	Catherine	18				
	William	14				
916	Henry MYERS	46	Farmer	1,500	700	
	Elizabeth	46				
	Ruth MYERS	23				

	Name	Age	Occupation	Real	Pers.	Birthplace
	Ann	18				
	William	14				
	Nathan	11				
	Hetty	9				
	Mary	7				
	Stephen	4				
	Milly	2				
917	Josiah JOHNSON	25	Tenant		150	
	Anna	32				
	Elizabeth	14				
	Louisa	7				
	Martha	2				
918	Ann CAMERON	70	Farmer	2,000	1,350	
	Marion (m)	32				
	Jane	24				
	George	6				
	William	3				
	John	1				
919	John HENRY	28	Tenant		75	
	Ann	25				
	Mary	2				

Page 135   11 July 1860

	Name	Age	Occupation	Real	Pers.	Birthplace
	William	10/12				Tenn.
920	Bluford BIRD	49	Farmer	3,000	950	
	Susan	46				
	Jacob BIRD	25			300	
	Jane BIRD	24				
	Polly BIRD	21				
	Margarett	19				
	James	16				
	Rhoda	14				
	Daniel	13				
	Rachel	10				
	William	8				
	Warren	5				
	Milly	3				
921	Ann HEADRICK	70	Farmer	2,000	400	
	John	18				
	Elizabeth HEADRICK	23	Help			
922	Nancy HEADRICK	29	Tenant			
	John	7				
	Ann	4				
	William	2				
923	Eli CAYLER	51	Farmer	1,500	1,000	
	Susan	50				
	George TAYLOR	25			400	
	William CAYLER	24			350	
	Catharine	18				
	John	12				
	Eli	10				
	Daniel	9				

District 15   P.O.: Tuckqualeechee

	Name	Age	Occupation	Real	Pers.	Birthplace
924	George CAYLER	45	Farmer	2,000	600	
	Ann	44				
	John	16				
	Martha	9				
925	Daniel CAYLER	25	Tenant		350	
	Ellen	26				
926	Jacob FRESHOUR	25	Farmer	1,000	450	
	Elizabeth	23				
	Samuel DAVIS	4	Indentured			
927	Stephen GIPSON	68	Farmer	1,000	1,550	N. Car.
	Polly	70				

Page 136   12 July 1860

	Name	Age	Occupation	Real	Pers.	Birthplace
	Stephen	19				Tenn.
	William	17				
	Dolly	9				
	Mary	6				
928	John GIPSON	26	Tenant		500	
	Katherine	26				N. Car.
	Delila	5				
	Sally	2				Tenn.
929	Samuel GIPSON	24	Tenant		200	
	Clementine	17				
	Stephen	2				
	Sally	6/12				
	Gaham GIPSON	33			75	
930	Bomen BIRD	69	Tenant		50	N. Car.
	Rachel	69				
	Mary	35	(Idiot)			Tenn.
	Biddy	10				
	James	2				
	John BIRD	28	Labourer		10	
931	John WALKER	44	Farmer	1,000	600	
	Mary	41				
	Elizabeth	19				
	Anna	16				
	Rhoda	14				
	John	12				
	Isaack	10				
	Mary	9				
	Henry	8				
	Sidney (f)	6				
	Peter	4				
	Jeptha (m)	1				
932	William WALKER	22			300	
	Nancy	19				
	George	2				
933	George KAYLOR	85	Farmer	1,600	1,200	Penn.
	Nancy	75				N. Car.
	John KAYLOR	48				Tenn.

| District 15 | | | | | P.O.: Tuckqualeechee | |

Name	Age	Occupation	Real	Pers.	Birthplace
Martha	40				
Braxton	16				
Eli	14				

Page 137 · 12 July 1860

Name	Age	Occupation	Real	Pers.	Birthplace
Noah	12				Tenn.
Perry	8				
934 Joseph WALKER	19	Tenant		75	
Ann	18				
935 Levi DUNN	46	Farmer	2,000	1,300	
Elizabeth	46				
Rhoda	16				
Giles	12				
Sidney	10				
Levi	6				
Nancy	2				
Hetty J. WALKER	20	Help			
936 William DUNN	25	Tenant		700	
Elizabeth	24				
Jonas	4				
Franky (f)	2				
Elizabeth	3/12				
937 Daniel DUNN	20	Tenant		500	
Betsy	21				
938 George FAN	30	Tenant		25	
Nancy	30				
Rachel	7				
James	5				
Martha	4				
Sarah	1				
939 Jonas JENKINS	33	Farmer	1,300	600	N. Car.
Susan	29				Tenn.
Mary	10/12				
940 William BRICKEY	25	Farmer	2,000	1,400	
Susan	22				
941 John STINSON	50	Tenant		700	
Ann	54				
Peter	17				
William	14				
John	12				
Ibby	11				
942 William WALKER	72	Farmer	2,000	900	
Elizabeth	67				Va.
Joseph WALKER	24			800	Tenn.
Sally	30				

Page 138 · 12 July 1860

Name	Age	Occupation	Real	Pers.	Birthplace
Mary	4				Tenn.
Susan	1/12				

	Name	Age	Occupation	Real	Pers.	Birthplace
943	William WALKER Jr.	30	Tenant		700	
	Barbary	27				
	Thomas	8				
	Mary	6				
	William	4				
	Levi	6/12				
944	Tyre WALKER	26	Tenant		700	
	Elizabeth	22				
	Phebe	6				
	Ann	4				
	Martha	1				
945	Fredrick EMITT	70	Farmer	4,000	650	
	Drucilla	69				Va.
	Andrew	34			650	Tenn.
	Sarah	19				
	John	1				
	Mary MYERS	15	Indentured			
	Mindy COPE	8				
946	John EMITT	41	Tenant		750	
	Nancy	36				
	Rhoda	15				
	Polly	13				
	Daniel	11				
	Perlina	9				
	Fredric	7				
	Susan	5				
	John	2				
947	Thomas HENRY	33	Tenant		100	
	Jane	36				
	Mariah Olizabeth (twins)	11				
	William Headrick (twins)	11				
	Levi	8				
	Edward	6				
	Tempe (f)	4				
	Rachel	2				
948	Richard BURNS	31	Farmer	2,000	2,500	
	Lydia	21				
	Johnson	8				

Page 139   12 July 1860

	Name	Age	Occupation	Real	Pers.	Birthplace
	Mary	6				Tenn.
	Aaron	4				
	James	1				
	Elizabeth BURNS	53				
949	Thomas WEAR	30	Miller		2,000	
	Mary	22				
	Richard	2				
950	William MYERS	45	Farmer	5,000	2,000	
	Mary	40				
	John	28				
	Jane	16				

District 15   P.O.: Tuckqualeechee

	Name	Age	Occupation	Real	Pers.	Birthplace
	Daniel	14				
	Sidney (f)	12				
	Nancy	10				
	Susan	5				
	Mary	2				
951	Abraham TIPTON	28	Farmer	600	200	
	Susan	27				
	William	3				
	Daniel	1				
	Jane MYERS	57				
952	John MYERS	33	Farmer	2,000	100	
	Mary	30				
	Susan	7				
	John	6				
	James	4				
	Elizabeth	2				
	Elizabeth TIPTON	33				
	Adaline	16				
953	Daniel MYERS	40	Farmer	1,500	500	
	Matildy	42				
	Jane	21				
	John	19				
	Saml	17				
	Elizabeth	15				
	Ann	13				
	Mary	11				
	William	9				
	Thomas	7				
	Daniel	5				

Page 140   12 July 1860

	Name	Age	Occupation	Real	Pers.	Birthplace
	Catherine	3				Tenn.
	Peter	1				
	Peggy	2	Home			
954	Mary WEBB (m)	74	Farmer	10,000	7,100	
	Fanny	50				Ga.
	Jane	18				Tenn.
	Robt	15				
	David	13				
	Perry TIPTON (mwy)	23		4,000	250	
	Emeline	17				
955	Mery WEBB (m)	30	Tenant			
	Betsy	30				
	Benjamin	16				
	David	14				
	Sarah	12				
	Merry (m)	10				
	Betsy	8				
	William	6				
	Caldona	4				
	Alfred	6/12				

District 15   P.O.: Tuckqualeechee

	Name	Age	Occupation	Real	Pers.	Birthplace
956	Lynch WEBB	29	Tenant			
	Sarah	34				
	Martha	18				
	John	16				
	Ann	13				
	Merry (m)	11				
	Rebecca	7				
	Dolly	5				
	Lynch	4				
957	Adam MAY	60	Tenant		50	Va.
	Betsy	37				Tenn.
958	Henry WEBB	24	Tenant			
	Polly	18				
	Rebecca PETERSON	17				
959	Geo FRESHOUR	55	Farmer	1,600	1,500	
	Alice	53				
	Thomas FRESHOUR	23			500	
	Elizabeth	16				
	William Wallace	13				
	Daniel	8				

Page 141   12 July 1860

	Name	Age	Occupation	Real	Pers.	Birthplace
960	Dan HEADRICK	45	Farmer	2,000	1,100	Tenn.
	Mary	40				
	Peter HEADRICK	21				
	Jackson	19				
	Elizabeth	16				
	William	14				
	James	12				
	Jacob	10				
	Patsey	8				
	Dolly	6				
	Sarah (Twins)	3				
	Emiline (Twins)	3				
961	Adam DOWEL	50	Tenant		200	N. Car.
	Rebecca	40				
	Lucy	17				
	Nancy	15				
	Elizabeth	13				
	Pink (f)	11				
	Cassander	5				
962	John McCAMPBELL	28	Miller & Farmer	800	40	Tenn.
	James McCAMPBELL	80			500	Va.
	Elizabeth Mc	55				Tenn.
	Mary McCAMPBELL	25				
	Isaack McCAMPBELL	32			150	
	Elizabeth	20				
	Minnis McCAMPBELL	22				
	Samuel	19				
	James	3				
	Robert McCAMPBELL	60	Miller & Herdsman			Va.

District 15   13 July 1860

	Name	Age	Occupation	Real	Pers.	Birthplace
963	Caleb FANCHER	29	Farmer	800	800	Tenn.
	Milly	30				
	Nancy	7				
	John	5				
	William	4				
964	William LAUSOM	28	Farmer	100	250	
	Elizabeth	24				
	William	1				
965	William CHAMBERS	30	Tenant		250	
	Laura	25				
	Andrew	3				
Page 142						13 July 1860
	Nancy	2				Tenn.
	James	6/12				
966	Mary LOSSON	54	Farmer	2,600	750	
	John	26				
	Jacob	21				
	Rhoda	19				
	Thomas	16				
967	Ezekiel BIRD	32	Tenant		125	N. Car.
	Nancy	32				Tenn.
	Rachel	9				
	William	7				
	Eleanor	3				
	George Washington	4				
	Isaack	3				
	John	1				
968	Joseph LAMBERT	51	Farmer	600	300	
	Sarah	32				
	Catherine	10				
	Robert PETERSON	23	Labourer			
969	John CHAMBERS	55	Farmer	2,500	1,000	
	Rhoda	50				
	John	19				
	Sidney (f)	16				
	Lydia	13				
	Benjamin	12				
	Andrew	9				
970	Sam McCHANAHAN	53	Tenant		300	
	Sarah	45				
	James	19				
	Rebecca	14				
	Mary	12				
	Martha	10				
	David	8				
	Sarah	5				
	Lena	3				

District 15   P.O: Tuckqualeechee

	Name	Age	Occupation	Real	Pers.	Birthplace
971	Elija OLIVER	30	Farmer	500	340	
	Mary	30				
	Martha	9				
	John	7				
	William	4				

Page 143   13 July 1860

	Mary	3/12				Tenn.
972	Col H. TIPTON	37	Farmer	5,000	3,700	
	Catherine	29				
	Patsey	11				
	Alice	9				
	Louisa	7				
	Mary	4				
	Susan	1				
	William TIPTON	19	Help			
	Thomas LAMBERT	10	"			
973	Phebe SCOTT	85	Farmer	2,000	650	
	Jane	42				
	Joseph SCOTT	23				
	Elizabeth	19				
	Mary	2				
	John JOHNSON	25			150	
	Ann	32				
	Elizabeth	12				
	Elzena (f)	7				
	Martha	2				
974	John FRAZIER	65	Tenant		250	
	Agnes	69				
	Peggy	43				
	John	21				
	George	14				
975	William RORIX	54	Farmer	300	1,800	
	Ann	44				
	Addison	21				
	Eveline	18				
	Sarah	16				
	William	14				
	Leon	12				
	Isaack	10				
	Louisa	8				
	John	6				
	Joseph Alexander	4				
	Charles	1				
976	George FEAREL	48	Farmer	2,000	1,450	
	Margarett	42				
	William FEAREL	23			50	

Page 144   District 16   P.O.: Cades Cove   13 July 1860

	Jane	21				Tenn.
	James	20				
	Althea	19				

District 16   P.O. Cades Cove

	Name	Age	Occupation	Real	Pers.	Birthplace
	Rachel	18				
	Lucy	16				
	Elizabeth	13				
	John	11				
	Louisa	8				
	George Washington	4				
	Caledonia	1				
977	James LEDBETTER	65	Bell Maker		50	N. Car.
	Martha	60				
	James	18				
	Francis (m)	16				
	Matthew	12				
978	Charles PEARSON (?)	55	Tenant	2,000	300	
	Martha	45				
	Theodore	15				
	Adaline	14				
	Adolphus	12				
	Benjamin	9				Tenn.
	Sidney (m)	8				
	Susan	6				
	Martha	2/12				
979	Henry McCOLLOUGH	40	Tenant		1,000	
980	Dewitt GHORMLY	34	Farmer	1,000	300	
	Jane	28				
	Sudina	9				
	Jasper	6				
	Hugh	4				
	John	2				
	Baby (f)	6/12				
	Mary McCALDEN	36				
	William ARMSTRONG	15	Home			
981	John COOPER	53	Tenant		300	N. Car.
	Margarett	40				
	Mary	10				Tenn.
	Sally	8				
	Swinton	7				
	Dorcas	5				
Page 145						13 July 1860
	Polly	2				Tenn.
982	Martha JOHNSON	53			150	
	Milly	18				
	John	16				
	Elizabeth	12				
	William	4				
983	Curren LEMON	40	Farmer	1,600	1,100	
	Elvira	36				N. Car.
	Leonidas	16				
	Columbus	13				Tenn.
	Samuel	12				

District 16   P. O.: Cades Cove

Name	Age	Occupation	Real	Pers.	Birthplace
Emeline	10				
Mary	8				
Thomas	6				
Parma (f)	4				
John	2				
984 Cyrus REAGEN	64	Farmer	3,000	1,400	
Elizabeth	56				
William REAGEN	21		250		
James	19				
Hetty	13				
985 James GREER	70	Miller		75	Va.
Rachel	60				
Catherine	18				Tenn.
986 Hannah GREER	55			25	
Hetty	10				
Emily	8				
Catherine	9/12				
987 John OLIVER	80	Farmer	500	500	N. Car.
Lurany	62				Tenn.
William	21			125	
Sarah TURMAN	31				
988 Lazrus OLIVER	33	Tenant		250	
Mary	36				
Martha DAVIS	6	Home			
William THOMAS	14	"			
Caroline McDANIEL	18	Help			
989 Walter GREGORY	26	Tenant		500	
Ruth	25				
James	6				

Page 146   13 July 1860

Name	Age	Occupation	Real	Pers.	Birthplace
Mary	3				Tenn.
Lurany	1				
990 Henry SHIELDS	40	Farmer	500	500	
Martha	38				
Mary	18				
George	16				
David	14				
Ruth	12				
Wit	10				
Jesse (m)	8				
Rebecca	6				
Martha	4				
991 Fredrick SHIELDS	48	Farmer	300	400	
Mary	46				
Martha	19				
Matildy	17				
Jonathan	16				
Elizabeth (Twins)	14				
Zachariah	14				

	Name	Age	Occupation	Real	Pers.	Birthplace
	Elijah	12				
	Mary (Twins)	10				
	Lazarus	10				
	Ruth	8				
	David	6				
	Margarett	4				
	William	2				..
992	Nathan SPARKS	33	Tenant		1,200	N. Car.
	Jane	25				
	James	7				
	Margarett	5				
	Lucy	1				
	John	6/12				
993	Charles FISHER	50	Tenant		600	
	Amanda	54				N. Car.
	Nancy	18				
	Isaack	15				
	Adaline	13				
	Benjamin	12				
994	John W. SPARKS (Mwy)	22			300	
	Mary	18				
995	John A. SPARKS (Mwy)	19	Tenant		400	Tenn.
	Mary	18				
996	George ROWAN	74	Farmer	3,000		Va.
	Susan	51				Tenn.
	Thomas CAMEL	24				
	Chasley Rowan	45	(Weak Mind)			N. Car.
997	William CAMEL	47	Farmer	500	350	Tenn.
	Sarah	33				
	Elija	6				
	Ephraim	1				
	Joel JOHNSON	30	Labourer			
998	Smith CAMEL	33	Tenant		20	
	Rebecca	36				N. Car.
	Joseph	7				Tenn.
	Nancy	5				
	Thomas	4				
999	Riley POWEL	47	Farmer	2,000	1,500	N. Car.
	Harriet	45				
	George	20				
	William	15				
	Mary	12				
	Matildy	10				
	Henry	5				Tenn.
	Leonidas	3				
1000	John TIPTON	50	Tenant		100	
	Naomi	27				
	Hampton	10				
	John	6				
	Isaack	4				
	Butler	1				

District 16   P.O.: Cades Cove

	Name	Age	Occupation	Real	Pers.	Birthplace
1001	Absolom ABBOTT	55	Tenant		50	
	Ann	50				
	Frank ABBOTT	25			60	
	Julia	15				
	Vitty (?) (m)					
1002	Peter CABLE	67	Farmer	1,200	1,225	N. Car.
	Lavina	34				Tenn.
1003	Daniel LOSSON	33	Farmer	2,000	1,600	
	Mary	33				
	Mary	8				

Page 148   13 July 1860

	Name	Age	Occupation	Real	Pers.	Birthplace
	Leaner (f)	7				Tenn.
	Elvira	5				
	Lydia	3				
	Daniel	4/12				
	James LANE	21				
1004	Archibald STEWARD	32	Tenant		300	
	Martha	29				
	Mary	8				
	Elizabeth	6				
	Joseph	4				
	Eliza	2				
1005	Martin STEWARD	55	Tenant		200	
	Mary	50				
	Susan	18				
	Angeline	16				
	Mary	15				
1006	Andrew GREER	36	Tenant		200	
	Catherine	31				
	Selah (f)	13				
	Betsy	10				
	Rachel	8				
	Susan	6				
	Jane	4				
	John	2				
1007	Danl D. FOUTE	59	Farmer	30,000	8,400	
	Dorcas	54				N. Car.
	Jane	27				Tenn.
	Boaz	20				
1008	Mathew WHITEHEAD	33	Tenant		600	
	Mary	30				
	Saml	10				
	Margarett	8				
	Wiley	6				
	Daniel	4				
	John	2				
1009	Lea DOWEL	23	Tenant		50	N. Car.
	Fanny	24				
	Alexander	2				Tenn.

District 16   P.O.: Cades Cove
_____

	Name	Age	Occupation	Real	Pers.	Birthplace
1010	James DOWEL	30	Tenant		100	N. Car.
	Vicey	30				

Page 149   13 July 1860

	Name	Age	Occupation	Real	Pers.	Birthplace
	Melville	9				N. Car.
	Katy	7				
	Ransome	3				
	Eli	7/12				Tenn.
1011	Adam DOWEL	40	Tenant		200	N. Car.
	Cynthia	40				
	Dorcas	20				
	Elizabeth	18				
	Fieldey (m)	17				
	Alfred	15				
	Pauline	10				
	Minerva	8				
	Nelson DOWEL	25	Labourer			
1012	Calvin POST	55	Fruit Grower	500		N. York
	Martha	40				Tenn.
	Calvin	13				
	Rebecca	10				
	Martha	8				
	Florence	6				
	Eugene (f)	4				
	William	6/12				
1013	James WILLIAMS	34	Tenant		300	
	Susan	42				
	William	11				
	Ransome	9				
	Albert	8				
	Lafayette	6				
	James	4				
	Barckley	2				
1014	William ANTHONY	25	Tenant		150	
	Mary	21				
	James	4				
	Baby (f)	1				
1015	John ANTHONY Jr.	30	Tenant		150	
	Elizabeth	37				
	William	7				
	John	5				
	Elgen (m)	3				
	Martha	1				
1016	John ANTHONY, Sr.	65	Farmer	700	400	So. Car.

Page 150   14 July 1860

	Name	Age	Occupation	Real	Pers.	Birthplace
	Isabel	60				So. Car.
	Lucy	27				Tenn.
	Armuta (f)	21				

District 16   P. O.: Cades Cove

	Name	Age	Occupation	Real	Pers.	Birthplace
1017	Thomas HERREN	24	Tenant		200	
	Maria	23				
	Jane	3				
	Mary	1				
1018	Robert BURCHFIELD	79	Farmer	1,500	500	N. Car.
	Mary	44				
	John	16				Tenn.
	Russel	14				
	Charles	13				
	Noah	11				
	Susan	7				
	Drury	5				
1019	Nathan BURCHFIELD	25	Tenant		150	N. Car.
	Elizabeth	25				Tenn.
	John	7				
	Elizabeth	5				
	Mandy	3				
	Robert	1				
1020	Berter BURCHFIELD	28			150	N. Car.
	Elizabeth	25				**Tenn.**
	Leah	7				
	Tennessee (f)	6				
	Josiah	4				
	Robert	2				
1021	Russel GREGORY	70	Farmer	2,000	1,000	N. Car.
	Susan	72				
	Elizabeth	36				
	Angeline	17				Tenn.
1022	Drury GREGORY	40	Tenant		900	N. Car.
	Martha	25				
	Houston	17				
	Lena	15				
	Ebenezer	14				
	William	7				
	John	5				
	Calvin	3				
	Jane	7/12				

Page 151   14 July 1860

	Name	Age	Occupation	Real	Pers.	Birthplace
1023	Bennet BURCHFIELD	33			300	Va.
	Arrena	31				N. Car.
	Margarett	13				
	Emeline	12				
	John	10				Tenn.
	Martin	8				
	Bennett	7				
	Jane	3				
1024	James HENRY	38	Farmer	4,500	3,500	
	Martha Jane	28				So. Car.
	William	7				
	Hetty	6				
	John	4				

The Town of Maryville, Blount County, Tennessee

      356 Whites

       17 Free Colored

     120 Slaves

The Town of Rockford, Blount County, Tennessee

     210 Whites

      27 Slaves

and has 1 N. S. Prst. Church

        1 Meth.   "

        2 Sabbath Schools

    Young Men's Christian Association

    and deserves a place on the map.

District 10   (Louisville)   P. O.: Louisville

	Name		Age	Occupation	Real	Pers.	Birthplace
Page 1							1 June 1860
1	Joseph	HART	42	Carpenter	500	200	Tenn.
	Elizabeth J.	"	37				"
	Wm. A.	"	16				"
	Emily E.	"	14				"
	Susan M.	"	11				"
	John C.	"	5				"
	Martha E.	"	6/12				"
2	Andrew J.	DUNN	31	Boatman		100	Tenn.
	Sarah E.	"	25				"
	Susan F.	"	9				"
	Samuel	"	7				"
	John M.	"	2				"
	No Name (f)	"	2/12				"
3	James W.	STONE	31	Painter		200	Tenn.
	Sarah J.	"	27				"
	Saml L.	"	10				"
	Laura A.	"	3				"
	Leonidas	"	4/12				"
4	James D.	TEMPLES	25	Tailor	250	150	Tenn.
	Victoria J.	"	21				"
	Isabora M.	"	2				"
	Nancy SMITH		26				N. C.
5	Jordan	Shaver	52	Shoe Maker	300		N. C.
	Sarah	"	52				"
	Melvin JERRAD (mul)		33				"
	Rhoda SHOEMAKER		18				"
6	Bingham	SMITH	75				N. C..
	Elizabeth	"	69				"
7	H. Talbot	COX	44	Merchant	42,000	62,000	Tenn.
	Lucy A.	"	38				"
	Nathaniel H.	"	10				"
	Eliza O.	"	8				"
	John C.	"	6				"
	Mary P.	"	4				"
	Sarah E.	"	3				"
	Charles C.	"	1				"
	Peter NANCE		86				Va.
	Wm. GOODLIN		21	Clerk			Tenn.
	Geo. M.	"	17				"
8	Nancy COX		55		700	3,000	Tenn.
Page 2			50				1 June 1860
9	G. Heart	CHAFFIN	50	Physician	2,500	3,000	N. C.
	Eliza L.	"	62				Va.
10	James M.	GEORGE	29	Waggon Maker	800	200	Tenn.
	Tilitha C.	"	21				"
	Sarah E.	"	3				"
	Adeline	"	1				"
	C. M.	GEORGE	25	Student			"
	David E.	LEBOW	21	Com. S. Teacher			"

	Name		Age	Occupation	Real	Pers.	Birthplace
11	Jackson L.	COX (mwy)	28	Merchant		2,000	Tenn.
	Rosatha C.	"	18				Conn.
12	Leonidas A.	GAMBLE	30	Dentist		600	Tenn.
	Eliza E.	"	30				
	Patton	"	5				
	William	"	3				
	Samuel	STEELE	66				Va.
13	Sally	COX (mul)	18				Ala.
	James D.	" (mul)	2/12				Tenn.
14	Robert	HOOD	41	Laborer		200	Tenn.
	Elianor	"	31				"
	Sarah I.	"	12				"
	Oney E. (f)	"	11				"
	Mary	"	9				"
	Aaron	"	8				"
	David	"	6				"
	Seth R.	"	5				"
	Hannah A.	"	6/12				"
15	Henry	BURIM	55	Farmer	7,500	17,500	Tenn.
	Nancy	"	42				"
	John	"	9				"
	Mark K.	"	7				"
	Henry	"	5				"
	Otey	" (m)	3				"
	Susan	"	11				"
	H. L. SINGLETON		18	Student			"
16	Ann	LAW	57	Instructress	800	500	England
	Ann	"	19				"
	Edmond	"	17				"
	Fanny	"	15				"
17	Thomas	BAINETT	80			300	Pa.
	Sarah	"	70				Tenn.

Page 3   1 June 1860

	Name		Age	Occupation	Real	Pers.	Birthplace
18	Abram	HEARTSILL	48	Master Mill Wright	2,500	3,000	Tenn.
	Napolian A.	"	18				"
	Ann B.	"	16				"
	T. Archimides	"	14				"
	John R.	"	12				"
	Jo. E. L.	" (m)	9				"
	Polly RANKIN		65				Pa.
19	Wyley	McDONALD	24	Plastier	300	250	Va.
	Alonira A.	"	23				Tenn.
	Emory A.	"	4				"
	Giraldus	"	2				"
	Heazia	CASTILL (f)	38				"
20	Marian	THOMAS (m)	28	Miller		200	Tenn.
	Malinda	"	24				"
	William A.	"	5				"
	James A.	"	3				"
	Mary F.	"	1				"

District 10   (Louisville)   P. O.: Louisville

	Name		Age	Occupation	Real	Pers.	Birthplace
21	James	NIPPER	35	Laborer		150	Tenn.
	Elizabeth	"	35				"
	Tabbitha	"	12				"
	Elizabeth	"	9				"
	Evaline	"	7				"
	Samuel	"	5				"
	Washington	"	6/12				"
22	James F.	FLANAGIN	33	Chair Wright		200	Va.
	Nancy	"	34				N. C.
	Mary A. E.	"	10				Tenn.
	John F.	"	9				"
	William J.	"	8				"
	Nancy J.	"	6				"
23	Samuel B.	HART	24	Com S. Teacher	500	200	Tenn.
	Almira J.	"	18				"
	Ann E. SINGLETON		11				"
24	Charles SPILLMAN		46	Blacksmith		150	Tenn.
	Foraba	"	45				N. C.
	Magnolia	"	17				Tenn.
	Samantha	"	15				"
	Marion C.	" (m)	13				"
	Eliza C.	"	7				"
25	Palmer	COX (bl)	50	Laborer	200	150	Tenn.

Page 4   1 June 1860

	Name		Age	Occupation	Real	Pers.	Birthplace
26	Martha	WHEELER	47			100	Tenn.
	William	"	18				"
	Sarah J.	"	16				"
	James M.	"	13				"
	Rufus	"	9				"
27	Wm. T.	HEARTSILL	37	Carpenter	500	400	Tenn.
	CAroline	"	34				"
	Mary A.	"	8				"
	Francis M.	" (m)	5				"
	Martha J.	"	1				"
	Paralee	"	7/12				"
28	Abner L.	HEARTSILL	32	Carpenter	600	500	Tenn.
	Mary M.	"	36				"
	Samuel A.	"	2				"
	L. C.	DELASHMIT	25	Meth. Minister		300	"
29	George	RAMSEY	35	Cooper	300	200	Ireland
	Mary	"	25				"
	William H.	"	4				N. Y.
	Joseph S.	"	11/12				Tenn.
	Joseph	FRAME	55	Dyer			Ireland
30	Washington S. DEARRING		24	Merchants Clerk		400	Tenn.
	Martha A.	"	18				"
	Cyntha A.	"	15				"
	Thomas L.	"	13				"

	District 10 (Louisville)					P.O.: Louisville

	Name		Age	Occupation	Real	Pers.	Birthplace
31	John	NORRIS	34	Cooper		150	Ireland
	Hannah	"	26				"
	William H.	"	8				N. Y.
	Mary J.	"	5				S. C.
	Josephine	"	4				"
32	Joseph A.	BROWN	37	Carriage Smith	800	1,000	Canada West
	Margaret J.	"	30				Tenn.
	William J.	"	13				Canada
	Charlotte H.	"	12				"
	John T.	"	9				"
	Martha C.	"	4				Tenn.
	Mary I.	"	2				"
	Jack	OWENS (mul)	21				"
33	George W.	CASTEEL	41	Laborer		200	Tenn.
	Eliza C.	"	25				"
	William E.	DALTINY	7				"

Page 5   1 June 1860

	Name		Age	Occupation	Real	Pers.	Birthplace
34	Josiah T.	LOVE	31	Physician	1,000	500	Tenn.
	Martha	"	35				"
	Cyrus R.	"	9				"
	Ambrose H.	"	3				"
	Emma	"	1				"
35	Andrew	TEDFORD (mul)	41	Carpenter	1,000	250	Tenn.
	Hannah	" (mul)	41				"
	Abigale	" (mul)	12				"
	Hannah R.	" (mul)	11				"
	Wilmonia P.	" (mul)	8				"
	Scott R.	WARREN (mul)	22	Porter			"
36	Samuel K.	FINLEY	30	Merchant	2,000	6,000	Tenn.
	Mary J.	"	28				"
	Narcissa E.	"	20				
	John P.	KENY	58	Mechanic	2,000		Va.
37	David	MEAD	48	Farmer	4,000	2,000	N. Y.
	Hannah T.	"	47				Conn.
	Homer G.	"	23	Merchant	2,000	500	
	Euphemia E.	"	18				
38	Elizabeth FRENCH		49			200	Tenn.
	Learner	"	19	Boatman			"
	Henry L.	"	12				"
							"
39	Samuel P.	Viles	28	Blacksmith		200	Tenn.
	Mary E.	"	26				"
	Lucy B.	"	5				"
	Robert P.	"	3				"
	Martha J.	"	1				"
40	James H.	HENRY	23	Stone Cutter		500	Tenn.
	Amanda C.	"	19				
	Gustavus A.	"	1				

District 10 (Louisville)   P.O.: Louisville

	Name		Age	Occupation	Real	Pers.	Birthplace
41	P. Green	FARR	30	Laborer		100	Tenn.
	Martha J.	"	21				"
	Nancy Y.	"	7/12				"
42	Benjamin F.	OWENS	39	Cabinet Maker	3,000	1,500	Tenn.
	Emily	"	39				"
	Mary E.	"	16				"
	Patrick H.	"	14				"
	Margaret E.	"	12				"
	Isaac F.	"	10				"
	Horace P.	"	8				"

Page 6   1 June 1860

	Name		Age	Occupation	Real	Pers.	Birthplace
	Sarah C.	OWENS	5				Tenn.
	No Name	" (f)	9/12				"
	Samuel	"	19	Cabinet Apprentice			"
	Elizabeth SOUTHERLAND		69				"
43	William R.	WILKERSON	33	Ferryman	300	200	N. C.
	Elizabeth J. C.	"	32				Tenn.
	Sarah A. D.	"	6				"
44	Joseph B.	CUMMINS	41	Sawyer	300	400	Tenn.
	Elizabeth	"	42				N. C.
	William F.	"	18	Laborer			Tenn.
	Mary J.	"	16				"
	Margaret A.	"	14				"
	John T.	"	13				"
	Charles B.	"	9				Ill.
	Sarah F.	"	6				Tenn.
45	Smith	KEELER	27	Shoe Maker	200	2,000	Conn.
	Mary R.	"	27				N.Y.
	Joseph C.	"	4				"
	William A.	"	2				"
	No Name	" (f)	1/12				Tenn.
	Mary HALLETT		60				N.Y.
	David H. HAIGHT		20	Shoe Maker			"
46	Smith	KEELER	38	Shoe Maker	700		Conn.
	Amanda	"	38				N.Y.
	William H.	"	13				Conn.
	Sarah J.	"	11				"
	Mary A.	"	9				"
	Fernando D.	"	5				"
	Estella	"	3				"
47	Martha	TALLENT	77			100	Md.
	Jesse	" (m)	36	Laborer			Tenn.
48	Elizabeth	SAFFELL	70		5,000	3,000	Tenn.
	Henry C.	"	56	Lawyer	10,000	1,500	"
49	John	TALLENT	49	Laborer		100	Tenn.
	Elizabeth	"	48				"
	Sarah J.	"	20				"
	Jonathan	"	19				"
	John P.	"	17				"

District 10 (Louisville)   P.O.: Louisville

Name		Age	Occupation	Real	Pers.	Birthplace
Sullens	"	14				"
Mary E.	"	13				"

Page 7   1 June 1860

Name		Age	Occupation	Real	Pers.	Birthplace
Jacob M.	TALLENT	11				Tenn.
Martha C.	"	9				"
Aaron P.	"	6				"
James H.	"	3				"
50 John	ROLLINS (bl)	86			75	Md.
Esther	" (bl)	76				"
Jennette G.	" (bl)	44				"
51 John	WILKINSON	37	Laborer		200	Va.
Sarah J. C.	"	39				"
Catharine	"	15				"
Francis V.	" (f)	9				"
John F.	"	3				"
52 S. H.	CLODFELTER	33	Blacksmith	300	300	Tenn.
Catharine	"	35				Va.
53 Charles P.	SAFFELL	34	Farmer	15,000	1,000	Tenn.
Marianne M.	"	26				
Samuel W.	"	9				
Nancy E.	"	7				
Octavia L.	"	5				
William G.	"	2				
Joseph SHAVERLY		25				Switzerland
54 John	SINGLETON	33	Physician	1,000	3,000	Tenn.
Elizabeth M.	"	29				"
Margaret R.	"	9				"
Mary M.	"	7				"
John Ross	"	3				"
Malvina J.	"	9/12				
55 John A.	PATTON	49	Merchant	600		Tenn.
John C.	LOVE	25	"	2,000	15,000	"
56 Horace	FOSTER	44	"	20,000	4,000	N. Y.
Elizabeth	"	37				Tenn.
Samuel	"	17				"
Frank D.	"	15				"
Mary L.	"	11				"
Martha	"	9				"
Alice	"	6				"
Ursula	"	3				"
Horace L.	"	1				"
57 James R. L.	ASKIN	41	Carpenter	300	200	S. Ca.
Mary I.	"	36				Tenn.

Page 8   1 June 1860

Name		Age	Occupation	Real	Pers.	Birthplace
Mary E.	ASKIN	17				Tenn.
Margaret A.	"	14				"
Charles	"	12				"
James R.	"	6				"

District 10   (Louisville)   P. O.: Louisville

	Name		Age	Occupation	Real	Pers.	Birthplace
	Alice G.	"	4				"
	Samuel G.	"	7/12				"
58	William	COLBURN	61	Farmer	3,000	2,000	Va.
	Catharine	"	47				Tenn.
	Samuel W.	"	28				"
	Elizabeth	"	25				"
	William B.	"	21				"
59	Leamer B.	SAFFELL	49	Farmer	4,500	1,000	Tenn.
	Sarah A.	"	43				"
	Ellen N.	"	18				"
	Isabella D.	"	15				"
	Samuel W.	"	13				"
	Lilly	"	3				"
	Anna L.	"	9/12				"
	Rufus K.	SCRUGGS	26	Meth. Min & Teacher			"
	George D.	GILBERT	16	Student		2,500	"
60	Elifus	HUNTER	57	Farmer		500	Tenn.
	Margaret	"	52				"
	Catharine	"	30				"
	Sarah J.	"	28				"
	Minda R.	"	12				"
	Nancy C.	"	7				"
61	Hiram	HEARTSILL	53	Teacher	2,000	500	Va.
	Amanda M. F.	"	46				Tenn.
	Willie B. W.	"	19	Merchant Clerk			"
	Isaac N.	"	17				"
	Mary R.	"	15				"
	Ann Eliza	"	13				"
	Matilda A. S.	"	10				"
	William A.	"	7				"
	Oliver M.	"	3				"
62	Willis	TALLY	23	Laborer		100	Tenn.
	Isabella	"	20				"
	Nancy E.	"	1				"
63	Unoccupied						
64	Unoccupied						

LOUISVILLE CONCLUDED

Page 9   2 June 1860

65	Arthur A.	KENNEDY	34	Miller	17,000	6,000	Tenn.
	Sarah C.	"	30				"
	Hetty H.	"	10				"
	John C.	"	7				"
	William	"	5				"
	Richard I.	"	2				"
	Kennedy	MALCOM	45				"
66	Hugh L.	SINGLETON	26	Farmer		200	Tenn.
	Josephine	"	26				"
	Walter K.	"	3				N. C.
	Mary	"	8/12				"

District 10   P. O.: Louisville

	Name		Age	Occupation	Real	Pers.	Birthplace
67	Joseph	SMITH	51	Carpenter		50	N. C.
	Martha	"	41				"
	John	"	11				Tenn.
	Mary	"	13				"
	Thomas	"	8				"
	Jesse	" (m)	7				"
	James	"	4				"
	Martha E.	"	7/12				"
68	Barton L.	WARREN	59	Farmer	14,000	18,000	Tenn.
	Evaline	"	51				"
	Marcus B.	"	21				"
	Octavia	"	17				"
	James	"	11				"
69	Isaac B	BYERLY	58	Farmer	6,000	500	S. C.
	Malinda	"	40				"
	Elizabeth M.	"	18				"
	Margaret C.	"	16				"
	James M.	"	14				"
	William J.	"	12				"
	Martin S.	"	7				"
	Jackson	FRENCH	28				"
70	Levi	ALLRIDGE	45	Farmer		300	Ga.
	Elizabeth	"	39				Tenn.
	John	"	18				"
	James	"	14				"
	George	"	12				"
	Sarah	"	7				"
71	Marcus L.	BYERLY	25	Farmer		500	Tenn.
	Catharine	"	24				N. C.

Page 10   2 June 1860

	Name		Age	Occupation	Real	Pers.	Birthplace
	Sarah E.	BYERLY	6/12				Tenn.
72	John F.	HENRY	52	Farmer	20,000	25,000	Tenn.
	Sarah M.	"	47				"
	James	"	61	Merchant		10,000	"
73	Williston M.	COX	44	Farmer	30,000	25,500	Tenn.
	Mary J.	"	34				"
	Isabella M.	"	12				"
	Eliza T.	"	10				"
	Caroline L.	"	8				"
	James K.	"	6				"
	Richard L.	"	4				"
	Fanny C.	"	2				"
74	John	KEY	38	Farmer	500	300	Tenn.
	Margaret	"	37				"
	Lewis C.	"	17				"
	Mary C.	"	15				"
	Martin R.	"	13				"
	Caldonia A.	"	11				"
	Elizabeth L.	"	9				"

District 10   P.O.: Louisville

	Name		Age	Occupation	Real	Pers.	Birthplace
	Dorcas S.	"	7				"
	William A.	"	5				"
	Hannah C.	"	2				"
75	Andrew	KEY	80	Farmer	1,600	200	Va.
	Rosanna	"	65				Pa.
76	Price	TERRY	44	Farmer		200	Tenn.
	Elizabeth	"	39				"
	William P.	"	18				"
	Willie C.	" (m)	16				"
	Hannah J.	"	14				"
	Louisa M.	"	12				"
	Jesse B.	"	10				"
	Sarah	"	8				"
	Mary	"	6				"
	Margaret R.	"	4				"
	Josiah	"	3				"
77	James L.	BONHAM	35	Farmer	300	300	Tenn.
	Elizabeth L	"	33				"
	Nancy O.	"	13				"
	Hugh M.	"	11	-			"
	Mary I.	"	9				"

Page 11   4 June 1860

	Name		Age	Occupation	Real	Pers.	Birthplace
	James B.	BONHAM	6				Tenn.
	Arizona B.	"	2				"
	Henry L.	"	2/12				"
	Benjamin	"	87				Va.
	Olive	"	82				Va.
78	William H.	ROGERS	47	Meth Minister	3,500	2,500	Tenn.
	Wm. H. Bascom		8				"
	Adrian R.	"	6				"
	Leon O.	"	3				"
79	Richard C.	GEORGE	23	Farmer		1,0C0	Tenn.
	Catharine	"	22				"
	Samuel L.	"	2				"
	Josiah R.	"	3/12				"
	Josiah R.	BADGETT	23	Laborer			"
	Wright	BOND	16	"			"
80	Grinsfield	TAYLOR	74	Farmer	6,000	6,000	Va.
	Susannah	"	72				Tenn.
	William R.	"	30				"
	Mary E.	"	23				"
81	William D.	GILLESPIE	32		500	1,000	Tenn.
	Mary I.	"	28				"
	Ann E.	"	5				"
	John M.	"	2				"
82	Alexander	GILLESPIE	57	Farmer	6,000	1,000	Tenn.
	Louisa E. B.	"	47				"
	Sarah J.	"	25				"
	Mary J. W.	"	23				"
	Glasgow S.	"	19				"

District 10　　　　　　　　　　　　　　　　　　　　　　　　　　P.O.: Louisville

	Name		Age	Occupation	Real	Pers.	Birthplace
83	Marian A.	ORR	26	Laborer		100	Tenn.
	Nancy P.	"	29				"
	Mary J.	"	3				"
	Nancy C.	"	6/12				"
84	Wayne	GIDIAN	47	Farmer		1,000	Tenn.
	Mary J.	"	43				"
	William	"	25				"
	Martha A.	"	23				"
	John B.	"	21				"
	Thomas F.	"	19				"
	James N.	"	15				"
	Hugh C.	"	11				"

Page 12　　　　　　　　　　　　　　　　　　　　　　　　　　　　　　4 June 1860

	Name		Age	Occupation	Real	Pers.	Birthplace
	Stepehn K.	GIDIAN	6				"
	Elias	"	2				"
85	George A.	McLIN	39	Farmer	9,500	5,000	Tenn.
	Amanda J.	"	25				"
	Charles E.	"	1				"
	Jas. H.	McCONNELL	21	Laborer			"
	Robt.	KIDD	21	"			"
	William	"	23	"			"
86	John D.	PARHAM	35			100	Tenn.
	Elizabeth A.	"	36				"
	Catharine J.	"	12				"
	Martha A.	"	10				"
	Nancy C.	"	9				"
	William A.	"	8				"
	Isabella I.	"	5				"
	Mary T.	"	2				"
87	Stephen K.	HITCH	30	Laborer		100	Tenn
	Charlotte A.	"	32				"
	Elias A.	"	10				"
	Mary E.	"	7				"
	James C.	"	5				"
	Nancy A.	"	2				"
	Emory A.	"	1/12				"
	Louisa J.	McCLURE	18	Domestic			"
88	John	STINNETT	65	Laborer		100	Tenn.
	Tempa	"	25				"
	Rebecca	"	23				"
	William	"	30				"
	Harriet	"	29				"
89	Madison	COX	46	Farmer	10,000	10,000	Tenn.
	Eliza	"	29				"
	John R.	"	1				"
	Susannah		78				Va.
	James M.	SINGLETON	24	Mer Clerk	6,300	3,000	Tenn.
	Harrison	"	20	Student			"
90	James	FERGUSON	53	Sawyer		200	Tenn.
	Isabella C.	"	34				"
	Esther A.	"	13				"
	Susannah J.	"	10				"
	Saphrona	"	8				"

Page 13　　　　　　　　　　　　　　　　　　　　　　　　　　　　　　4 June 1860

	Name		Age	Occupation	Real	Pers.	Birthplace
	Orpha C.	FERGUSON	6				Tenn.
	James M.	"	3				"
	Mary V.	"	2/12				"

	Name		Age	Occupation	Real	Pers.	Birthplace
91	James K.	COX	49	Farmer	2,000	2,500	Tenn.
	Sarah E.	"	26				"
	Susannah K.	"	1				"
92	Abram	DYER	60	Farmer		200	Tenn.
	Nancy	"	58				"
	Daniel R.	"	36		3,000	1,000	"
	Jacob	"	25				"
	Sarah A.	MERONEY	24				"
93	James	HERRON	21	Laborer		50	Tenn.
	Artimiram	"	18				"
94	Wm. W.	TAYLOR	44	Farmer	600	600	N. C.
	Elizabeth A.	"	39				Tenn.
	George W.	"	17				"
	Joseph A. T.	"	15				"
	Frances J.	" (f)	8				"
	Frances	" (f)	78				N. C.
95	David	TAYLOR	47	Farmer	5,000	3,000	Tenn.
	Arminta	"	43				"
	Marcus L.	"	19				"
	Elizabeth J.	"	17				"
	Lycurzas W.	"	15				"
	Calvin E.	"	13				"
	Robert S.	"	11				"
	Cornelia H.	"	9				"
	Grinsfield	"	7				"
	David A.	"	5				"
96	Fulton J.	WHITTENBURG	32	Laborer		100	Tenn.
	Nancy	"	35				"
	Magnolia A.	"	10				"
	Mary J. C.	"	6				"
	Nancy I.	'	3				"
	Martha	"	4	(Idiot)			"
	Flora A.	"	1/12				"
97	Henry	BROWN	26	Laborer		150	Baden
	Elizabeth W.	"	23				Tenn.
	Mary A.	"	1				"
	Emily	"	7/12				"

Page 14   4 June 1860

	Name		Age	Occupation	Real	Pers.	Birthplace
98	Francis A.	KIDD	33	Farmer	300	900	Tenn.
	Mary A.	"	34				"
	Samuel P.	"	1				"
99	Amb. C.	WHITTENBURG	38	Farmer	2,000	1,000	Tenn.
	Orpha	"	39				"
	Mary E.	"	11				"
	Wesley L.	" (twins)	9				"
	Ruth V.	"	9				"
	Joshua L. W.	"	5				"
	Donald L.	"	3				"
100	John	McCULLOUGH	56	Farmer	750	1,000	Tenn.
	Hannah H.	"	54				"
	Joshua J.	"	22	Laborer			"
	Mary A.	"	21				"
	Cyrus H.	"	14				"
101	Rhoda	PHELPS	48	Farmer		500	Tenn.
	William	"	30				"
	Sarah S.	"	24				"
	Richard D.	"	21				"
	John M.	"	18				"

	Name		Age	Occupation	Real	Pers.	Birthplace
	George H.	"	14				"
	Hiram T.	"	12				"
	Frances E.	" (f)	6				"
102	Barton	MILLICAN	39	Shoemaker		200	Tenn.
	Margaret	"	38				"
	Hugh F.	"	18	Laborer			"
	Martha A. E.	"	15				"
	Samuel H.	"	14				"
	Tilitha	"	13				"
	James M.	"	11				"
	Margaret J.	"	1				"
103	Jethro G.	HINTON	27	Farmer	1,000	500	Tenn.
	Mary A.	"	30				"
	James L.	"	7				"
	George W.	"	10/12				"
	Joshua L.	"	30	Distiller	1,000	50	"
	Amy	BAILY	59				"
104	John W.	BAILY	28	Farmer	1,000	200	Tenn.
	Elizabeth A.	"	20				"
	Sarah C.	"	7				"

Page 15   5 June 1860

	Name		Age	Occupation	Real	Pers.	Birthplace
	Aston T.	BAILY	5				Tenn.
	Erasmus H.	"	3				"
	Alexander C.	"	1/12				"
105	Martin	BONHAM	85			200	Va.
	Orpha	"	79				Md.
106	Abram N.	LAW	45	Farmer	1,600	800	Tenn.
	Sarah A.	"	45				Va.
	Stephen C.	"	25	Com S. Teacher			Tenn.
	Clementine O.	"	11				"
107	Wm. W.	ANDERSON	49	Farmer	2,500	1,000	Tenn.
	Euphemia J.	"	43				"
	Martha E.	"	21				"
	Robert M.	"	20				"
	Margaret O.	"	18				"
	Myriam A.	"	14				"
	William E.	"	9				"
	Mary E.	"	3				"
108	Wm. E.	TALBOTT	28	Farmer	1,600	1,000	Tenn.
	Eugenia H.	"	22				"
	Margaret L.	"	48				"
109	John	BROWN	54	Farmer	1,300	1,000	Tenn.
	Nancy	"	54				"
	Mary A.	"	19				"
	Nancy E.	"	16				"
	Dorothy C.	"	14				"
	William A.	"	10				"
	Catharine	HIX	79				Va.
	Dorothy	"	42				Tenn.

District 10   P.O.: Louisville

	Name		Age	Occupation	Real	Pers.	Birthplace
110	Alexander	LUNSFORD	30	Farmer		300	Tenn.
	Ann M.	"	36				"
	Mary W.	BROWN	50				"
111	Josiah	BALLENGER	30	Farmer		100	Tenn.
	Rebecca M.	"	26				"
	Dempsy A.	"	3				"
	William C.	"	2				"
	Dewitt C.	"	4/12				"
112	Andrew K.	BROOKS	26	Farmer		500	Tenn.
	Sarah	"	29				Pa.
	William T.	"	5				Tenn.
	Susan J.	"	4				"

Page 16   5 June 1860

	Name		Age	Occupation	Real	Pers.	Birthplace
	Margaret E.	BROOKS	4				Tenn.
	Fred A.	"	1				"
113	Jo. B.	BROWN	40	Farmer	1,400	500	Tenn.
	Aseneth	"	36				"
	Sarah E.	"	16				"
	George A.	"	14				"
	John C.	"	12				"
	Isaac N.	"	10				"
	Francis M.	" (m)	8				"
	Mary A.	"	6				"
	Harriet I.	"	4				"
	Benj. S.	"	2				"
	James B.	"	5/12				"
114	Isaac W.	BROWN	34	Farmer	800	500	Tenn.
	Eliza A.	"	36				"
	Margaret B.	"	8				"
	Amanda C.	"	6				"
	Nancy E.	"	1				"
	Peter	KEY	39	Farmer	600		"
115	Aaron	TALLENT	63	Farmer		400	Tenn.
	Bestena	"	57				N. C.
	James H.	"	30				Tenn.
	Mary E.	"	20				"
	John R.	"	18				"
	Jonathan S.	"	14				"
116	Terrance O.C.	DAVIS	35	Farmer	1,600	400	Tenn.
	Rebecca J.	"	22				"
	James A.	"	3				"
	William H.	"	2				"
	Minerva A.	"	2/12				"
	Nathan A.	BOATMAN	20	Laborer			"
117	Dempsey	BALLENGER	61	Farmer	450	200	N. C.
	Sarah	"	57				Va.
	Mary	"	38				Tenn.
	Ann	"	36				"
	Jane	"	24				"
	Martha	"	22				"

	Name		Age	Occupation	Real	Pers.	Birthplace
118	G. G.	O'CONNER	33	Farmer	1,500	400	Tenn.
	Elizabeth A.	"	33				"
	Martha E.	"	9				"

Page 17   5 June 1860

	Name		Age	Occupation	Real	Pers.	Birthplace
	Saml M.	O'CONNER	6				Tenn.
	William T.	"	3				"
	Mary J.	"	1				"
	No Name	" (f)	1/12				"
119	Margaret	DYER	63	(Pauper)			Tenn.
	Jane	"	38				"
	Elizabeth	"	22				"
120	Elizabeth	MYERS	58	Farmer	3,000	5,000	N. C.
	John C.	"	33				Tenn.
	Dorcas M.	"	25				"
	Philiph L.	"	23				"
121	Robert W.	HUTSELL	46	Farmer		200	Va.
	Sarah	"	37				"
	William	"	20				"
	Margaret A.	"	18				"
	John L.	"	16				"
	Benj F.	"	14				"
	Susannah L.	"	12				"
	Isabella	"	10				"
	Joseph M.	"	6				Tenn.
	Malinda H.	"	4				"
	Hester E.	"	2				"
	Mary V.	"	2/12				"
122	Jonas	JENKINS	46	Farmer	2,000	1,000	N. C.
	Ellen	"	47				Tenn.
	Jame A.	"	18				"
	Saml H.	"	16				"
	David T.	"	13				"
123	A. O.	GEORGE	56	Farmer		200	Tenn.
	Mary A.	"	33				"
124	George T.	DAVIS	21	Laborer		200	Tenn.
	Martha J.	"	17				"
125	John B.	COX	34	Farmer	6,000	7,000	Tenn.
	Ann M.	"	25				"
	Saml. T.	"	47				"
	Sarah A.	"	26				"
126	Cyrus S.	COX	28	Farmer		500	Tenn.
	Nancy E.	"	23				"
	Melville B.	"	5				"
	Mary J.	"	3				"

Page 18   6 June 1860

	Name		Age	Occupation	Real	Pers.	Birthplace
	Charles K.	COX	1				Tenn.
127	Edward	HUNT	28	Laborer		100	N. C.
	Margaret F.	"	29				Tenn.

District 10   P.O.: Louisville

	Name		Age	Occupation	Real	Pers.	Birthplace
	William R.	"	8				"
	Sarah E. N.	"	5				"
	James B.	"	3				"
	Martha A. B.	"	1				"
128	Sarah	BOATMAN	45			100	Tenn.
	Nathan	"	20				"
	Rachel T.	"	18				"
	William M.	"	16				"
129	William	CASLEY	77	Farmer	2,500	700	Va.
	Jane	"	74				Tenn.
	Martha J.	"	42				"
	Isabella F.	"	40				"
	Margaret E.	"	30				"
	Wm.	PRITCHARD	23				"
130	Edward	GOURLEY	77			300	S. C.
	Elizabeth	"	67				N. C.
131	John C.	GOURLEY	32	Farmer	10,000	10,000	Tenn.
	Lucy A.	"	28				"
	Marcellus E.	" (m)	10				"
	Avery	"	6				"
	Ransom	"	5				"
	Lenora	"	3				"
	Alexander	"	2				"
132	David T.	HAYNES	46	Brick Mason		300	Va.
	Malvina A.	"	36				Tenn.
	Amanda T.	"	11				"
	Caroline	"	4				"
	Marcella	" (f)	2				"
	Cassander	"	3/12				"
	Elizabeth	TIPTON	77				Va.
133	William	HENDERSON	54	Farmer	16,000	20,000	Tenn.
	Mary	"	52				"
	Mary	"	19				"
	Marcella	" (f)	17				"
	Albert G.	"	15				"
	Blanche	"	13				"
	Mathew R.	"	12				"

Page 19   6 June 1860

	Name		Age	Occupation	Real	Pers.	Birthplace
	Geo. W.	HENDERSON (twins)	10				Tenn.
	Wm. H.	"	10				"
134	Alexander	BROWN	28	Laborer		100	Tenn.
	Mary J.	"	24				
	Sarah D.	"	3				
	Eliza A.	"	6/12				
135	Isaac	WRIGHT	49	Farmer	4,000	1,500	Ky.
	Susan	"	48				S. C.
	John W.	"	18				Tenn.
	Jesse F.	" (m)	11				"
	Isaac T.	"	9				"

District 10   P.O.: Louisville

	Name		Age	Occupation	Real	Pers.	Birthplace
	Eliza A.	"	6				"
	Martha E.	"	3	(Idiot)			"
136	Benj.	LONGBOTTOM	29	Laborer		50	N. C.
	Elizabeth	"	33				Tenn.
	Saml. F.	"	10				"
	Sarah J.	"	9				Ala.
	John M.	"	7				Tenn.
	James A.	"	5				"
	Nancy I.	"	3				Mo.
	Mary E.	"	1				"
	Isabella C.	"	25				Tenn.
137	Ezekiel	WINCHESTER	52	Laborer		50	N. C.
	Charlotte	"	35				Tenn.
	John	"	17				"
	David	"	14				"
	James	"	12				"
	Mary	"	10				"
	Douglass	"	6				"
	Samuel	"	4				"
	Caroline N.	"	2				"
138	Andrew	FRENCH	44	Laborer		500	Tenn.
	Mary	"	34				"
	Sarah A.	"	16				"
	Elbert P.	"	14				"
	Wright	"	11				"
	Colonel M.	"	10				"
	John	"	6				"
	Marcus	"	3				"
	No Name	" (f)	1/12				"
Page 20							6 June 1860
139	Michael	HARVEY	50	Farmer	1,500	800	Tenn.
	Sarah	"	50				N. C.
	Clark	"	22	Laborer			Tenn.
	Sarah A. E.	"	17				"
140	Smith	TAILY	59			150	Va.
	Nancy	"	58				"
	Narcissa A.	"	19				Ga.
	Amanda C.	"	15				Tenn.
	Smith H.	"	14				"
141	Ann C.	JEFFRIES	64		1,000	800	Tenn.
	Martin L.	"	28				"
	James	"	24				"
	Nathaniel	"	22				"
	Marcus L.	"	26				"
	Jennetta	"	18				"
	James A.	BOYD	19	Laborer			"
142	Mary B.	PRATER	43		25,000	35,000	Tenn.
	Hugh W. B.	"	16				"
	George W.	"	13				"

District 10   P. O.: Louisville

	Name		Age	Occupation	Real	Pers.	Birthplace
143	James A.	PRATER (mwy)	22	Farmer		14,000	Tenn.
	Astre A.	"	17				"
144	Absalam	MATLOCK	40	Farmer	10,000	5,000	Tenn.
	Margaret J.	"	34				"
	Ann Polixini	"	14				"
	William R.	"	12				"
	Jane L.	"	10				"
	Avery L.	"	8				"
	Robert M.	"	6				"
	John R.	"	3				"
	Mary C.	"	1				"
	Saml	HOLTSINGER	21	Student			"
	Robert	PARK	26	"			"
	Elbert	STEPHENS	21	"			"
	Talbott	NAFF	15	"			"
	Wesley H.	DOAK	20	"			"
	Benj. F.	TAYLOR	16	"			"
145	Polly A.	DAVIS	28			50	Tenn.
	James P.	"	3				"
	Harvy B.A.	"	1				"
146	James A.	ROACH	32	Laborer		100	Ga.

Page 21   7 June 1860

	Name		Age	Occupation	Real	Pers.	Birthplace
	Martha J.	ROACH	21				Ga.
	Mary A. E.	"	3				Tenn.
	Isaac L.	"	1				"
147	James	BAKER	28	Farmer		1,100	Va.
	Elizabeth	"	33				Tenn.
	Henry	"	16				"
	Thomas	"	12				"
	John	"	5				"
	Margaret	"	3				"
	Nancy	"	1				"
	Wm.	MANN	22	Laborer			"
148	John	RUSSELL	64	Farmer	37,200	22,500	Tenn.
	John	McDADE	21	Laborer			"
	George	"	17	"			"
	John	TALLENT	17	"			"
149	George M.	BLAIR	18	Student			Tenn.
	Chas. C.	ALEXANDER	17	"			"
	James M.	BLAIR	16	"			"
	E. W.	JOHNSON	16	"			Ga.
150	John W.	BOYD	27	(Prof. Ment. & Mor. Sci.)	12,000	2,500	Tenn.
	Mahulda J.	"	25				"
	Alice E.	"	2				"
	John L.	"	1				"
	Benton	McCALEB	20	Student			"
151	Wm. A.	BLAIR	24	Prof Mathematics		2,500	Tenn.
	Sarah A.	"	28				"
	Jane	"	1				"

	Name		Age	Occupation	Real	Pers.	Birthplace
152	Solon	McCROSKEY	30	Cum. Pres. Minister	4,000	3,500	Tenn.
	Nancy J.	"	31				"
	Sarah G.	"	9				"
	John A.	"	7				"
	George G.	"	5				"
	Saphrona A.	"	3				"
	Saml N.	"	5/12				"
153	James G.	RUSSELL	36	Farmer	6,000	5,000	Tenn.
	Sarah C.	"	25				"
	Colvill M.	"	6				"
	Ann E.	"	2				"
	John F.	"	10/12				"
	Andrew	RUSSELL	24	Laborer		2,000	"

Page 22   7 June 1860

	Name		Age	Occupation	Real	Pers.	Birthplace
154	Elizabeth	HOOKS	50			100	N. C.
	Mary	"	27				Tenn.
	James L.	"	23				"
	Marcus L.	"	21				"
	Martha J.	"	19				"
	Joseph M.	"	17				"
	Theodore	"	8				
155	Thomas G.	TEFERTELLER	40	Farmer		300	Tenn.
	Terressa	"	40				"
	Marcellus M.	" (m)	20				"
	John W.	"	18				"
	Polly A.	"	16				"
	Rachel E.	"	15				"
	William L.	"	12				"
	Margaret A.	"	9				"
	James A.	"	7				"
	Henry Y.	"	6				"
	Cyrina C.	" (f)	4				"
	Thomas	"	2				"
	Martha L.	"	4/12				"
156	John	McGLOTHLIN	49	Farmer		400	Ireland
	Mary	"	50				Va.
	John Wm.	"	21				"
	Cornelius	"	15				"
	Wesley	"	14				"
	Charles R.	"	12				"
	Margaret C.	"	7				"
	Elizabeth	SHINALT	60				"
157	Patrick	VaNALEY	50	Gardner		100	Ireland
	Rachel	"	52				Va.
	James	"	18				"
	Charles A.	McCLURE	21				Tenn.
	Rebecca A.	RICHARDS	18				"
	Mary J.	PAUL	19				"

District 5   P.O.: Friendsville

	Name		Age	Occupation	Real	Pers.	Birthplace
Page 23							7 June 1860
158	William	JEFFRIES	32	Farmer			Tenn.
	Elizabeth	"	30				"
	Ann E.	"	2				"
	William T.	"	1				"
	Benjamin	"	20				"
159	George W.	DALTON	48	Laborer		100	Va.
	Mary	"	45				"
	Martha A.	"	16				Tenn.
	Polly E.	"	15				"
	Elizabeth	"	12				"
	Rebecca	"	9				"
	Jame T.	"	7				"
	William A.	"	5				"
	Millard F.	"	3				"
160	John	STRANGE	25	Laborer		100	Tenn.
	Milly	"	18				"
	William H.	"	4				"
	James H.	"	2				"
	Martha A.	"	1/12				"
161	John W.	TALIFERRO	32	Farmer	2,500	1,600	Tenn.
	Elizabeth J.	"	26				"
	Mary L.	"	3				"
	No Name	" (f)	1				"
	James	PELFRY	19	Laborer			"
	Hiram	CAMPBELL	39	Tabacconist			N. C.
	James	CLOUCH	21				Ky.
162	Parker	EDMONSON	59	Farmer	500	500	Va.
	Jane	"	54				Tenn.
	Benjamin	"	30				"
	Elizabeth A.	"	24				"
163	John	TALIAFERRO	62	Farmer	50,000	17,000	N. C.
	Martha	"	50				Tenn.
	James D.	"	21				"
	George	"	18				"
	Sarah E.	"	16				"
	Margaret J.	"	14				"
	Mary	"	12				"
164	Wm. Y.	WARREN	53	Farmer	5,000	3,000	Tenn.
	Mary	"	52				Va.
	Samuel V.	"	20				Tenn.
Page 24							8 July 1860
	Sarah A.	WARREN	18				Tenn.
	Henry E.	"	17				"
	Barton L.	"	14				"
	John F.	"	12				"
	Leonidas T.	"	10				"

District 5   P.O.: Friendsville

	Name		Age	Occupation	Real	Pers.	Birthplace
165	James	PRATER	39	Farmer	5,000	7,000	Tenn.
	Mary J.	"	35				"
	Annie C.	"	10				"
	Samuel L.	"	8				"
	Isabella J.	"	6				"
	Cordelia M.	"	2				"
166	Jacob	LINGENFELTER	62	Laborer		100	Va.
	Jane	"	61				Tenn.
	Mary J.	"	25				"
	Nancy A.	"	23				"
	Martha E.	"	20				"
	Thompson G.	"	17				"
	H. M.	LUNSFORD	9				"
	Phebe K. A.	KEY	6				"
167	F. M.	BOWERMAN	36	Farmer		7,000	Tenn.
	Joseph	KEY	51	Blacksmith			"
168	Alexander	ISH	70	Farmer	17,000	30,000	Tenn.
	Elizabeth S.	"	54				"
	Benjamin A.	"	18	Student			"
	John F. J.	"	16	"			"
	James F.	DANFORTH	14	"			Mo.
	Sarah A.	FROST	40				Tenn.
	James B.	LACKEY	31	Physician		10,000	Va.
169	Wesley N.	KEY	41	Farmer	3,180	250	Tenn.
	Catharine	"	26				"
	Mary A.	"	3				"
	David W.	"	2				"
170	David	KEY	66	Farmer		1,000	Tenn.
	Nancy	"	66				"
	Thomas K.	"	29				"
	Elizabeth	"	27				"
	John J.	"	21				"
171	Naomi	MILLS	55	Farmer	2,360	500	N. C.
	Huldah J.	"	15				Tenn.
	Saml B.	BRIGHT (mwy)	24	Farmer		100	"

Page 25   8 June 1860

	Julia	BRIGHT (mwy)	20				Tenn.
172	John	SMITH	44	Farmer		200	Tenn.
	Mary	"	45				"
	Daniel	"	15				"
	Priscilla E.	"	14				"
	Malinda	"	13				"
	Joel	"	11				"
	Nancy J.	"	7				"
	Sarah E.	"	5				"
	Mary M.	"	2				"
	Elizabeth	PERKYPYLE	26				"
	Isaac W.	"	1				"

1860 U. S. CENSUS OF BLOUNT COUNTY, TENNESSEE

	Name		Age	Occupation	Real	Pers.	Birthplace
173	Andrew J.	PHELPS	25	Farmer		200	N. C.
	Sarah J.	"	22				Tenn.
	Isaac W.	"	5				"
	Hugh H.	"	(2				"
	George T.	"	(2				"
	James S.	"	6/12				"
	Catharine N.	JOHNSON	15				"
174	Hiram	PHELPS	65	Farmer		300	N. C.
	Sarah	"	64				"
	Mildred	"	34				"
	Catharine	"	32				"
	John L.	"	28				"
	Ruffin	"	22				"
	Elizabeth L.	"	16				"
175	James P.	DAVIS	29	Farmer		200	Tenn.
175	Josiah	HICKMAN	23	Laborer		100	Tenn.
	Margaret J.	"	25				"
	Catharine A.	"	2				"
	John A.	"	7/12				"
177	Moriah	RICHARDS	52			100	Tenn.
178	Michael	BOWERMAN	70	Farmer	11,200	21,175	Pa.
	Isaac W.	"	28				Tenn.
	Ann B.	HUDSON	46			4,000	"
	Saml P.	"	20				"
	George W. BOWERMAN(mwy)		30				"
	Hester A.	"	20				"
179	P. M.	BOWERMAN	40	Farmer	3,000	3,000	Tenn.
	William	GAUT	26	Mill Wright			"

	Name		Age	Occupation	Real	Pers.	Birthplace
180	William	HICKMAN	27	Miller		100	Tenn.
	Mary C.	"	28				"
	John A. E.	"	2				"
	Mary C.	"	7/12				"
181	Uriah A.	ROUSER (mwy)	25	Mill Wright		400	Md.
	Mary E.	"	16				Tenn.
182	Jona.	ANDERSON	45	Laborer		100	Tenn.
	Sarah A.	"	43				
	Barthena E.	"	9				
	James C.	"	7				
	William T.	"	2				
183	Ralph	PIRKYPYLE	57	Laborer		100	Tenn.
	Rebecca H.	"	29				"
	Nancy M.	"	18				"
	Lucinda	"	16				"
	James B.	"	10				"
	John	"	7				"
	Michael	"	5				"
	Mary E.	"	3				"
	Rachel P.	"	1/12				"

District 5   P. O.: Friendsville

	Name		Age	Occupation	Real	Pers.	Birthplace
184	Elizabeth T.	WARD	26				"
	David W. A.	"	1				"
	Sarah A. E.	"	2/12				"
	Elizabeth	LYLE	75				N.C.
185	John E.	DAVIS	36	Farmer	800	400	Tenn.
	Sarah E.	"	22				
	Wm. E. A. A.	"	6				
	Peggy Ann	"	4				
	James C. P.	"	3				
	Samuel H.	"	1				
186	William E.	DAVIS	74	Farmer	800	500	S. C.
	Mahala	"	66				N. C.
	Mary A.	"	28				Tenn.
	Henry H.	"	18				"
	Sarah J.	"	5				"
187	William D.	BRIGHT	54			200	Tenn.
	Sarah	"	47				"
	Wm. N. M.	"	16				"
	Alex R.	"	15				"
	Nancy J.	"	13				"

Page 27   9 June 1860

	Name		Age	Occupation	Real	Pers.	Birthplace
	Martha C. A.J.J.	BRIGHT	8				Tenn.
188	Robert E.	JOHNSON	46	Farmer	2,000	1,500	Tenn.
	Jane	"	46				"
	Martha E.	"	24				"
	Margaret E.	"	22				"
	William H.	"	21				"
	Isabella M.	"	18				"
	Emmit A.	"	15				"
	Mary J.	"	11				"
	John R.	"	9				"
	Joseph M.	"	3				"
189	Catharine	JOHNSON	57			200	Tenn.
	Caroline S.	"	34				"
	Alexander J.	"	21				"
190	Wm. M.	STEELE	34	Farmer	2,500	400	Tenn.
	Sarah E.	"	33				"
	Cornelius W.	"	5				"
	Leander S.	"	4				"
	Mary E.	"	3				"
191	James	KEY	63	Farmer	1,400	1,000	Tenn.
	Ursula	"	63				"
	James	"	28			8,000	"
	Phebe K.	ELLIS	24				"
	Sarah E.	"	2				"
	Enoch	KEY	20				"

	Name		Age	Occupation	Real	Pers.	Birthplace
192	Nancy W.	STONE	47			200	Tenn.
	Samuel	"	24				"
	Wm. Z. T.	"	12				"
	Pinckney	"	8				"
	Martha E.	"	2				"
193	Rebecca	SPEARS	39			50	Tenn.
	Saml H.	"	16				"
	Nancy E.	"	12				"
	Elkana S.	"	10				"
	Robert T.	"	8				"
	William	"	3				"
194	Jesse	JAMES	65	Farmer	6,000	1,500	Va.
	Polly	"	62				Tenn.
	Benj. P.	"	21				
	Mary M.	"	11				

Page 28   9 June 1860

	Name		Age	Occupation	Real	Pers.	Birthplace
	Elizabeth	CASWELL	67				Va.
195	Henry	PESTERFIELD	72	(Pauper)			Pa.
	Eleanor	"	76	(")			N. C.
196	Rachel M.	CATON	26				N. C.
	Mary E.	"	7				Tenn.
	Martha E.	"	5				"
	William V.	"	1				"
	Margaret	TUCK	33				N. C.
197	George	PESTERFIELD	49	Laborer		150	Ohio
	Tempy	"	32				Tenn.
	Stephan A.	"	21				"
	A. Rebecca	"	18				"
	Melinda C.	"	13				"
	George D.	"	12				"
	James W.	"	9				"
	Malinda	"	6				"
	William R.	" (Twins)	3				"
	Henry L.	"	3				"
198	Alexander	BOYD	30	Shoe Maker		100	Tenn.
	Minerva J.	"	36				"
	Celia L.	"	11				"
	James C.	"	8				"
	William A.	"	5				"
	Richard C.	"	3				"
	Isaac G.	"	1				"
199	Robert	SPEARS	76	(Pauper)			N. C.
	Polly F.	"	74	(")			Va.
	Patsey	"	35	(")			N. C.
	John	"	25				Tenn.
	Lucy	" (mwy)	21				"
	Isabella E.	"	15				"
	William W.	"	10				"
200	Joseph	MISER	33	Farmer	3,500	1,000	Tenn.
	Mary	"	31				"

District 5   P.O.: Friendsville

	Name		Age	Occupation	Real	Pers.	Birthplace
	George H.	"	10				"
	Lucy A.	"	8				"
	Thomas A.	"	7				"
	Sarah J.	"	5				"
	John J.	KEY	23				"
	Jerusha	" (f)	20				"
Page 29							**11 June 1860**
201	William N.	PRICE	28	Farmer	1,000	1,000	Tenn.
	Martha J.	"	24				"
	George L.	"	3				"
	Columbus A.	"	1				"
202	George W.	PRICE	58	Laborer		200	Tenn.
	Mary W.	"	65				Va.
	Mary A.	"	25				Tenn.
	Henry H.	"	20				"
	Whitehill P.	"	16				"
203	Wm. M.	BRICKNELL	41	Farmer	3,000	1,350	S. C.
	Sarah	"	50				Tenn.
204	Samuel P.	MYERS	29	Blacksmith		350	Tenn.
	Mary	"	30				"
	Henry	"	3/12				"
205	Harvey B.	McCLURE	35	Laborer		350	Tenn.
	Mary	"	35				N. C.
	George W.	"	8				Tenn.
	Hiram F.	"	6				"
	John B.	"	2				"
206	John	MOORE	39	Farmer	2,500	1,000	N. C.
	Dealtha	"	39				Tenn.
	George	"	12				"
	Margaret	"	10				"
	Elizabeth	"	8				"
	Mary	"	9				"
	James	"	7				"
	Jennett	"	2				"
207	Francis	MISER	57	Farmer	5,000	3,000	Tenn.
	Isabella C.	"	26				"
	Benj. F.	"	24	Com. S. Teacher			"
	John H.	"	22				"
	Pleasant	"	21				"
	Lucretia F.	BICKNELL	5				"
208	George W.	MISER	36	Farmer		1,000	Tenn.
	Nancy J.	"	32				"
	Henry A.	"	6				"
	Sarah A.	"	5				"
	Hannah F.	"	1				"
209	Julia	ANDERSON	60			100	Tenn.
	Cyntha A.	"	20				"

District 5   P.O.: Friendsville

	Name		Age	Occupation	Real	Pers.	Birthplace
Page 30							11 June 1860
	George	ANDERSON	14				Tenn.
210	Wm. T.	JOHNSON	31	Saddler	6,000	3,000	Tenn.
	Caroline J.	"	26				"
	Barton W.	"	7				"
	Ellen A.	"	4				"
	Evaline L.	"	11/12				"
	Martha	AKRIDGE	17				"
211	Michael	KIPANE	29	Stone Cutter		150	Ireland
	Nancy	"	29				"
	Margaret	"	4				Va.
	Mary A.	"	1				Tenn.
212	H. L. W.	HACKNEY	39	Farmer	3,500	3,000	Tenn.
	Elizabeth H.	"	38				"
	Michael B.	"	12				"
	Malvin C.	KEY	18				"
	Elija J.	PRICHARD	26	(Idiot)			N. C.
213	John	STONE	61	Chair Maker	250	250	N. C.
	Isabella E.	"	47				Tenn.
	Baxter J.	"	9				"
	William J.	"	5				"
	Hugh M.	"	3				"
214	George	HACKNEY	47	Farmer	1,000	3,000	Tenn.
	Susan	"	35				"
	James T.	"	11				"
	Wm. H.	"	9				"
	Mary J.	"	8				"
	Sally A.	"	6				"
	Aaron T.	"	4				"
	Amanda C.	"	2				"
	No Name	" (f)	5/12				"
215	Thomas	HICKMAN	77			150	N. C.
	Polly	"	59				S. C.
	Elizabeth	"	26				Tenn.
216	Thomas M.	JONES	55	Farmer	2,500	2,000	Tenn.
	Jane	"	52				"
	Mary A.	"	22				"
	George W.	"	21				"
	Aaron H.	"	17				"
	Sarah E.	"	15				"
	Levi J.	"	12				"
Page 31							11 June 1860
217	David	MORGAN	37	Friends Minister	4,000	2,000	Tenn.
	Lucinda	"	36				"
	Emily	"	13				"
	Timanda	" (f)	12				"
	Allen	"	9				"
	Thompson	"	8				"
	Caroline	"	6				"

#	Name		Age	Occupation	Real	Pers.	Birthplace
218	Thomas	LEE (MWY)	25	Merchant	75	1,000	Tenn.
	Ruth B.	"	21				"
	Albert	JONES	22	Mer. Clerk			"
219	Francis	HACKNEY	43	Farmer	6,000	2,000	Tenn.
	Ann	"	44				"
	Lucinda J.	"	18				"
	Nancy E.	"	16				"
	Mary A.	"	14				"
	George T.	"	12				"
	Henry C.	"	10				"
	Aaron L.	"	24	Laborer	300		"
	Wm. A.	ROBINSON	25	Brick Mason		1,000	"
	Jeptha W.	MORGAN	24	Prof. Languages		300	"
	Aaron	JONES	18	Student	2,500	500	"
220	Lewis	WADE	55	Cabinet Maker		500	Va.
	Elizabeth	"	49				"
	Emaline P.	"	20				"
	Lewis D.	"	15				"
	Spiral T.	" (m)	13				"
	Malinda J.	"	12				"
	Mary A.	"	11				"
	Charles W. T.	"	1				Tenn.
221	James C.	BEALS	23	Miller	200	250	Tenn.
	Susannah	"	26				"
	Catherine E.	"	2				"
	James F.	"	22	Student			"
222	Aaron T.	HACKNEY	28				Tenn.
	Arabella E.	"	25				"
	James L.	"	5				"
	Gustavus A.	"	4				"
	Henry A.	"	1				"
	No Names	" (m)	2/12				"
	George W.	KEY	11				"

#	Name		Age	Occupation	Real	Pers.	Birthplace
223	David	HACKNEY (mwy)	29			150	Tenn.
	Hannah E.	"	28				"
	Hiram H.	"	7				"
	John W.	"	5				"
	Isaac P.	"	3				
224	John	HACKNEY	52	Farmer	7,000	2,000	Tenn.
	Phebe	"	53				"
	Aaron	"	24				"
	Levi	"	20				"
	Edith L.	"	18				"
	Saphrona P.	"	16				"
	John L.	"	13				"
225	Anderson T.	BEALS (mwy)	21	Laborer		3oo	Tenn.
	Elizabeth J.	"	22				"

District 5 (Friendsville)   P.O.: Friendsville

	Name		Age	Occupation	Real	Pers.	Birthplace
226	David	POLAND	27	Blacksmith	700	600	Tenn.
	Prudence C.	"	27				"
	William L.	"	11/12				"
227	James C.	ALLEN	53	Merchant	7,000	6,000	Tenn.
	Mary	"	18				
	Rebecca	"	14				
	Lucinda	"	11				
	David C.	"	7				
228	David	JONES	30	(Teacher Friends Inst.)	1,900	500	Tenn.
	Rebecca P.	"	31				"
	James M.	"	7				"
	Elisha R.	"	5				"
	Francis A.	" (m)	3				"
	Martha E.	"	1				"
	Rebecca	"	71				N.C.
	Nancy	"	26				Tenn.
229	Wm. Rufus	JONES	36	Waggon Maker	3,000	1,000	Tenn.
	Mary	"	36				"
	Sarah A.	"	12				"
	Susan J.	"	7				"
	Nancy T.	"	5				"
	Saml L.	"	1				"
	Jno H.	POLAND	25	Waggon Maker			"
	Benj. C.	BRIGHT	22	Laborer			"
230	Samuel L.	GREER (mwy)	26	Com. S. Teacher	600	250	Tenn.
	Elizabeth C.	"	21				"
Page 33							12 June 1860
231	Alexander	JONES	36	Farmer		250	Tenn.
	Mahala J.	"	30				"
	William C.	"	11				"
	Isaac M.	"	10				"
	John L.	"	7				"
	Lloyd B.	"	4				"
	Mary E.	"	2				"
	Sarah A.	"	4/12				"
232	Nancy	HENDERSON	47	Farmer	800	1,000	Va.
	Josiah	"	24				Tenn.
	George W.	"	20				"
	Lucinda E.	"	17				"
	Mary A.	"	14				"
	Edward	"	10				"
	Nancy C.	"	7				"
	Michael	"	3				"
233	Francis A.	JONES	53	Farmer	2,500	1,500	Tenn.
	Mary A.	"	30				"
	William L.	"	28				"
	Albert	" (Twins)	22				"
	Eliza	" (Twins)	22				"
	Lucretia	"	15				"
	Ransom P.	"	20				"
	Joseph M.	"	11		2,500	500	"

District 5   P.O.: Friendsville

	Name		Age	Occupation	Real	Pers.	Birthplace
234	Sarah	ELLIS	64	Farmer	2,000	1,000	N. C.
	Nancy J.	"	24				"
	Francis B.	" (m)	23				"
	Jacob	"	21				"
235	Richard T.	JONES	48	Waggon Maker	2,500	1,000	Tenn.
	Jane L.	"	46				N. C.
	Palmyra	" (f)	24				Tenn.
	Francis A.	" (m)	20				"
	Martha A.	"	17				"
	William R.	"	15				"
	Sarah J.	"	11				"
	Ephraim L.	"	9				"
	Richard T.	"	7				"
	David M.	"	5				"
236	Pleasant M.	JONES (mwy)	22	Waggon Maker			Tenn.
	Rebecca	"	22				"

Page 34   12 June 1860

	Name		Age	Occupation	Real	Pers.	Birthplace
	Benj. P.	JONES	10/12				Tenn.
237	Thomas	FERGUSON	61	Farmer	1,000	600	Tenn.
	Nancy	"	58				"
	Robert A.	"	27				"
	James M.	"	25				"
	Albert	"	22				"
	Texiana	" (f)	18				"
	Mary	"	16				"
238	David H.	MOORE	36	Farmer	1,000	600	Tenn.
	Rachel	"	28				Ill.
	Mary E.	"	6				Tenn.
	John R.	"	4				"
	Luna A.	" (m)	1				"
	Sarah A.	HAMMER	14				"
239	William	AKRIDGE	23	Farmer		300	Tenn.
	Rebecca	"	20				"
	Nathan	"	1				"
	Mary E.	"	3/12				"
	Hiram	SMITH	35	Laborer			N. C.
240	Elizabeth	AKRIDGE	48			250	S. C.
	Martha	"	15				Tenn.
	Hannah G.	"	14				"
	Judson	"	11				"
	Tennessee	" (f)	8				"
241	Mary	JONES	54	Farmer	1,000	600	Tenn.
	David M.	MILLS	22				"
	Lucinda	JONES	17				"
	Newton	"	15				"
242	Mary	SMITH	44	Farmer	5,000	2,000	Tenn.
	Gilbert	BLANKENSHIP	19				"
	Alexander	"	16				"
	Joseph	"	14				"

District 5   P.O.: Friendsville

	Name		Age	Occupation	Real	Pers.	Birthplace
	Mary J.	"	9				"
	Cicero	SMITH	1				"
243	William	HENDERSON	22	Farmer	2,200	500	Tenn.
	Lucinda E.	"	17				"
	John C.	"	5/12				"
244	Thomas	JONES	58	Cooper	500	150	Tenn.
	Lucreta	"	64				N. C.
245	John	DELANEY	34	Laborer		200	Tenn.

Page 35   12 June 1860

	Name		Age	Occupation	Real	Pers.	Birthplace
	Susan	DELANEY	22				Tenn.
	Elizabeth A.	"	8				"
	James H.	"	5				"
	Melvina A.	"	3				"
	Britta T.	" (f)	2				"
246	Robert	McGHEE	49	Laborer		100	Tenn.
	Delitah	"	46	(Blind)			N. C.
	John	"	19				Tenn.
	Charles	"	15				"
	Rachel	"	12				"
	Mahala	"	9				"
	Elizabeth A.	PHILIPS	24				"
	Ann E.	"	2				"
	Malinda	PETERSON	74				N. C.
247	James C.	SHARP	33	Farmer	1,140	500	Tenn.
	Sarah E.	"	33				"
	William T.	"	8				"
	Mary L.	"	6				"
	Alice P.	"	5				"
	Susannah E.	"	3				"
	Lilian G.	"	2				"
248	A. L.	SPARKS	26	Farmer		250	Tenn.
	Nancy J.	"	26				"
	Cordelia F.	"	6				"
	Rosabella	"	5				"
	Herbert T.	"	3				"
	Sam P.	"	1				"
249	William	MARSHAL	38	Farmer	500	1,000	Tenn.
	Rachel	"	35				"
250	Elisha B.	MOORE	27	Farmer	700	400	Tenn.
	Sarah R.	"	21				"
	James E.	"	2/12				"
251	Elisha	ANDERSON	32	Farmer	1,500	1,200	Tenn.
	Mary R.	"	39				"
	Wm. N.	"	17				"
	Hannah E.	"	14				"
	James B.	"	2				"
252	James	BARNS	28	Brick Mason		250	Tenn.
	Caroline E.	"	28				"
	William H.	"	10				"

	Name		Age	Occupation	Real	Pers.	Birthplace
Page 36							13 June 1860
	John C.	BARNS	7				Tenn.
	James R.	"	3				"
	Campbell L.	"	8/12				"
253	Samuel U	RANKIN	63	Farmer	1,000	1,000	Pa.
	Isabella G.	"	53				Tenn.
	Martha E.	"	18				"
	James H.	"	16				"
	Caladonia L.	"	7				"
254	James	MOORE	65	Farmer	2,500	2,000	N. C.
	Elizabeth	"	37				"
	Jane P.	"	34				Tenn.
	Wm. W.	KEY	16				"
255	And. J.	SMITH	45	Farmer	3,000	2,000	Tenn.
	Elizabeth C.	"	20				"
	Hester A.	"	19				"
	Martha C.	"	15				"
	Richard A.	"	13				"
	Nicholas L.	"	12				"
	Thomas N.	"	8				"
	Jackson L.	"	7				"
256	Michael	MISER	41	Farmer	3,000	3,000	Tenn.
	Susan	"	41				N. C.
	James H.	"	18				Tenn.
	Mary E.	"	17				"
	George M.D.	"	15				"
	Martha E.	"	12				"
	Phebe C.	"	9				"
	Pleasant P.	"	7				"
	Isthena A.	" (f)	5				"
257	Peter	KEY	50	Farmer	500	800	Tenn.
	Avis B.	"	53				"
	Columbus	"	18				"
	Ruth	"	15				"
	Wesley	"	12				"
258	Alvan R.	JAMES	41	Farmer	1,500	700	Tenn.
	Salina	"	26				"
	Mary E. V.	"	2/12				"
	Maston A.	KEY	6				"
259	David	HUMPHREYS	76				Tenn.
	Jane	"	43				
Page 37							13 June 1860
	Sarah A.	HUMPHREYS	14				Tenn.
	Mary A.	"	12				"
	Miranda J.	"	6				"
260	Jesse H.	JAMES	23	Farmer		500	Tenn.
	Ava J.	"	24				"
	Elizabeth C.	"	3				"

District 5   P.O.: Friendsville

	Name		Age	Occupation	Real	Pers.	Birthplace
	John C.	"	1				"
	Elizabeth	STONE	35				"
261	William	ANDERSON	30	Farmer		400	Tenn.
	Rachel D.	"	36				"
	Margaret D.	"	5				"
	David A.	"	3				"
262	Geo. W.	BRICKNELL	30	Farmer	1,200	1,500	Tenn.
	Sarah J.	"	31				"
	William P.	"	6				"
	Lucretia	"	4				"
	Frank L.	" (twins)	1				"
	Hannah L.	"	1				"
263	William	JONES	46	Farmer	2,500	1,500	Tenn.
	Ruth	"	46				"
	Joan	"	16				"
	Ignatius	"	14				"
	Ephraim G.	"	13				"
	Sarah	"	11				"
	Marthisa	"	6				"
	Sam Houston	"	2				"
264	Oscar	PRICHARD	25	Laborer		100	N. C.
	Martha J.	"	26				Tenn.
	Alford J.	"	7				"
	Julia A.	"	4				"
	Susan E.	"	3				"
	Hannah A.	"	4/12				"
265	Merada A.	LANE	34	Farmer	2,500	1,500	Tenn.
	Nancy	"	31				"
	Sarah E.	"	11				"
	James	"	8				"
	Seymour T.	"	4				"
	Laura A.	"	3				"
	Margaret V.	"	5/12				"
	Robert	ALLFORD	35	Laborer			"

Page 38   13 June 1860

266	Margaret	LANE	59	Farmer	3,000	1,000	Tenn.
	Sarah	"	36				"
	Rosannah	"	25				"
	William M.	"	23				"
	John T.	"	22				"
	Martha A.	"	20				"
	James P. H.	"	19				"
	Rachel G.	"	16				"
	Jack	CONARD (bl)	60				"
	Wyley	McADOO (mu)	30				"
267	John	ANDERSON	26	Laborer		200	Tenn.
	Eleanor J.	"	23				"
	George M.D.	"	11/12				"
268	Allen R.	DYER	33	Farmer	1,000	1,000	Tenn.
	Martha A.	"	32				"
	Feliz P.	"	11				"

	Name		Age	Occupation	Real	Pers.	Birthplace
	Lucretia F.	"	8				"
	Nancy J.	"	6				"
	James H.	"	3				"
	Sarah J.	"	1				"
	Mary	"	18				"
269	Felix A.	DYER	31	Farmer	1,500	800	Tenn.
	Sarah F.	"	29				"
270	Harvey T.	MAXWELL	32	Farmer	1,500	600	Tenn.
	Mary C.	"	29				"
	William N.	"	7				"
	Andrew B.	"	6				"
	James F.	"	4				"
	Margaret E.	"	1				"
271	Jonathan	LEE	41	Farmer	1,500	1,200	Tenn.
	Sarah	"	37				"
	Elizabeth	"	15				"
	John L.	"	13				"
	Ezra H.	"	11				"
	Grenville S.	"	8				"
	William F.	"	6				"
	Elihu M.	"	3				
272	Alexander VARNUM	(mul)	30	Farmer		250	N. C.
	Mary Ann	" (mul)	35				"

CLOSE OF 5th DISTRICT

	Name		Age	Occupation	Real	Pers.	Birthplace
273	Alexander	CROMWELL	74		50	100	N. C.
	Margaret	"	70				"
	Sarah	CALDWELL	32				Tenn.
274	Sarah	PASS	38	Farmer		500	N. C.
	Danl W.	PERKINS	17				Tenn.
	Levi M.	"	15				"
	Jonathan R.	"	13				"
	Susan J.	PASS	7				"
	Arminta C.	"	2				"
275	John	GREER	49	Farmer	3,000	3,000	Tenn.
	Annice	"	46				"
	Isabella J.	"	22				"
	Joseph M.	"	17				"
	James A.	"	14				"
	Nathaniel H.	"	10				"
	Annice E.	"	7				"
	Sarah K.	DAVIS	17				"
276	Joseph AMBURN (mwy)	"	18	Laborer		50	Tenn.
	Elizabeth J.	"	18				"
277	James	PHILIPS	41	Farmer	1,500	1,000	Tenn.
	Eliza	"	30				Va.
	Henry	"	11				Tenn.
	Moriah J.	"	10				"
	Anna B.	"	74				"

	Name		Age	Occupation	Real	Pers.	Birthplace
278	James B.	COHORN	30	Farmer	1,500	1,000	Tenn.
	Hetty A.	"	26				
	James H.	"	8				"
	Mary J.	"	7				"
	Gustavus A.	"	5				"
	Catherine L.	"	3				"
	Nancy C.	"	1				"
	Robert	McCULLY	22	Laborer			"
	Mira	BRACKET	11				"
279	John J.	GREER	21	Farmer	1,500	1,500	Tenn.
	Margaret J.	"	28				"
	Elizabeth C.	"	24				"
	Nancy C.	"	19				"
	Martha J.	"	17				"
280	Edmond	TUCKER	31	Laborer		500	Tenn.
	Louisa	"	25				"

Page 40   14 June 1860

	Name		Age	Occupation	Real	Pers.	Birthplace
	James W.	TUCKER	3				Tenn.
281	Sarah	BRACKET	43				Tenn.
	Mary J.	"	15				
	Nancy E.	"	13				"
	Elmira A.	"	12				"
	Arrena	" (f)	10				"
	Sarah M.	"	8				"
	Eliza A.	"	6				"
	James L.	"	5				"
	Annice J.	"	4				"
282	John P.	RHEA	28	Farmer	2,500	1,000	Tenn.
	Mary M.	"	27				"
	Sarah A.	"	3				"
	Joseph E.	"	2/12				"
	Mary	"	59				"
283	Lewis	JONES	29	Laborer		200	Tenn.
	Hannah	"	34				"
	John E.	"	13				"
	James B.	"	4				"
	Nancy E.	"	2				"
284	John	FULLER	45	Laborer		300	N. C.
	Ailsey	"	34				"
	Eliza J.	"	21				Tenn.
	Susan C.	"	19				"
	Elizabeth A.	"	14				"
	Melissa R.	"	11				"
	Saml W.	"	9				"
	John R.	"	7				"
	George W.	"	5				"
	Margaret A.	"	4				"
	Sarah L.	"	3				"
	Mary A.	"	1				"

	Name		Age	Occupation	Real	Pers.	Birthplace
285	George	DUNCAN	55	Farmer	2,500	3,000	Tenn.
	Nancy	"	55				"
	Louisa M.	"	23				"
	Richard J.	"	22				"
	Luana M.	"	6				"
	Reddin	RAINWATER	17				"
286	James	WILLIAMSON	33	Farmer	1,000	1,500	N. C.
	Melena	"	29				Tenn.

Page 41   14 June 1860

	Name		Age	Occupation	Real	Pers.	Birthplace
	Martha J.	WILLIAMSON	10				Tenn.
	John	"	7				"
	James H.	"	2				"
	Mary E.	"	1/12				"
287	John J.	HUDGEONS	41	Farmer	3,500	3,000	Mo.
	Eliza	"	42				Tenn.
	Hester A.	"	19				"
	Sarah M.	"	17				"
	Mary E.	"	14				"
	Melissa P.	"	5				"
	Elvira T.	"	2				"
	Selah	"	60				Va.
288	Nelson	CRISP	48	Laborer		400	N. C.
	Visa J.	"	25				Tenn.
	Ailsey	"	10				
	George	"	6				
	Caladonia	"	3				
	Sarah	"	1				
289	Hezekiah	KIZER	49	Farmer	3,000	2,000	N. C.
	Polly A.	"	46				"
	Joseph A.	"	21				Tenn.
	Sarah E.	"	18				"
	Mary J.	"	12				"
	Margaret L.	"	8				"
290	John W.	KIZER	23	Farmer	2,500	900	Tenn.
	Sarah A.	"	21				"
	Hezekiah R.	"	1				"
291	Ephraim H.	DUNLAP	72	Farmer	1,000	800	S. C.
	Sarah B.	"	69				N. C.
	Elizabeth A.	"	30				Tenn.
	Sarah E.	"	29				"
	Aaron T.	"	8				"
292	Ephraim H.	DUNLAP (mwy)	27	Laborer		350	Tenn.
	Anna	"	17				"
293	Edward	TUCK	72	Farmer		150	Va.
	Lucinda	"	71				"
	Robert	"	39				"
294	Henry	TUCK	33	Farmer	2,500	1,500	Va.
	Nancy	"	32				Tenn.
	Lucinda	"	13				"

District 4   P.O.: Unitia

	Name		Age	Occupation	Real	Pers.	Birthplace
Page 42							14 June 1860
	Martha E.	TUCK	11				Tenn.
	And. J.	"	7				"
	James M.	"	5				"
	Edward	"	3				"
	Henry	"	9/12				"
295	Isaac	ROBINSON	37	Farmer	1,000	600	Tenn.
	Polly	"	27				"
	James M.	"	14				"
	Mary J.	"	11				"
	Elizabeth T.	"	4				"
	Samuel D.	"	1				"
296	Wm.	McROY	34	Laborer		500	Tenn.
	Kissiah M.	"	39				N. C.
	Mary R.	"	9				Tenn.
	Nancy J.	"	7				"
	Sarah M.	"	5				"
	Mary	"	85				Va.
297	Isaack W.	COHORN	40	Farmer	10,000	4,000	Tenn.
	Mark K.	"	10				"
	Martha G.	"	8				"
	James K.	"	6				"
	Silas A.	"	4				"
298	Joseph	DUBERRY (mwy)	21	Farmer		500	Tenn.
	Martha J.	"					"
	Modenia A.	" (f)	4/12				"
299	David	TAYLOR	50	Farmer	2,500	1,500	N. C.
	Kissiah	"	33				Tenn.
	Sarah A.	"	20				"
	Ann E.	"	17				"
	Ellen B.	"	14				"
	Emily L.	" (twins)	10				"
	Henry	"	10				"
	Horace J.	"	9				"
	James V. R.	"	5				"
	Margaret J.	"	3				"
	Alpha	CARSON	26				"
	Margaret	EWING	74				Pa.
300	John	TRUE	27	Laborer		50	Tenn.
	Martha J.	"	26				"
	Daniel J.	"	8				"
Page 43							15 June 1860
	Joseph N.	TRUE	7				Tenn.
	John W.	"	5				"
	Nancy C.	"	2				"
	Margaret L.	"	4/12				"
301	James A.	ALEXANDER	54	Farmer	3,000	1,500	Tenn.
	Jane	"	48				"
	Hannah E.	"	22				"

District 4   P.O.: Unitia

	Name		Age	Occupation	Real	Pers.	Birthplace
	John D.	"	20				"
	Francis M.	"	18				"
	Margaret L.	"	16				"
	Clarinda C.	"	13				"
	James E.	"	10				"
	William J.	"	9				"
	Mary Ann	"	3				"
302	Edwin G.	JONES	28	Farmer	800	500	Tenn.
	Lucinda	"	24				"
	Martha J.	"	5				"
	Isaac	KING	50	Laborer		250	"
303	Margaret	FERGUSON	41		900	300	Tenn.
	Nancy J.	"	40				"
	Josiah	"	13				"
	Martha E.	"	8				"
304	James	BURNHAM	25	Laborer		200	Ky.
	Charity	"	25				Tenn.
	Sarah E.	"	4				"
	Harrieta	"	1				"
305	Joseph D.	ALEXANDER	31	Farmer	1,000	600	Tenn.
	Lucinda	"	33				"
	Margaret F.	"	9				"
	Amanda B.	"	7				"
	Robert H.	"	3				"
	James N.	" (twins)	3				"
	Hamilton W.	"	2/12				"
306	Holder R.	PARSONS	33	Farmer		500	Tenn.
	Penelope	"	26				"
	John C.	"	13				"
	Newton A.	"	5				"
	Daniel T.	"	1				"
307	Saml	ALEXANDER	49	Farmer	1,300	500	Tenn.
	Ann	"	43				"

Page 44   15 June 1860

	Name		Age	Occupation	Real	Pers.	Birthplace
	Mary E.	ALEXANDER	20				Tenn.
	William	"	15				"
	George W.	"	13				"
	James	"	11				"
308	Abram	MELSON	37	Laborer		50	Tenn.
	Rebecca	"	34				"
	Riley J.	"	3				"
	Larkin	"	6/12				"
309	Joseph	GIDER	54	Farmer	1,800	1,000	Va.
	Ann E.	"	36				"
	Sarah E.	"	13				Tenn.
	Lucinda	"	10				"
	James E.	"	8				"
	Joseph H.	"	4				"
	John W.	"	2				"
	No Name	" (m)	1				"

	Name		Age	Occupation	Real	Pers.	Birthplace
310	James M.	THOMPSON	30	Laborer		100	Tenn.
	Sarah J.	"	25				"
	Francis M.	" (m)	10				"
	Spencer	"	6				"
	Joseph H.	"	1				"
	Sarah F.	"	4				"
311	Saphen	KING	57	Farmer		500	Va.
	Winniford	"	53				Tenn.
	Lucinda	"	14				"
	Harriet	"	11				"
	Francis	" (f)	6				"
312	John W.	HARMON	35	Farmer		350	Tenn.
	Margaret E.	"	32				"
	Nancy E.	"	12				"
	James	"	10				"
	Arminta	"	8				"
	Dialtha J.	"	6				"
	Simeon H.	"	4				"
	Juletta M.	"	2				"
313	Wm. M.	CHAPMAN	35	Farmer		500	Tenn.
	Susannah	"	43				"
	Hester J.	"	14				"
	Rebecca M.	"	12				"
	Harvey C.	"	8				"

Page 45   15 June 1860

	Name		Age	Occupation	Real	Pers.	Birthplace
314	Isabel M,	HUMPHREYS	45	Farmer	6,000	2,000	Tenn.
	William C.	"	22				"
	Samuel A.	"	20				"
	James M.	"	17				"
315	Lucineda	ONEAL	25			50	Tenn.
	James M.	"	12				"
	Minerva J.	"	10				"
	Marvin	"	6				"
	William H.	"	1				"
316	Samuel H.	BEALS	22	Farmer		1,000	Tenn.
	Sarah	"	22				"
	Albert L.	MAUPIN	23	Student			"
317	Joel	CRISP	53	Farmer		500	N. C.
	Adaline	"	27				Tenn.
	Caroline	"	2				"
	Sarah J.	"	8/12				"
318	Benjamin	DOCKERY	45	Laborer		100	N. C.
	Nancy	" (mul)	43				"
	Elizabeth	" (mul)	18				Tenn.
	Wilburn	" (mul)	13				"
	Emaline D.	" (mul)	9				"
	Peggy J.	" (mul)	4				"
319	William	DOCKERY (mul)	17				Tenn.
	Peggy	"	21				"
	Sarah E.	" (mul)	4/12				"

District 4   P.O.: Unitia

	Name		Age	Occupation	Real	Pers.	Birthplace
320	Margaret	HUMPHREYS	61	Farmer	1,000	500	Pa.
	Aaron T.	DUNLAP	36				Tenn.
	Louisa E.	"	28				"
	Isabella C.	"	2				"
	Alice G.	"	2/12				"
	Jane	PRIVETT	17	Dom.			"
321	Jno. P.	CHAPMAN	62	Farmer		1,000	Va.
	Sarah H.	"	58				Tenn.
	Elizabeth J.	"	28				"
	Robert E.	"	23				"
	Eliza E.	"	21				"
	Pleasant M.	"	19				"
	Sarah L.	"	16				"
	Bonaparte	"	9				"
	Thomas	"	3				"

Page 46   15 June 1860

	Name		Age	Occupation	Real	Pers.	Birthplace
322	Saml	HUMPHREYS	45	Farmer	1,000	1,000	Tenn.
	Mary B.	"	45				"
	Mary J. A.	"	4				"
323	Thomas S.	KEITH	27	Laborer		500	N. C.
	Louisa	"	28				"
	William A.	"	3				"
	Mary E.	"	1				Tenn.
324	Amzi	KIZER	26	Farmer		600	Tenn.
	Phebe J.	"	21				"
	Melissa P.	"	3				"
	John J.	"	1				"
325	Jane	TUCK	57	Farmer	1,000	600	Va.
	David	"	21				Tenn.
	Moses	"	18				"
	Mary	"	26				"
	Susan	"	55				Va.
326	Hezekiah	TUCK	31			400	Tenn.
	Margaret	"	25				"
	Mary J.	"	6				"
	Sarah E.	"	4				"
	John T.	"	2/12				"
327	Alford C.	McINTURF	26	Miller		500	Tenn.
	Mary	"	21				"
	Perssia E.	"	5				"
	William R.	"	4				"
	James I.	"	3				"
	No Name	" (m)	2/12				"
328	James	HUNT	48	Farmer	4,000	2,000	N. C.
	Edith	"	33				Tenn.
	William	"	11				"
	Samuel	"	9				"
	James	"	5				"
	Amos	"	3				"
	Alexander	"	1				"

District 4   P.O.: Unitia

	Name		Age	Occupation	Real	Pers.	Birthplace
	Erskine	"	3/12				"
	Nancy J.	CALDWELL	12				"
329	George	HUNT	22	Farmer		500	Tenn.
	Sarah	"	25				"
	Nancy J.	"	1				"
	Columbus B.	"	6/12				"

Page 47   16 June 1860

330	Andrew	ROSE	40	Farmer	600	500	S. C.
	Susannah	"	40				Va.
	Elizabeth J.	"	18				Tenn.
	Luvica	"	13				"
	Dialtha	"	11				"
	Pressia A.	"	6				"
	Edith S.	"	3				"
	William	CALDWELL	8				"
331	Clementine	TUCK	37			50	Ga.
	Nancy A.	"	17				Tenn.
	Grigory	"	1/12				"
332	Enoch	LEACH	48	Hatter		100	Md.
	Elizabeth A.	"	18				Tenn.
	Sarah J.	"	17				"
	Nancy H.	" (twins)	15				"
	James C.		15				"
	Susan	"	14				"
	Mary E.	"	12				"
	Martha	"	11				"
	Josiah	"	10				"
	John W.	"	9				"
	Thomas E.	"	7				"
	Eliza C.	"	6				"
	Rosannah	"	4				"
	Amanda F.	"	2				"
333	Thomas	PARSON	52	Farmer		400	N. C.
	Mary	"	50				Tenn.
	John P.	"	23	Blacksmith			"
	William H.	"	21				"
	David	"	19				"
	Ralph	"	17				"
	Silas	"	14				"
	Francis M.	" (m)	12				"
	Sarah E.	"	6				"
334	Elizabeth	DUNLAP	45			300	Tenn.
	Francis A.	" (m)	19				"
	William R.	"	16				"
	James K.	"	9				"
	David H.	"	6				"
	Sarah J.	"	4				"

Page 48   16 June 1860

	Uritha M.	DUNLAP	1				Tenn.

District 4   P.O.: Unitia

	Name		Age	Occupation	Real	Pers.	Birthplace
335	Mary	GREER	50	Farmer	2,500	2,500	N. C.
	Sarah	"	45				"
	Martha	"	43				"
	Kessiah T.	KING	19				Tenn.
336	Lewis	WILLIAMSON	30	Farmer	1,500	1,200	Tenn.
	Nancy A.	"	32				"
	Hester A.	"	6				"
	Eliza J.	"	4				"
	Isaac A.	"	1				"
	Nancy W.	"	52				"
337	Lockey	JOHNSON (f)	35			200	Tenn.
	Nancy C.	"	15				"
	William P.	"	12				"
	Mary L.	"	10				"
	Asydia A.	" (f)	7				"
	Elizabeth C.	"	5				"
	Lockey E.	" (f)	3				"
	Robert G.	"	1				"
338	Joseph	JONES	40	Farmer	1,600	1,500	Tenn.
	Joana	"	38				"
	Jane	ENSLEY	53				"
	Wm. H.	"	20				"
339	Levi C.	PERKINS	73	Miller	5,000	1,000	Va.
	Mary A.	"	71				"
	Kessiah	"	35				Tenn.
340	Levi	PERKINS	32	Farmer		600	Tenn.
	Margaret A.	"	29				"
	Margaret E.	"	9				"
	Andrew	"	8				"
	James L.	"	5				"
	David L.	"	3				"
	William R.	"	1				"
	Sarah E.	FERGUSON	18				"
341	Gertrude	JONES	39	Farmer	3,600	2,000	Tenn.
	Loranzo B	"	20				"
	Elisha D.	"	18				"
	Huldah J.	"	16				"
	Joanna N.	"	13				"
	Ruth D.	"	10				"
Page 49							16 June 1860
	Henry T.	JONES	7				Tenn.
	Joseph H.	"	4				"
342	Ephraim W.	LEE	24	Farmer		800	Tenn.
	Sarah E. T.	"	21				"
	David	SMITH	14				"
343	Samuel	DONALDSON	44	Farmer	3,000	2,000	Tenn.
	Rachel A.	"	39				"
	Mary E.	"	14				"
	Nancy E.	"	12				"

	Name		Age	Occupation	Real	Pers.	Birthplace
	Frieling Suysen "		9				"
	James H.	"	6				"
	John W.	"	4				"
	Buenavista	" (f)	3/12				"
344	Saml. A. J.	BROOKS	23	Laborer		100	Tenn.
	Amanda J.	"	21				"
	James H.	"	4				"
	Ralph	"	3				"
	Delancy B.	"	1				"
345	Heartsill	BORING	44	Farmer	3,000	2,700	Tenn.
	Emaline	"	37				"
	Joseph A.	"	16				"
	Mary M.	"	14				"
	Eliza J.	"	12				"
	Hester A.	"	8				"
	Tennessee	" (f)	5				"
	James R.	"	3				"
	Blount H.	"	1				"
346	Wm. J.	HACKNEY	46	Farmer	500	500	Tenn.
	Martha L.	"	44				N. C.
	Susan J.	"	20				Tenn.
	Francis N.	" (m)	17				"
	Aaron T.	"	13				"
	Martha A.	"	12				"
347	Nancy	TUCKER	62			200	Va.
	Richard	"	27				Tenn.
348	Ephraim	LEE	80	Hatter	4,000	1,700	N. C.
	Ephraim	LEE	31	Farmer			Tenn.
	Elizabeth	"	29				"
	Nancy J.	"	6				."
	Sarah A.	"	4				
Page 50							18 June 1860
	Hannah	LEE	2				Tenn.
	Eli	PARSONS	17				"
349	William	HENSON	25	Laborer			Tenn.
	Mary	"	20				"
	Sally A.	"	4				"
	John	"	2				"
350	Thomas N.	ALLEN	49	Farmer	3,500	1,600	Tenn.
	Elizabeth	"	39				"
	Amanda	"	16				"
	Julia	"	14				"
	Edwin	"	11				"
	Emily	"	9				"
	Elizabeth	"	7				
	Thomas	"	2				

District 4   P.O.: Unitia

	Name		Age	Occupation	Real	Pers.	Birthplace
351	Henry	SMITH	42	Laborer		125	Tenn.
	Jane	"	23				"
	Mary C.	"	4				"
	Benj. M.	"	1				"
352	Joseph	KIZER	45	Farmer		1,200	N. C.
	Mary	"	44				Tenn.
	Sarah M.	"	15				"
	Dolly J.	"	10				"
	William	"	7				"
353	Joseph	KIZER	45	Farmer		1,200	N. C.
	Mary	"	44				Tenn.
	Sarah M.	"	15				"
	Dolly J.	"	10				"
	William	"	7				"
353	John	JONES	56	Farmer	5,000	1,000	Tenn.
	Catharine	"	32				Ireland
	Euphemia	"	12				Tenn.
	Nancy	"	10				"
	Eliza J.	"	8				"
	Margaret E.	"	5				"
	Andrew Johnson	"	1				"
	James	PARKS	19	Laborer			"
354	John W.	HAMILL	29	Carpenter	350	700	Tenn.
	Mary A.	"	27				"
	Nancy J.	"	6				"
	Robert F.	"	7/12				"
355	Melinda	TUCK	37	Farmer	300	150	Tenn.
	Isaac W.	"	10				"
	Lucinda A. B.	"	6				"
356	Elijah	WALKER	70	Farmer	10,000	20,000	Pa.
	Nancy	HAMILL	50				Tenn.

Page 51   19 June 1860

	Name		Age	Occupation	Real	Pers.	Birthplace
357	David	WALKER	75	Farmer	5,000	3,000	Pa.
	Robt. F.	"	42		5,500	2,000	Tenn.
	Margaret E.	"	27				"
	Laura	"	1				"
	Elijah	"	39	Farmer	3,500	5,200	"
	Amanda E.	"	30			600	"
	Joseph	SMITH	19	Laborer			"
358	Campbell	BADGETT	34	Blacksmith		300	Tenn.
	Cynthia A.	"	36				"
	Harriet E.	"	12				"
	Martha A.	"	10				"
	Mary E.	"	7				"
	Lucy A.	"	5				"
	Mary A.	"	64				Va.
359	Eliza	PRIVETT	47			150	Tenn.
	Robert	"	20				"
	Jane	"	18				"

	Name		Age	Occupation	Real	Pers.	Birthplace
	John	"	14				"
	Doctor	"	12				"
	Isaac	"	7				"
360	James	DUNLAP	40	Farmer		900	Tenn.
	Aritta	"	29				"
	Samuel D.	"	7				"
	Isaac W.	"	4				"
361	Harlan	MATHIS	63	Farmer		3,000	Tenn.
	Nancy	"	59				N. C.
	Joseph	"	35	Farmer	9,500	3,600	Tenn.
	Ruth	HARRINGTON	23	Dom.			"
	Charles	RICHARDS	16	Laborer			"
	Joseph	FORTNER	18	"			"
362	Isaac M.	CASTON	30	Farmer	3,000	900	Tenn.
	Hannah E.	"	28				"
	William K.	"	9				"
	James T.	"	8				"
	Joseph V.	"	7				"
	Hugh B.	"	4				"
	Sarah E.	"	1				"
	Texiana	" (f)	2/12				"
	Eliza	"	52				"
363	Elisha A.	JONES	28	Farmer		500	"

Page 52   19 June 1860

	Name		Age	Occupation	Real	Pers.	Birthplace
	Elizabeth	JONES	27				Tenn.
	Joseph L.	"	2				"
	Sarah E.	"	9/12				"
364	Wm. M.	WILLIAMS	19	Laborer		300	Tenn.
	Lucinda C.	"	18				"
	Mary P.	"	1/12				"
365	T.D.W.C.	MAUPIN	28	Farmer		600	Tenn.
	Phebe J.	"	28				"
	James R.	"	2				"
	Susan M.	"	5/12				"
366	George	BISHOP	31	Carpenter		300	S. C.
	Susan	"	28				N. C.
	Catharine	"	18				Tenn.
367	Matilda	MYERS	41				Va.
	Philip	"	27				(Blank)
	Ellen	"	22				(Blank)
	Susannah	"	20				(Blank)
	Jane	"	18				(Blank)
	Margaret J.	"	14				(Blank)
368	John	GRIFFITTS	55	Farmer	16,000	14,500	Tenn.
	Nancy D.	"	44				"
	John L.	"	19				"
	Sarah E.	"	13				"
	Hugh B.	"	8				"
	Jane	MALCOM	22	Dom.			"

	Name		Age	Occupation	Real	Pers.	Birthplace
369	James	GRIFFITTS	46	Farmer	12,550	9,075	Tenn.
	Mary P.	"	42				"
	William H.	"	17				"
	Amanda E.	"	13				"
	Jacob D.	"	9				"
	Mary	"	83				N. C.
	James	WILLIAMSON	40	Laborer			Ireland
370	Joseph D.	STANFIELD	27	Sawyer	1,500	500	Tenn.
	Sarah	"	27				
	James C.	"	1				
371	Henry SKIPRETH	(bl)	50	Tanner		200	Tenn.
	Hannah	" (bl)	57				"
372	John A.	WALKER	36	Book & Shoe Maker		300	N. C.
	Martha J.	"	32				Tenn.
	George H.	"	10				"

Page 53   19 June 1860

	Name		Age	Occupation	Real	Pers.	Birthplace
	Mary C.	WALKER	7				Tenn.
	Josephine	"	5				"
	Martha M.	"	8/12				"
373	Isaac M.	HAIR	52	Blacksmith		400	Tenn.
	Mary	"	47				"
	Isaac T.	"	22				"
	Mary J.	"	9				"
374	Sarah	STANSBERRY	61			400	N. C.
	Theresa L.	"	24				"
	John L.	"	22				"
375	David	THOMPSON	35	Laborer		350	Tenn.
	Martha A.	"	38				"
	Anderson L.	"	13				"
	James L.	"	10				"
	George W.	"	8				"
	John P.	"	6				"
	Sarah J.	"	3				"
	Nancy C.	"	6/12				"
376	Granville W.	WHITEHEAD	27	Brickmason		350	Tenn.
	Martha J.	"	23				"
	Elijah D.	"	1				"
377	Wm. E.	SHEDDAN	30	Com. S. Teacher		500	Tenn.
	Nancy J.	"	24				Ala.
	William K.	"	1				Tenn.
378	Thomas	WHITEHEAD	37	Brickmason		500	Tenn.
	Mary	"	41				"
	William L.	"	13				"
	Jacob P.	"	11				"
	James G.	"	9				"
	Nancy J.	"	7				"
	John H.	"	5				"
	Sarah C.	"	3				"
	Hannah L.	"	1				"

District 4   P.O.: Unitia

	Name		Age	Occupation	Real	Pers.	Birthplace
379	Robinson	GRAHAM	24	Blacksmith		350	Va.
	Martha E.	"	21				Tenn.
	Dora E.	"	1				"
380	William	BARNHILL	73			25	N. C.
381	Mathew	GOODMAN	21	Laborer		50	Tenn.
	Elizabeth	"	18				N. C.
	Peter M.	"	1				Tenn.
Page 54							19 June 1860
382	James W.	HAIR	25	Blacksmith		500	Tenn.
	Mary J.	"	23				"
	James B.	"	5				"
	Sarah A.	"	3				"
383	Alexander	ROSS	48	(Bap. Min. & Carpenter)	1,500	800	Tenn.
	Margaret	"	43				N. C.
	John W.	"	22	Blacksmith		150	Tenn.
	Robert A.	"	15				"
	Mary J.	"	12				"
	Thomas C.	"	10				"
	Caleb J.	"	5				"
384	David W.	ROSS (mwy)	20	Carpenter		250	Tenn.
	Sarah E.	"	17				"
385	Thomas	GOODMAN	40	Laborer		100	Tenn.
	Mary	"	38				"
	James	"	19				"
	John	"	17				"
	William	"	15				"
	Elizabeth	"	13				"
	Mary J.	"	11				"
	Charles	"	9				"
	Nancy A.	"	7				"
	Joseph M.	"	5				"
	Peter C.	"	2				"
386	Hugh B.	LEEPER	68	Farmer	10,500	16,500	Pa.
	Esther	"	58				N. C.
387	Sanders M.	LEEPER	40	Merchant	10,500	14,000	Ga.
	Rebecca L.	"	32				Tenn.
	Ann E.	"	13				"
	James L.	"	12				"
	Mary L.	"	10				"
	Hugh B.	"	6				"
	John T.	"	3				"
	Allen C.	"	1				"
	Mira M.	ESKRIDGE	16				"
388	William H.	O'NEAL (mul)	21	Laborer		100	Tenn.
	Ailsey E.	"	19				"
	Mary O.	" (mul)	6/12				"
389	Elijah W.	ALLEN	31	Miller		250	Tenn.
	Margaret	"	24				"

District 4   P.O.: Unitia

	Name		Age	Occupation	Real	Pers.	Birthplace
							19 June 1860
Page 55							
	Hugh B.	ALLEN	4/12				Tenn.
390	Stepehen	MATHIS	32	Merchant	4,000	1,500	Tenn.
	Mesina A.	"	31				"
	Robert	"	5				"
	Nancy L.	"	3				"
	Lara B.	"	1				"
	Agnes	HOPE	68				"
	Rachel	WHITEHEAD	20				"
	John W.	BROOKS	25	Carpenter		400	"
391	James H.	DONALDSON	48	Merchant			Tenn.
	Lucinda	"	40				"
	Martha J.	"	17				"
	Sarah A.	"	15				"
	James H.	"	6				"
	Nora S.	"	2				"
	Malvina T.	"	2/12				"
392	William P.	LEWIS	26	Farmer		1,500	Tenn.
	Nancy	"	26				"
	Henry	"	6				"
	Isaac	"	4				"
	Catharine	"	2				"
	David B.	"	1/12				"
393	William P.	LEWIS	52	Farmer	3,500	5,800	N. C.
	Delilah	"	42				Tenn.
	Samuel	"	24		1,000	100	"
	Robert	"	20	Med. Student			"
	Joshua	"	16				"
	Thomas	"	14				"
	Mary A.	"	11				"
	William	"	9				"
	Alva M.	" (m)	7				"
394	John	GRIFFITTS	50	Farmer	3,500	1,600	Va.
	Phebe M.	"	35				Tenn.
	David	"	24				"
	Sarah	"	19				"
	Simeon	"	17				"
	John V.	"	12				"
	James A.	"	9/12				"
395	Stephen	NEWBERRY	42	Laborer		500	Tenn.
	Barbara	"	38				S. C.
							20 June 1860
Page 56							
	James	NEWBERRY	19				Tenn.
	John	"	17				"
	Mary	"	15				"
	Richard	"	13				"
	George	"	11				"
	Sarah	"	9				"
	Allen	"	6				"
396	John	GOSSAGE	35	Laborer		100	Tenn.
	Delilah	"	33				"
	George A.	"	15				"
	Sarah A.	"	13				"
	John	"	11				"
	Andrew J.	"	9				"
	Matilda E.	"	7				"

District 4   P.O.: Unitia

	Name		Age	Occupation	Real	Pers.	Birthplace
	James K. Polk	"	5				"
	William B.	"	1				"
397	Wesley D.	KEY	25	Laborer		800	Tenn.
	Letha	"	24				N. C.
	Thompson	"	5				Tenn.
	James	"	4				"
	Silas	"	1				"
	Samuel	BIDDOX	16				N. C.
398	Samuel	JONES	62	Farmer	3,000	1,300	Tenn.
	Hannah	"	59				"
	Ruth	"	38				"
	Emmit	"	19				"
	Miriam A.	HACKNEY	30				"
	William B.	"	7				
	Hannah E.	"	6				"
399	Alexander	ENSLEY	34	Farmer	2,500	1,500	Tenn.
	Dorinda	"	26				"
	Nancy E.	"	10				"
	Ephraim L.	"	6				"
	James	"	4				"
	Francis M.	" (m)	2				"
	Mary A.	"	5/12				"
400	Calvin T.	LEWIS	29	Farmer		1,500	Tenn.
	Jane	"	27				"
	Hannah J.	"	3				"
	Elizabeth	JONES	69				"

Page 57   20 June 1860

	Name		Age	Occupation	Real	Pers.	Birthplace
	Sarah J.	LEWIS	2/12				Tenn.
	Joseph	KEY	10				"
401	Merida	O'ONEAL (m)	60	Laborer		50	Va.
	Polly	"	58				"
	Newton	"	17				Tenn.
	Alvin	"	15				"
	Riley	"	14				"
	Samuel	"	9				"
402	David T.	BRIGHT	26	Laborer		50	Ala.
	Martha	"	29				Tenn.
	John	"	2/12				"
	Sally	DOTSON	21				"
403	Calvin	PARKS	33	Farmer		250	Tenn.
	Vina	"	31				"
	Abner	"	11				"
	Mary J.	"	7				"
	Susan	"	1				"
404	Abner	PARKS	75	Waggon Maker	4,500	1,200	Va.
	Levina	"	73				"

	Name		Age	Occupation	Real	Pers.	Birthplace
405	Samuel	FRENCH	38	Farmer		1,300	Tenn.
	Salina	"	29				"
	Malvina	"	11				"
	Caldonia	"	10				"
	John	"	6				"
	Samuel	"	3				"
	Albert	"	10/12				"
406	Joseph	PARKS	33	Farmer		500	Tenn.
	Nancy J.	"	35				"
	Nanch A. H.	"	8				"
	Robert H.	"	5				"
	Thaddeus C.	"	2				"
	Livinia R.	"	4/12				"
407	Samuel	LINGINFELTER	30	Farmer		700	Tenn.
	Elizabeth A.	"	28				"
	Mary A.	"	9				"
	James R.	"	8				"
	George C.	"	5				"
	Isaac S.	"	11/12				"
408	Walter H.	KEEBLE	45	Farmer		1,000	Tenn.
	Mary	"	41				"

Page 58   20 June 1860

	Name		Age	Occupation	Real	Pers.	Birthplace
	John	KEEBLE	21				Tenn.
	Nancy	"	20				"
	Samuel	"	18				"
	Mary	"	15				"
	Richard	"	12				"
	Jane	"	5				"
409	Merchant	BALDWIN	58	Farmer		600	Tenn.
	Martha	"	43				"
	Rebecca E.	"	22				"
	Henry C.	"	21				"
	Driny P.	" (m)	13				"
	Charlotte A.	"	12				"
	Sarah E.	"	11				"
	Robert G.	"	9				"
	Luna H.	" (m)	5				"
	Susan E.	"	2				"
410	Francis R.	HACKNEY	33	Farmer	7,000	1,500	Tenn.
	Mary J.	"	23				"
	John	"	3				"
	Rachel	"	61				N. C.
411	Solomon	DOCKERY (mul)	34	Laborer		100	Tenn.
	Viney	" (mul)	34				N. C.
	William P.	" (mul)	10				"
	Harriet M.	" (mul)	9				"
	John	" (mul)	7				"
	James I.	" (mul)	6				Tenn.
	Jackson	" (mul)	5				"
	Joseph	" (mul)	4				"

District 4   P.O.: Unitia

	Name		Age	Occupation	Real	Pers.	Birthplace
	Miller E.	" (mul)	2				"
	Lucretia E.	" (Mul)	2/12				"
412	William H.	MELSON	31	Laborer		150	Tenn.
	Rohama	"	22				N. C.
	Harlan	"	6				Tenn.
	Angelina	"	2				"
	Joseph	"	1/12				"
413	William	COPPOCK	45	Farmer	1,250	500	Tenn.
	Ellen	"	36				"
	Ann E.	"	13				"
	Robert D.	"	10				"

CLOSE 4th DISTRICT

Page 59   District 3   P.O.: Unitia   21 June 1860

	Name		Age	Occupation	Real	Pers.	Birthplace
414	Green	PASS	36	Laborer		100	N. C.
	Nancy A.	"	22				Tenn.
	William P.	"	13				"
	Jesse	" (m)	15				"
	Mary A.	"	12				"
	Nancy E.	"	8				"
	Thomas A.	"	7				"
	Fannel T.	" (m)	4				"
	Sarah M.	"	2				"
	Rose E.	"	2/12				"
415	Chesley	CRISP	55	Farmer		1,000	N. C.
	Mahala	"	55				"
	Sarah A.	"	21				Tenn.
	Joel A. J.	"	18				"
	Joshua H.	"	16				"
	Wm. B.	"	14				"
	Geo. W.	"	12				"
	Margaret L.	"	10				"
	Mary J.	"	8				"
416	James T.	CRISP	22	Laborer		250	Tenn.
	Martha	"	27				"
	Andrew J.	"	7/12				"
417	Saml. C.	WILLIAMS	64	Farmer	8,000	11,500	Va.
	Martha	"	45				Tenn.
	Joel H.	"	23			250	"
	Lilburn R.	"	22			600	"
	Levi J.	"	21			150	"
418	James W.	BUSSELL	69	Farmer	5,500	14,500	Va.
	Judah	"	65				N. C.
	Cred H.	"	20				Tenn.
419	Jonathan	PERKINS	41	Farmer		600	Tenn.
	Mary	"	42				N. C.
	Amanda J.	MOORE	6				Tenn.
420	Reuben	THOMAS	36	Laborer		300	Tenn.
	Sabra	"	27				"

	Name		Age	Occupation	Real	Pers.	Birthplace
421	Rice L.	CRISP	29	Farmer		800	N. C.
	Sarah J.	"	22				Tenn.
	Susan	"	6				"
	Caldonia	"	4				"
	Sarah J.	"	2				"

Page 60   21 June 1860

	Name		Age	Occupation	Real	Pers.	Birthplace
	Lucinda	CRISP	1				Tenn.
	Sarah	"	77				S. C.
	Francis M.	KING	24	Laborer		200	Tenn.
422	Riley	GRAVES	35	"		100	Tenn.
	Elizabeth	"	32				"
	Elizabeth	"	12				"
	Rebecca C.	"	9				"
	James A.	"	6				"
	John A.	"	2				"
423	Silas	GRAVES	43	Laborer		150	Tenn.
	Nancy A.	"	48				"
	Barbara A.	"	13				"
	Eliza J.	"	10				"
	Martha A.	"	8				"
	Nancy C.	"	3				"
424	John C.	WYLEY	23	Farmer	3,500	10,000	Tenn.
	Mary A.	"	23				Va.
	John	SEMPSON	19				"
425	Joseph F.	DAWSON	25	Farmer		4,000	Tenn.
	Mary M.	"	20				"
	James W.	"	2				"
426	Simeon	GRITTITTS	31	Farmer	200	300	Ky.
	Elizabeth	"	18				N.C.
	Robert	"	2				Tenn.
427	Calvin	MYZELL	33	Farmer	1,000	700	N. C.
	Sarah	"	29				Tenn.
	William L.	"	8				"
	Mary J.	"	6				"
	James M.	"	5				"
	Joseph M.	"	3				"
	Albert F.	"	9/12				"
428	Edmond	WAYMOND	30	Farmer	1,040	1,000	Tenn.
	Eliza	"	26				"
	Mary A.	"	5				"
	Martha E.	"	4				"
	Nora S.	"	11/12				"
429	Mary	WYLEY	59		10,000	3,580	Tenn.
	Mary E.	SMITH	12				"
430	Jackson R.	WYLEY	28	Farmer	9,000	10,000	Tenn.
	Anna Mary	"	2				"

District 3   P.O.: Unitia

	Name		Age	Occupation	Real	Pers.	Birthplace
Page 61							21 June 1860
431	John G.	STEWART	38	Farmer	2,500	4,200	Tenn.
	Harriett N.	"	33				"
	Elizabeth B.	RHEA	20				"
432	Samuel	PERKINS	30	Farmer		500	Tenn.
	Jane	"	29				"
	Lockey V. (f)	"	6				"
	Francis V.(f)	"	3				"
	Arminta C.	"	3/12				"
433	William	LUNDY	34	Laborer		700	Tenn.
	Rachel	"	34				"
	James Y.	"	8				"
	Mordica (m)	"	7				"
	Mary K.	"	2				"
434	Isaac	DOUTHET	42	Physician	7,000	2,750	Tenn.
	Elizabeth W.	"	28				"
	John	"	7/12				"
435	James	McKINLEY	75	Laborer		600	Va.
	Sarah	"	50				Tenn.
	Thomas	"	20				
436	John	McDANIEL	26	Laborer		150	Tenn.
	Jane	"	22				"
	James T.	"	8/12				"
	James	McKINLY	16				"
	Peter	"	14				"
	William	"	10				"
437	John H.	JACKSON	37	Farmer	13,750	8,200	Tenn.
	Aries A.	"	31				"
	James J.	"	15				"
	Josiah L.	"	11				"
	Samuel P.	"	9				"
	George W.	"	6				"
	No Name (m)	"	1				"
438	Philip J.	KIZER	30	Laborer		200	N. C.
	Eliza J.	"	30				Tenn.
	John	"	17				"
	William	"	9				"
	Martha	"	3				"
	Laura	"	11/12				"
	Sarah E.	"	12				"
	Jacob	"	18	Laborer			"
Page 62							22 June 1860
439	Birce	CASTON	44	Farmer	1,300	1,000	N. C.
	Martha	"	38				Tenn.
	Terressa A.	"	19				"
	Caswell	"	17				"
	Francis (m)	"	14				"
	John J.	"	11				"
	James J.	"	5				"
	Price	"	2				"
	No Name (f)	"	1/12				"

	Name		Age	Occupation	Real	Pers.	Birthplace
440	John W.	GRIFFITTS	29	Farmer	500	400	Ky.
	Mary E.	"	21				Tenn.
	James H.	"	2				"
	Nancy A.	"	9/12				"
441	John	CASTON	50	Farmer	2,500	1,500	N. C.
	Sarah	"	44				Tenn.
	William T.	"	24				"
	Francis M. (m)	"	20				"
	Eliza J.	"	16				"
	Margaret C.	"	13				"
	Mary A. P.	"	11				"
	John H.	"	8				"
	Katharine	JONES	25		100	300	"
	Samuel H.	"	2				"
442	Jesse	HAMMER	74	Farmer	2,000	400	N. C.
	Hannah	"	58				(Blank)
	Hiram P.	"	20				(Blank)
	Celia L.	"	19				(Blank)
443	Jesse L.	HAMMER	30	Farmer	500	250	Tenn.
	Mary Ann	"	20				"
	Martha J.	"	1				"
444	Thomas C.	HAMMER	23			250	Tenn.
	Harriet	"	21				"
	James H.	"	2				"
445	Henry	DIFORD	51	Farmer		350	N. C.
	Esther W.	"	38				Tenn.
	George W.	"	17				"
	Hannah J.	"	16				"
	Margaret A.	"	14				"
	Mordica A.	"	10				"
	James H.	"	2				"

Page 63   22 June 1860

	Name		Age	Occupation	Real	Pers.	Birthplace
446	William	GALLION	26	Laborer		175	Tenn.
	Mary	"	23				"
	James R.	"	1				"
	Thomas M.	"	10				"
447	Marion M.	SHIPLEY	25	Farmer		400	Tenn.
	Ruth A.	"	21				"
	Tamar C.	"	4				"
	Joseph E.	"	2				"
	John B.	"	10/12				"
448	Conway	STONE	64	Farmer	1,500	500	N. C.
	Rachel	"	61				Tenn.
	Mahala J.	"	32				"
	Hugh C.	"	29				"
449	Jane	BROOKS	50	Farmer	500	500	Tenn.
	Eleanor C.	"	18				"
	Victoria	"	16				"
	Hester	"	14				"
	Madison	"	12				"

	Name		Age	Occupation	Real	Pers.	Birthplace
450	Elizabeth	BROOKS	58	Farmer	1,000	400	Tenn.
	Marion J.	"	37				"
	Eliza J.	"	25				"
451	Samuel H.	BROOKS	24	Laborer		100	Tenn.
	Martha	"	20				"
	Sarah E.	"	9/12				"
452	Benj. F.	HENDERSON	43	Laborer		300	Tenn.
	Susan J.	"	39				"
	Mary L.	"	1/12				"
	Ellen	CASTON	52				N. C.
453	John	McCASLAND	62	Farmer	3,000	2,300	N. C.
	Polly	"	51				Tenn.
	John	"	21				"
	Lucinda	"	17				"
	James	"	12				"
	Jeremiah	"	10				"
	Lydia A.	"	8				"
454	Sarah G.	GOURLEY	58	Farmer	2,500	1,250	Tenn.
	Ellen	BROOKS	48				Va.
455	James	HOOPER	20	Farmer	700	200	Tenn.
	Nancy J.	"	18				"
	Rebecca	LAIN	19				"

Page 64   22 June 1860

	Name		Age	Occupation	Real	Pers.	Birthplace
456	Jacob	PRESLEY	25	Laborer		150	Tenn.
	Sarah A.	"	18				N. C.
	William F.	"	1				Tenn.
457	Columbus	KEY	21	Laborer		500	Tenn.
	Margaret	"	28				"
	John M.	"	1				"
458	Charles	WAYMAN	53	Farmer		1,200	N. C.
	Elizabeth	"	41				Tenn.
	Polly A.	"	26				"
	Mary E.	"	18				"
	Nancy J.	"	17				"
	James E. O'B	"	13				"
	William T.	"	15				"
	Rebecca L.	"	4				"
	Elija L.	"	2				"
459	Joseph	ABBOTT	53	Laborer		150	N. C.
	Margaret	"	51				Tenn.
	Nancy C.	"	23				"
	Abner T.	"	21				"
	Stanhope C.	"	16				"
	Moses M.	"	10				"
460	Samuel B.	ABBOTT	26	Laborer		100	Tenn.
	Emily A.	"	29				"
	Sarah C.	"	1				"

District 3   P.O.: Unitia

	Name		Age	Occupation	Real	Pers.	Birthplace
461	Levin	MYZELL	36	Farmer	4,500	800	N. C.
	Phebe C.	"	31				Tenn.
	Sarah M.	"	12				"
	John C.	"	9				"
	Nancy E.	"	7				"
	William A.	"	5				"
	Millard F.	"	3				"
	Laura J.	"	2/12				"
462	Martin	GRIFFITTS	35	Farmer	1,000	1,200	Va.
	Elizabeth J.	"	32				"
	John F.	"	13				"
	George W.	"	11				"
	Granville T.	"	9				"
	Alexander D.	"	1				"
463	Spencer	THOMPSON	66	Laborer		500	N. C.
	Susan	"	59				Tenn.

Page 65   23 June 1860

	Name		Age	Occupation	Real	Pers.	Birthplace
	Mary A.	THOMPSON	29				Tenn.
	Larkin	"	20				"
	Elizabeth	" (twins)	15				"
	Margaret J.	" (twins)	15				"
	Nathaniel H.	" (mwy)	26				"
	Miriam A.	" (mwy)	22				"
464	David L.	TULLOCK	48	Carpenter	500	500	Scotland
	Nancy A.	"	24				Tenn.
	David L.	"	3				"
	Hester A.	"	6/12				"
465	John	STALEY	60	Farmer	2,500	1,200	Va.
	Mary A.	"	56				"
	James D.	"	19				Tenn.
	Martin V.	"	14				"
	William M.	"	10				"
	Sarah A.	"	17				"
466	Hiram	HARLESS	32	Laborer		500	N. C.
	Francis A.	"	29				Tenn.
	Joseph L.	"	5				"
	Sarah R.	"	3				"
	Orlina T.	"	9/12				"
467	Thomas	LAIN	20			100	Tenn.
	Elizabeth	"	18				Va.
	Sarah A.	"	1				Tenn.
468	Strut	LAIN	56	Farmer	1,000	500	N. C.
	Matilda	"	47				Va.
	Minerva	MYZELL	14				Tenn.
469	William	LAIN	28			100	Tenn.
	Rebecca	"	28				"
	James	"	8				"
	John	"	6				"
	Strut	"	4				"

District 3   P.O.: Unitia

	Name		Age	Occupation	Real	Pers.	Birthplace
	Pasley	" (m)	2				"
	No Name	" (f)	2/12				"
470	Albert W.	GREGORY	25	Physician		500	Va.
	Frances S.	" (f)	12				"
	Paul M.	"	10				"
	Elizabeth	"	7				"
471	George	GRIFFITTS	51	Farmer	9,000	5,500	Tenn.
	Martha	"	51				"

Page 66   23 June 1860

	Name		Age	Occupation	Real	Pers.	Birthplace
	John R.	GRIFFITTS	22				Tenn.
	Julia A.	"	19				"
	Nancy C.	" (Twins)	13				"
	Mary J.	"	13				"
	George M.	"	10				"
	Harvey	REID	15				"
	Mary	LUNSFORD	35	(Pauper)			"
472	John D.	JONES	34	Farmer	3,000	1,875	Tenn.
	Ann	"	33				"
	Sarah E.	"	9				"
	Joseph P.	"	3				"
	No Name	" (f)	5/12				"
	Elizabeth	"	70				N. C.
473	John H.	LONG	64	Farmer	350	900	Tenn.
	Agnes	"	58				Va.
	Sarah	"	28				Tenn.
	Isaac	"	21				"
	Rachel	"	18				"
	Rebecca	"	15				"
	Campbell	"	40				"
474	James	JONES	57	Farmer	200	400	Tenn.
	Sarah	"	54				"
	Elizabeth	"	34				"
	Aaron H.	CRUMLEY	14				"
475	Thomas M.	NICHOLSON	24	Farmer	400	200	Tenn.
	Catharine E.	"	25				"
	Joseph M.	"	2				"
	No Name	" (f)	1/12				"
476	James A.	PRATT	36	Farmer		1,000	N. C.
	Elizabeth	"	39				S. C.
	Hiram L.	"	14				Tenn.
	William E.	"	10				"
	Susan A.	"	9				"
	John H.	"	7				"
	Ann A. E.	"	4				"
477	James	MATHIS	38	Farmer	4,000	1,900	Tenn.
	Sarah L.	"	33				"
	Nancy A.	"	11				"
	Stephen H.	"	9				"
	Madison L.	"	7				"

District 3   P.O.: Unitia

	Name		Age	Occupation	Real	Pers.	Birthplace
Page 67							25 June 1860
	Isabella E.	MATHIS	5				Tenn.
	William N.	"	1				"
	Elizabeth T.	"	2/12				"
478	William	MILLS	30	Farmer	1,000	1,000	Ill.
	Terressa A.	"	25				Tenn.
	Mary J.	"	8				"
	Sarah A.	"	7				"
	Nancy E.	"	4				"
	Joseph R.	"	1				"
479	Rurel	O'NEAL (mul)	56	Laborer		200	Va.
	Mariah	"	50				"
	John	" (mul)	18				Tenn.
	Joseph	" (mul)	16				"
	Thomas	" (mul)	13				"
	David	" (mul)	11				"
	Pleasant	" (mul)	8				"
	Doctor B. M'C	" (mul)	5				"
480	John J.	HOOVER	47	Farmer	10,000	2,400	Tenn.
	Elizabeth	"	37				"
	Henry A.	"	24				"
	Mary	"	19				"
481	James	BROOKS	40	Laborer		150	Tenn.
	Sarah J.	"	25				"
	Adaline E.	"	4				"
482	Alexander	McGILL	39	Farmer	1,200	500	Tenn.
	Orlena	"	34				"
	James P.	"	11				"
	Samuel	"	9				"
	Mary A. C.	"	7				"
	John J.	"	5				"
	Cordetia A.	"	3				"
	Lucinda C.	"	1				"
483	Thomas A.	BALL	32	Laborer		350	Tenn.
	Elizabeth J.	"	32				"
	Samuel J.	"	2				"
484	Joseph	JONES	52	Farmer	3,500	1,500	Tenn.
	Tamar	"	45				"
	Harlan C.	"	19				"
	John W.	"	15				"
	Solomon S.	"	12				"
Page 68							25 June 1860
	Lydia H.	JONES	10				Tenn.
485	Josiah	POWERS	37	Laborer		600	Tenn.
	Malinda C.	"	29				"
	Margaret	"	12				"
	Ann	"	9				"
	Catharine	OWENS	70				Va.

District 3   P.O.: Unitia

	Name		Age	Occupation	Real	Pers.	Birthplace
486	James F. BLANKENBECKLER		28	Laborer		250	Va.
	Martha J.	"	21				Tenn.
	Virginia E.	"	10/12				"
	William	"	10				"
487	Bartley	BRIGHT	38	Farmer	1,500	800	Tenn.
	Nancy	"	29				"
	Mary E.	"	10				"
	Cyrus J.	"	8				"
	William J.	"	6				"
	Sarah A.	"	4				"
	Margaret	"	2				"
	Susan L.	"	6/12				"
488	James B.	JACKSON	30	Farmer	20,000	9,775	Tenn.
	Sarah E.	"	18				"
	William	THOMAS	17				"
489	Samuel	LAIN	27	Farmer		1,000	Tenn.
	Mary E.	"	23				"
	Aurelia F.	"	6				"
	Granville R.	"	3				"
	Sarah C.	"	6/12				"
	Mary	KEENE	66		1,500	1,000	Va.
490	John	GREENWAY	62	Farmer	12,000	1,500	Tenn.
	Rebecca	"	45				"
	Edward M.	"	22				"
	James A.	"	20				"
	Henry C.	"	18				"
	Belle Zora	"	16				"
	Josephine	"	13				"
	Terressa A.	"	10				"
	Sarah J.	"	7				"
	Elizabeth	"	29				"
491	Andrew	CARPENTER	31	Farmer	3,000	1,100	Tenn.
	Aretta J.	"	31				"
	Millard W.	"	7				"

Page 69   26 June 1860

	Name		Age	Occupation	Real	Pers.	Birthplace
	Nancy T.	CARPENTER	5				Tenn.
	Marietta	"	2				"
	No Name	" (m)	3/12				"
	Nancy	THOMPSON	47				"
	John T.	CARPENTER	19	Student			"
492	Mira	HUMPHREYS	39			100	Tenn.
	Milton	"	21				"
	Leonidas	"	13				"
	John C.	"	11				"
493	Jno. B.	SIMPSON	39	Farmer		675	Tenn.
	Susan B.	"	35				"
	Mary E.	"	15				"
	Nancy J.	"	13				"
	Charles R.	"	11				"
	Margaret A.	"	9				"

District 3   P.O.: Unitia

	Name		Age	Occupation	Real	Pers.	Birthplace
	James B.	"	6				"
	Jonathan D.	"	4				"
	Elihu A.	"	1				"
494	Mary	CARPENTER	45	Farmer	500	400	Tenn.
	Nancy	"	11				"
	Melvain	"	10				"
495	Leonidas	THOMPSON	22	Laborer		350	Tenn.
	Mary C.	"	22				"
	Margaret E.	"	2				"
	William R.	"	5/12				"
496	Josiah	JACKSON	60	Farmer	10,000	6,910	Tenn.
	Polly	"	61				"
	Josiah	"	24		4,000	200	"
	William	"	19				"
497	James W.	WEST	37			300	N. C.
	Sarah M.	"	37				Tenn.
	Mary A.	"	14				"
	Isabella M.	"	12				"
	James R.	"	8				"
	Elizabeth J.	"	6				"
	Alford W.	"	4				"
	William A.	"	1				"
498	Gilbert	BLANKENSHIP	68	Farmer	20,400	8,090	Va.
	Elizabeth L.	"	52				Tenn.
	Gilbert L.	"	17				"

Page 70   26 June 1860

	Name		Age	Occupation	Real	Pers.	Birthplace
	Jno. M.	BLANKENSHIP	14				Tenn.
	James A.	"	12				"
	Robert S.	"	8				"
	Lydia E.	HUGHS	17				Ala.
	Jas. K. Polk	"	15				"
	George	TIPTON	16	Student			Tenn.
499	John W.	GENTRY	27	Laborer		150	Tenn.
	Nancy E.	"	24				"
	Mina M.	" (f)	8				"
	Eliza L.	"	6				"
	Rebecca J.	"	4				"
	Angeline L.	"	2				"
500	James B.	SHIRLEY	29	Farmer		500	Tenn.
	Orpah	"	27				"
	Mary H.	"	5				"
	Sarah M.	"	3				"
	John M.	"	1				"
	Sarah E.	HINES	14				"
501	William H.	GRIFFITTS	36	Farmer	6,000	2,200	Tenn.
	Lucy A.	"	32				"
	John B.	"	11				"
	Joseph	"	8				"
	Robert	"	6				"

District 3   P.O.: Unitia

	Name		Age	Occupation	Real	Pers.	Birthplace
	Nancy E.	"	2				"
	Elizabeth	BISHOP	29				S. C.
	William	WOLF	24	(Idiot)			Tenn.
502	Joseph	BRUNER	61	Farmer	10,000	4,825	Blank
	Theresa	"	42				Va.
	Hugh K.	HUGHS	21				Tenn.
	Mary E.	"	18				"
	Enoch M.	"	15				"
	Thomas W. S.	"	11				"
	Robert P.	"	8				"
	Alexander	WILLIAMS	12				"
503	Milton S. HUMPHREYS (mwy)		21	Farmer		150	Tenn.
	Samatha	"	19				"
504	Thomas	WADDLE	54			250	N. C.
	Isabella	"	54				Tenn.
505	Thomas J.	WADDLE	33			250	Tenn.
	Mary A.	"	25				"

Page 71   26 June 1860

	Name		Age	Occupation	Real	Pers.	Birthplace
	Elvira C.	WADDLE	6				Tenn.
	Eliza E.	"	4				"
	No Name	" (m)	2/12				"
506	Matilda	ALEXANDER	42	Farmer	3,500	1,100	Va.
	Amanda A.	"	22				Tenn.
	Nancy E.	"	19				"
	James W.	"	17				"
	William B.	"	15				"
	George A.	"	13				"
	Virginia C.	"	11				"
	John	"	7				"
507	William C.	ISHOM (?)	23	Laborer		250	Tenn.
	Martha A.	"	22				"
	William L.	"	2				"
	Susan M. W.	"	9/12				"
508	Thomas	BLACKBURN	39	Farmer	4,000	1,500	Tenn.
	Louisa	"	25				"
	John M.	"	1				"
509	Thomas	LAIN	56			100	Tenn.
	Patsey	"	61				N. C.
510	David J.	LAIN	35			200	Tenn.
	Louisiana	"	26				"
511	Joseph W.	LAIN	33			100	Tenn.
	Artrmasia	"	28				"
	Martin R.	"	6				"
	Martha L.	"	8/12				"
	Walter	SAFFELL	70				Md.
512	Robt. H.	BLACKBURN	32	Farmer	4,000	1,700	Ga.
	Margaret	"	28				Tenn
	John L.	"	8				"

	Name		Age	Occupation	Real	Pers.	Birthplace
	William H.	"	4				"
	Margaret C.	"	2				"
	Lucinda	GIBSON	22				"
513	John	JONES	36	Farmer	3,500	1,125	Tenn.
	Ludinda	"	33				Ala.
	William A.	"	12				Tenn.
	Samuel L.	"	6				"
	David H.	"	1				"
514	Lewis	McMILLAN	54	Laborer		300	Ga.
	Margaret	"	52				Tenn.

Page 72   27 June 1860

	Name		Age	Occupation	Real	Pers.	Birthplace
	Elizabeth A.	McMILLAN	25				Tenn.
	James A.	"	24				"
	Dorcus M.	"	22				"
	John W.	"	21				"
	Nancy J.	"	18				"
	Allison W.	" (m)	15				"
	Silas M.	"	10				"
515	Malinda	KEENE	35	Farmer	3,000	1,150	Tenn.
	Gilbert P.	"	12				"
	Martha H.	"	8				"
	Theresa M.	"	6				"
	William H.	"	4				"
516	George	JOHNSON (mwy)	21				Tenn.
	Elizabeth	"	26				"
	Lydia	"	60				"
517	Harvey	THOMPSON	55	Farmer	1,600	1,100	Ga.
	Amnvira	"	33				Tenn.
	Samuel	"	23				"
	James M.	"	17				"
	Robt. A.	"	15				"
	Elizabeth J.	"	13				"
	William H.	"	11				"
	Hester A.	"	10				"
	Sarah M.	"	3				"
	Martha	"	1/12				"
518	William V.	GRIFFITTS	38	Farmer	2,000	1,125	Va.
	Saphrona	"	32				Tenn.
	James A.	"	8				"
	Henderson Y.	"	7				"
	Elizabeth M.	"	5				"
	John P.	"	2				"
	George N.	"	1				"
	Robert	WILSON	18	Laborer			"
519	John	LUNDY	84	Laborer		100	S. C.
	Elizabeth	"	59				"
	Thomas	REID	25	Laborer			Tenn.
	Anny P.	"	10				"
	Jemima E.	"	8/12				"

District 3   P.O.P Unitia

	Name		Age	Occupation	Real	Pers.	Birthplace
520	Willi m	FERGUSON	26	Laborer		100	Tenn.
	Matilda L.	"	20				"

Page 73   27 June 1860

	Name		Age	Occupation	Real	Pers.	Birthplace
	Andrew B.	FERGUSON	8/12				Tenn.
521	Francis	ALEXANDER	50	Farmer	4,000	1,800	Tenn.
	Margaret A.	"	42				Ala.
	Elizabeth J.	"	22				Tenn.
	John	"	18				"
	Andrew	"	16				"
	James H.	"	14				"
	Samuel G.	"	12				"
	William S.	"	10				"
	Josiah B.	"	3				"
	David V.	"	10/12				"
	Amanda	"	7				"
522	Jno. B.	BRIANT	46	Farmer	8,000	2,900	Va.
	Lydia	"	41				Tenn.
	Sarah A.	"	20				"
	Eliza J.	"	16				"
	Hester J.	"	11				"
	Ann E.	"	9				"
	James H.	"	6				"
	Mary E.	"	4				"
	Joseph T.	"	2				"
	Jno F.	NICHOLSON	21	Laborer			"
	Philip	MYERS	25	Laborer			N. C.
523	Samuel J.	GRIFFITTS	30	Farmer	4,500	1,900	Tenn.
	Ruth J.	"	32				"
	Lenora A.	"	4				"
	Mary A.	"	2				"
	Lucy C.	"	8/12				"
524	William	NELSON	70	Farmer		4,500	Tenn.
	Mary	"	74				"
	Jane	RENO	25				"
	Eliza Jane	"	2				"
525	Jno. C.	HUMPHREYS	29	Farmer	300	325	Tenn.
	Elizabeth J.	"	29				"
	Jno. M.	"	7				"
	Calvin J.	"	3				"
	Isabella J.	"	1				"
526	Addison P.	CHAPMAN	33	Farmer	2,500	1,375	Tenn.

CLOSE OF DISTRICT 3

Page 74   District 2   P.O.: Morganton   27 June 1860

	Name		Age	Occupation	Real	Pers.	Birthplace
527	Henry	LONG	58	Laborer		200	N. C.
	Hannah D.	"	34				"
	John J.	"	21				"
	Sarah D.	"	18				"
	James M.	"	17				"
	Eliza A.	"	13				"

	Name		Age	Occupation	Real	Pers.	Birthplace
	Fredric M.	"	11				Tenn.
	William H.	"	9				"
	Nancy L.	"	7				"
	Margaret M.	"	4				"
	Cordelia J.	"	2				"
528	William H.	SKINNER	24	Laborer		100	Tenn.
	Martha A.	"	18				Ga.
	Oma L.	"	2				N. C.
529	George	LONG	48	Laborer		100	Unknown
	Oma	"	52				"
	Catharine	" (Twins)	16				Ga.
	Louisa		16				"
	Elizabeth L.	"	10				"
530	Andrew L.	ANDERSON	50	Farmer	3,000	5,800	Tenn.
	Elizabeth R.	"	52		1,840		"
	William C.	"	23				"
	Samuel C.	"	18				"
531	Matthew	EDMONDS	60	Laborer		75	Tenn.
	Matilda	"	55				"
	Pleasant	"	22				"
	Isabella	"	16				"
	Martha G.	"	14				"
	Ellen	"	13				"
	George W.	"	11				"
	Robert	"	10				"
532	Mahala	MURRAY	38			350	Tenn.
	William	"	17				"
	Eagleton	"	15				"
	Amanda J.	"	10				"
	Newton M.	"	2				"
533	Joseph	TAYLOR	39	Farmer	2,000	600	Tenn.
	Mary A.	"	40				"
	Daniel A.	"	17				"
	Nancy J.	"	15				"

Page 75   28 June 1860

	Name		Age	Occupation	Real	Pers.	Birthplace
	Martha E.	TAYLOR	13				Tenn.
	Samatha	"	11				"
	James D.	"	9				"
	Ann E.	"	5				"
	John	"	2				"
	Andrew J.	"	9/12				"
	William	ELDER	11				"
534	Williamson	DAILY	26	Laborer		100	Tenn.
	Nancy	"	25				"
	John F.	"	5				"
	William W.	"	2				"
	Joseph T.	"	9/12				"
535	Wm. S.	ANDERSON	50	Farmer	2,500	1,000	Tenn.
	Nancy A.	"	35				"

	Name		Age	Occupation	Real	Pers.	Birthplace
	John R.	"	17				"
	Alvan L.	"	15				"
	Elizabeth J.	"	12				"
	Mary L.	"	10				"
	Candace M.	"	7				"
	Celestia A.	"	1				"
536	Larkin	THOMPSON	57	Farmer	2,000	1,600	Ga.
	Polly	"	51				Tenn.
	John R.	"	21				"
	Isaac W.	"	19				"
	Madison N.	"	17				"
	Nancy C.	"	15				"
	Sarah E.	"	13				"
537	Eagleton M.	CARSON	34	Farmer	2,000	1,250	Tenn.
	Martha J.	"	26				"
	Harriet E.	"	2				"
	Margaret	"	76				"
538	Isaac W.	ANDERSON	53	Farmer	1,000	600	Tenn.
	Matilda A.	"	43				"
539	B. H.	BLANKENSHIP	30	Farmer	4,000	1,200	Tenn.
	Sarah J.	"	25				"
	Nancy E.	"	7				"
	Gilbert A.	"	5				"
	William A.	"	3				"
	Mary J.	"	1				"
540	Daniel	WRIGHT	32	Laborer		200	S. C.

Page 76   28 June 1860

	Name		Age	Occupation	Real	Pers.	Birthplace
	Sapphira	WRIGHT	28				S. C.
	William H.	"	10				Tenn.
	Elizabeth J.	"	8				"
	Andrew G.	"	7				"
	Sally A.	"	5				"
	James A.	"	3				"
	Arclay H.	" (m)	2				"
541	Moses	CRAWLEY	38	Laborer		100	N. C.
	Polly	"	40				"
542	Pat D.	HAMMONTREE	26	Farmer	700	800	Tenn.
	Margaret	"	28				"
	Alexander	"	24				"
	William H.	"	4				"
543	Thomas	CONNER	48	Carpenter		250	Tenn.
	Dorcas	"	36				"
	Leonard	"	16				"
	Hugh	"	15				"
	Louisiana	"	9				"
	James	"	3				"
544	Wm. C.	CONNER	36	Farmer	2,500	3,000	Tenn.
	Nancy	"	25				Va.
	Jacob S.	"	7				"

District 2   P.O.: Morganton

	Name		Age	Occupation	Real	Pers.	Birthplace
	Claibourn W.	"	5				Tenn.
	Margaret H.	"	1				"
545	Leonard CONNER	(mwy)	19	Laborer		75	Tenn.
	Margaret "		22				N. C.
546	Peyton BLANKENSHIP		38	Farmer	4,500	1,280	Tenn.
	Martha E.	"	39				"
	Grizza	" (f)	16				"
	Louisa M.	"	13				"
	Blackmon M.	"	10				"
	Gilbert I.	"	5				"
547	William R. FULKERSON		23	Farmer	2,500	600	Tenn.
	Martha	"	22				"
	Eliza A.	"	10/12				"
548	Robert McTEER		64			250	Tenn.
	Ellen	"	67				Ireland
549	William B. CRAIG		22	Farmer		300	Tenn.
	Mary C.	"	24				"
	James C.	"	2				"

Page 77   28 June 1860

	Name		Age	Occupation	Real	Pers.	Birthplace
	Andrew G.	CRAIG	8/12				Tenn.
550	Margaret	DUNCAN	55			500	Tenn.
	Jno. W.	WOOD	24				"
	Hester A.	DUNCAN	17				"
	Decatur	"	13				"
	Josephine	"	12				"
	Philip W.	"	6				"
	James O.	"	5				"
551	Jno. Q. A.	KENNEDY	34	Farmer		500	Tenn.
	Elizabeth	"	34				"
	John W.	"	11				"
	Eliza E.	"	8				"
552	Benj.	DUNCAN (bl)	43			600	N. C.
	Nancy	" (bl)	37				Tenn.
	Granville	" (bl)	15				"
	Harriet	" (bl)	13				"
	John	" (bl)	10				"
	Joseph	" (bl)	7				"
	William	" (bl)	6				"
	Andrew	" (bl)	2				"
553	John	HAMMONTREE	45	Distiller		600	Tenn.
	Polly	"	43				"
	James	"	22				"
	Ailsey	"	21				"
	John	"	19				"
	Mary A.	"	17				"
	Hannah	"	14				"
	Andrew V.	"	12				"
	Elizabeth	"	8				"

	Name		Age	Occupation	Real	Pers.	Birthplace
	Nancy	"	6				"
	William J.	"	4				"
554	Joseph	HUMPHREYS	30	Laborer		300	Tenn.
	Rachel	"	28				"
	William J.	"	7				"
	Martha J.	"	4				"
	Margaret J.	"	2				"
	Mary A.	"	7/12				"
555	Marshal C.	TIPTON	33	Blacksmith		1,000	Tenn.
	Sarah J.	"	27				"
	Mary E.	"	4				"

	Name		Age	Occupation	Real	Pers.	Birthplace
	Louisiana	TIPTON	2				Tenn.
556	Jno. M.	HAMMONTREE	23	Blacksmith		600	Tenn.
	Elizabeth E.	"	17				"
	Thomas	"	1				"
557	Joseph B.	COBB	29	Farmer	1,500	1,255	Tenn.
	Evaline	"	25				"
	Isabel	"	1				"
	No Name	" (m)	3/12				"
558	Milas	JONES	33	Merchant	4,000	17,000	Tenn.
	Isabella	"	28				"
	Samuel A.	"	11				"
	Lilly E.	"	1				"
559	James C.	McTEER	40	Blacksmith	2,000	3,500	Tenn.
	Mary A.	"	31				
	Calvin	"	11				
	Minerva J.	"	8				
	Milas	"	7				
	Elvira	"	1				
560	Ambrose Y.	JONES	23	Mer. Clerk		1,100	Tenn.
	Ann E.	"	23				"
	James P. B.	"	5/12				"
561	Jno. M.	HEISKELL	44	Farmer	10,000	2,800	Va.
	Elizabeth A. R.	"	38				Ga.
	Wm. H. B.	"	19				Tenn.
	James K.	"	17				"
	Elizabeth M.	"	15				"
	Jno. M.	"	13				"
	Milton G.	"	11				"
	Mary C. P.	"	9				"
	Sarah R.	"	7				"
	Ann L.	"	5				"
	Addy F.	"	3				"
562	Jonas	RYAN	39	Laborer		200	N. C.
	Rebecca	"	36				Tenn.
	Jacob	"	16				"
	Malinda	"	11				"

District 2   P.O.: Morganton

	Name		Age	Occupation	Real	Pers.	Birthplace
	John	"	9				"
	Eliza	"	7				"
	Isabella	"	5				"
	John	BEST	13				"

Page 79   29 June 1860

	Name		Age	Occupation	Real	Pers.	Birthplace
	Nancy	BEST	10				Tenn.
	Caroline	"	7				"
563	Anderson	BURNS	39	Blacksmith		500	S. C.
	Phebe	"	35				"
	James A.	"	12				"
	Solomon S.	"	11				"
	Levina A.	"	10				"
	Mary N.	"	5				Tenn.
	Christopher	"	21	Blacksmith			S. C.
	David	KEYS	22	Laborer			"
564	Edwd.	WAYMAN	60	Carriage Maker	2,000	1,500	N. C.
	Elizabeth	"	59				"
	James L.	"	17				Tenn.
	Elizabeth	BARNHILL	14				"
565	Jno. S.	CUMMING	28	Carriage Maker		100	Tenn.
	Rachel L.	"	21				"
	Ann C.	"	2				"
	Sarah E.	"	1				"
566	Wm. G.	McKENZIE	30	Physician		3,000	Tenn.
	Elvira H.	"	19				"
	Jno. R.	"	25	Med. Student			"
567	Wm. L.	WAYMAN	29	Waggon Maker		150	Tenn.
	Mary E.	"	26				"
	John N.	"	5				"
	George M.	"	2				"
	John	SNIDER	21				"
568	Wm. C.	WARNACK	29	Tailor		150	Tenn.
	Elizabeth	"	26				"
	Samuel B.	"	10				"
	James L.	"	6				"
	Walter A.	"	4				"
	William M.	"	2				"
569	Jno. F.	HENDERSON	39	Tailor		400	Va.
	Sapphira	"	28				"
	Thomas D.	"	4				Tenn.
	John C.	"	1				"
570	Andrew F.	COWAN	30	Merchant	500	12,600	Tenn.
	Elizabeth J.	"	30				"
	Cherokee Pocahontas	"	2				"
571	Lewis O.	FOUVILLE	28	Trader	1,000	1,500	N. C.

Page 80   29 June 1860

	Name		Age	Occupation	Real	Pers.	Birthplace
	Lucinda	FOUVILLE	22				N. C.
	Walter C.	"	2				Tenn.
	Florence O.	"	1				"

-200-

	Name		Age	Occupation	Real	Pers.	Birthplace
572	Samuel	HENLEY	23	Merchant	7,775	11,100	Tenn.
	Thomas	"	25	Merchant	7,775	11,100	"
573	Asberry	HOWARD	27	Merchant		1,400	Tenn.
	Lucinda J.	"	25				"
574	William M.	JONES	32	Farmer	9,000	3,950	Tenn.
	Lavina	"	32				"
	Meredith E.	"	6				"
	Samuel T.	"	3				"
	Mary	"	1				"
	Wyley B.	COPPOCK	35	Dry Goods Clerk			"
	Nathan	WILSON	25	Laborer			S. C.
575	Jabes	COULSON	47	Merchant	4,500	39,600	Tenn.
	Jane	"	49				"
	Perez D.	"	20				"
	John C.	"	11				"
	Theodore M.	"	9				"
576	Amanda	HOOD	52			300	Tenn.
	John A.	"	16				"
	William H.	"	14				"
	Sydney C.	" (f)	12				"
	Rachel M.	TORBET	25				"
	Martha A.	"	3				"
	David B.	WELCH	25	Painter		1,000	N. C.
577	Saml J.	SPARKS	34	Saddler	600	400	Tenn.
	Mary A.	"	30				"
	James	"	9				"
	Winfield S.	"	7				"
	William	"	6				"
	Thomas	"	5				"
	Millard F.	"	3				"
	Daniel	"	2				"
	Sydney J.	"	3/12				"
578	William B. SCOTT (mul)		39	Saddler & Harness M.	400	500	N. C.
	Minerva	" (mul)	34				"
	Laura A.	" (mul)	15				"
	William B.	" (mul)	14				"
	Lawson CANSELLER (mul)		22	Laborer			Tenn.

Page 81   29 June 1860

	Name		Age	Occupation	Real	Pers.	Birthplace
579	John M.	HENSON	39	Ferryman		250	Tenn.
	Mary	"	27				S. C.
	George H.	"	1				Tenn.
	Elizabeth C.	"	5/12				"
580	Thomas R.	BLAIR	45	Tanner	1,500	5,500	Tenn.
	Athalinda	"	46				"
	Eliza J. R.	"	17				"
	Elizabeth L.M.	"	15				"
	Samuel P.	"	13				"
	Laura A.	"	4				"
581	Ann E.	McCLAIN	50	Farmer	5,500	10,500	Tenn.
	Mary E.	"	23				"
	Julia A.	"	22				"

	Name		Age	Occupation	Real	Pers.	Birthplace
	Lydia J.	"	20				"
	Martha C.	"	19				"
	Robert L.	"	18				"
	Rebecca	"	15				"
	Sarah A.	"	14				"
	Nancy L.	"	12				"
582	Ortey	COBB (f)	50	Farmer	5,000	5,270	Tenn.
	Thomas P.	"	22				"
	Samuel L.	"	20				"
	John O.	"	17				"
	William C.	"	13				"
	Henry C.	"	11				"
	Mira R. R.	"	6				"
	Calvin L.	"	27				"
	Julia H.	" (mwy)	24				"
583	Edmond	UNDERWOOD	24	Laborer		100	N. C.
	Sarah E.	"	20				Tenn.
	James M.	"	1				"
584	Moses	SCRUGGS	75	Farmer	4,000	8,850	N. C.
	Margaret	"	74				"
	Sarah E.	HOUSTON	12				Ga.
585	Barbara	LITNER (mul)	84			100	Va.
	Mary	" (mul)	12				Tenn.
	David	" (mul)	24				"
	Adeline	" (mul)	18				"
586	Nancy	SAUL (mul)	45			125	Va.
	Bartley	" (mul)	21				Tenn.

Page 82   29 June 1860

	Name		Age	Occupation	Real	Pers.	Birthplace
	Candacia	SAUL (mul)	16				Tenn.
	Sally H.	" (mul)	12				"
	Ludicia	" (mul)	8				"
	O'Connell	" (mul)	15				"
587	Mary	WEST	61			500	N. C.
	Alford	"	21				Tenn.
588	Franklin	WEST	28	Farmer		500	Tenn.
	Nancy	"	30				"
	Theodore	"	4				"
	Robert	"	3				"
	Lafayette	"	6/12				"
589	Bartley M.	RUSSELL	54	Farmer	10,000	1,000	Tenn.
590	John	FRANCE	69			400	Md.
	Abigail	"	41				Tenn.
	Samuel P.	"	16				"
	Ann E.	"	12				"
	John H.	"	10				"
	William S.	"	8				"
	Candais A.	"	4				"

District 2   P.O.: Morganton

	Name		Age	Occupation	Real	Pers.	Birthplace
591	Joseph	WALKER	24	Laborer		250	Tenn.
	Martha J.	"	23				"
	James H.	"	7				"
	John H.	"	5				"
	Calvin	"	1				"
592	Isaac D.	WEAR (mwy)	43	Farmer	7,500	7,470	Tenn.
	Susan A. J.	"	26				"
	Elizabeth L.	"	6				"
	Robert .	"	3				"
593	Sarah	HAWKINS	45			200	Tenn.
	Elvira	"	18				"
	Dolly	"	16				"
	Margaret	"	14				"
	Elizabeth	" (twins)	6				"
	Anna	"	6				"
	Hamilton	"	1/12				"
594	Joseph	McMILLAN	61	Laborer		150	Tenn.
	Milly	"	56				"
	Ann E.	"	14				"
	Polly	ROBINSON	90				Unknown
595	Elizabeth	TETER	20				Tenn.

Page 83   30 June 1860

	Name		Age	Occupation	Real	Pers.	Birthplace
	George	TETER	70				N. C.
596	John	McGHEE	37	Physician			Tenn.
	Amza	" (f)	34				"
	Margaret	"	11				"
	Mary	"	7				"
	Nancy A.	"	6				"
	Alexander	"	4				"
	John C.	"	2				"
597	William	YARBROUGH	55	Farmer	1,200	800	N. C.
	Sarah	"	59				Tenn.
	Wyley	"	29				"
	Eliza	"	24				"
	Nancy	"	21				"
	William	"	19				"
598	John	RIDER	69	Farmer	3,000	5,625	Tenn.
	David W.	"	18				"
	John M.	"	16				"
599	Beverage	LAWRENCE	66	Farmer	1,000	900	Ga.
	Kessiah A.	"	62				Tenn.
	Joseph	"	18				"
	Elizabeth	KING	18				"
600	James A.	BLACK	38	Farmer	4,000	7,425	Tenn.
	Rachel S.	"	24				"
	Orville B.	"	4				"
	Campbell H.	"	3				"
	Charlie R.	"	1				"

	Name		Age	Occupation	Real	Pers.	Birthplace
601	Isaac	BELT	63	Farmer		1,000	N. C.
	Pharaba	"	63				"
	Anderson	"	26				Tenn.
	John	"	24				"
	Sally	"	23				"
	Sophia	SPRADLIN	21				"
602	John	DAWSON	56	Farmer		1,770	Va.
	Elizabeth	"	49				"
	Elijah	"	20				Tenn.
	Alexander	"	18				"
	Williamson	"	16				"
603	Julia Ann	JACKSON (Bl)	50			100	Dist Columbia
	Geo. Washington	" (Bl)	14				Tenn.
	Chas. Houston	" (Bl)	12				"

Page 84   2 July 1860

	Name		Age	Occupation	Real	Pers.	Birthplace
	Litha Ann	JACKSON (Bl)	8				Tenn.
	Jos. Rawlings	" (Bl)	7				"
	Robt. Jackson	" (Bl)	5				"
604	Samuel	STOUT	46	Farmer	400	350	Tenn.
	Sarah	"	35				"
	Saraphina	"	15				"
	James D.	"	11				"
	John	"	8				"
	Nancy E.	"	6				"
	George W.	"	2				"
	Nancy	HAMMONTREE	81				N. C.
605	James	HAMMONTREE	61	Farmer	500	1,125	Tenn.
	Nancy	"	50				Ireland
	Mary	"	30				Tenn.
	Harvey	"	23				"
	Sarah	"	18				"
	Elizabeth	"	16				"
	Lucinda E.	"	14	(Blind)			"
	Lettitia	"	12				"
	William H.	"	5				"
606	Jere.	HAMMONTREE	57	Farmer	600	500	Tenn.
	Aisey	"	57				"
	Harvey	"	15				"
	Hiram	"	14				"
607	Saml N.	BICKNELL	25	Blacksmith		1,000	Tenn.
	Susan J.	"	24				"
	William	"	2				"
608	Robt.	THOMPSON	59	Farmer	10,000	10,225	Tenn.
	Nancy	"	54				"
	Nancy E.	"	16				"
	Robert H.	"	14				"
	John H.	"	12				"
	Mary	"	18				"
	Lorenzo W.	" (mwy)	22				"
	Mary	"	20				"

District 2   P.O.: Morganton

	Name		Age	Occupation	Real	Pers.	Birthplace
609	John	COLLINS	66			30	N. C.
	Rebecca	"	62				"
610	Philip	HAMMONTREE	61	Farmer	2,500	1,500	Tenn.
	Catharine	"	55				Ireland
	John C.	"	29				Tenn.

Page 85   2 July 1860

	Name		Age	Occupation	Real	Pers.	Birthplace
	Sarah E.	HAMMONTREE	25				Tenn.
	Thomas H.	"	24				"
	Rachel E.	"	22				"
	Philip E.	"	18				"
	Phebe C.	"	16				"
	Ann E.	"	13				"
	Dorcus	"	17				"
611	Emerson	HEDGECOCK	40			50	N. C.
	Sarah A.	"	46				S. C.
	John	"	18				Tenn.
	James	"	16				"
	David	"	14				"
	Taylor	"	11				"
	Catharine	"	8				"
	Sarah J.	"	5				"
	Louisa	"	2				"
612	John	THOMPSON	57	Farmer	5,000	3,725	Tenn.
	Margaret C.	"	31				"
	Harriet A. E.	"	12				"
	Millard B.	"	9				"
	Elizabeth T.	"	4				"
	John B.	"	2				"
	Martha N. J.	McALLEN	15				Mo.
613	Charles A.	IRVIN	44	Laborer		500	Ala.
	Nancy A.	"	22				Tenn.
	Margaret R.	"	16				"
	Phebe M.	"	14				"
	Sarah A.	"	12				"
	David H.	"	9				"
	Amanda E.	"	6				"
614	Pleasant S.	BYBY	23	Laborer		75	Tenn.
	Elizabeth	"	23				"
	Sarah J.	"	2				"
	John M.	"	5/12				"
	Sarah	"	74				N. C.
615	Charles	SHEDDAN	60	Farmer	5,000	2,300	Tenn.
	Ann M.	"	57				"
	John E.	"	24				"
	Lilitha A.	"	23				"
	Nancy C.	"	15				"

Page 86   2 July 1860

	Name		Age	Occupation	Real	Pers.	Birthplace
	Andrew L.	SHEDDAN	13				Tenn.

District 2   P.O.: Morganton

	Name		Age	Occupation	Real	Pers.	Birthplace
616	Thomas W.	SHEDDAN	34	Tanner		1,500	Tenn.
	Jane	"	30				"
	Chalres M.	"	8				"
	Patrick A.	" (Twins)	5				"
	Robert W.	"	5				"
617	John	EAKIN	73	Farmer	2,500	2,350	Tenn.
	Martha J.	"	27				"
	Hugh M.	"	22				"
	John W.	"	24				"
	Hetty A.	"	26				"
618	Joseph	RUNION	43	Farmer	1,500	1,000	Tenn.
	Elizabeth	"	41				"
	Sarah	"	16				"
	William B.	"	14				"
	James M.	"	11				"
	Alexander W.	"	9				
	Margaret E.	"	5				
	Samuel L.	"	2				
619	Robert	REID (mwy)	18				Tenn.
	Sarah A.	"	16				"
620	Jos. C.	McCONNELL	29	Farmer	5,000	2,745	Tenn.
	Mary J.	"	39				"
	Martha A.	"	32				"
	Elizabeth A.	"	30				"
	And.	RAINWATER	18				"
621	David C.	TALLY	30	Farmer		500	Tenn.
	Mary	"	30				"
	Joseph P.	"	10				"
	Martha	"	8				"
	John	"	7				"
	Tennessee	" (f)	5				"
	Mary J.	"	4				"
	Sarah	"	1				"
622	Edw. N.	CAYWOOD	36	Farmer	750	750	Tenn.
	Hetty B.	"	26				"
	Andrew V.	"	7				"
	William C.	"	5				"
	James M.	"	3				"
	John W.	"	1/12				"

Page 87   3 July 1860

	Name		Age	Occupation	Real	Pers.	Birthplace
623	A. H.	McCONNELL	41	Farmer	2,500	1,000	Tenn.
	Mary A.	"	34				"
	Joseph H.	"	14				"
	Elizabeth M.	"	11				"
	Amy J.	"	9				"
	Alexr. S.	"	3				"
	Susan	FULLER	16				"
624	John	McNABB	54	Farmer	3,500	2,000	Tenn.
	Elizabeth	"	48				"
							"
							"

District 2   P.O.: Morganton

	Name		Age	Occupation	Real	Pers.	Birthplace
	Mary E.	"	17				"
	James H.	"	14				"
	Alexander T.	"	12				"
	John N.	"	10				"
625	Martha	McNABB	34			500	Tenn.
	Mary E.	"	31				"
626	John	JENKINS	33	Waggon Maker	1,500	800	Tenn.
	Margaret	"	33				"
	Matthew W.	"	16				"
	Sarah E.	"	14				"
	Margaret J.	"	12				"
	Nancy L.	"	9				"
	James R.	"	4				"
	Lucinda A.	"	1				"
627	Samuel	OAR	75		500	250	Pa.
	Margaret	"	50				Tenn.
628	Martha	RAINWATER	40			150	Tenn.
	Thomas	"	15				"
	Reddin	"	13				"
	Jackson	"	12				"
	David	"	10				"
	William	"	9				"
629	Mary	ADAMS	60	Farmer	700	850	Va.
	Wyley	"	23				Tenn.
	Gillespie	"	22				"
630	James	COHORN	51	Blacksmith	500	800	Tenn.
	Ruhamah	"	47				"
	Martha L.	"	25				"
	Nancy M.	"	20				"
	Margaret E.	"	18				"
	Mary A.	"	14				"

Page 88   3 July 1860

	Name		Age	Occupation	Real	Pers.	Birthplace
	Jane M.	LOGAN	58				Tenn.
	David	RAINWATER	13				"
631	Andrew	VANCE	61	Minister U.S. Pres.	1,600	1,840	Va.
	Eliza J.	"	50				Ky.
	Ann E.	"	18				Tenn.
	Sarah E.	"	16				"
632	Joseph A.	TALLY	59	Miller		200	Va.
	Oney	"	54				Tenn.
	John	"	15				"
633	M. H.	STEPHENS	35	Farmer	2,000	16,775	Ireland
	Mary M.	"	29				Tenn.
	Molly M.	"	5				"
	Martha	"	1				"
	Blount	PAUL	23	Laborer			"

	Name		Age	Occupation	Real	Pers.	Birthplace
634	Saml	MONTGOMERY	35	Farmer	15,000	12,675	Tenn.
	Hetty A.	"	23				"
	Mary E.	"	7				"
	Eliza C.	"	5				"
	Andrew B.	"	2				"
635	Gillespy	WEST	28	Farmer	600	500	Tenn.
	Edna Ann	"	25				"
	William L.	"	8/12				"
636	James L.	WEST	22	Farmer		200	Tenn.
	Lucelia A.	"	24				Va.
	Elizabeth A.	"	68			250	"
637	James M.	HAIR	37	Farmer	1,000	600	Tenn.
	Sarah	"	34				"
	John R.	"	11				"
	Martha A.	"	9				"
	William	"	6				"
	Samuel	"	3				"
	Jacob W.	"	1				"
638	William L.	HALL	38	Farming	2,000	2,100	Tenn.
	Nancy E.	"	28				"
	Joseph C.	"	8				"
	James B.	"	6				"
	John R.	"	4				"
	Susan A.	"	1				"
639	Charles	STONE	39	Farmer		500	Tenn.
	Margaret	"	30				"

Page 89   3 July 1860

	Name		Age	Occupation	Real	Pers.	Birthplace
	Sarah A.	STONE	10				Tenn.
	Catharine T.	"	9				"
	Ann E.	"	7				"
	Mary A.	"	3				"
	James B.	"	1				"
640	William	ILES	65	Farmer	2,500	3,350	N. C.
	Jane	"	67				Va.
	William R.	ILES	45				N. C.
	Elizabeth	"	40				Tenn.
	Mary J.	"	15				"
	James L.	"	13				"
	John K.	"	11				"
	Tipton C.	"	9				"
641	Logan	BROWN	45	Laborer		100	N. C.
	Sarah A.	"	30				"
	Hannah C.	"	11				"
	John J.	"	9				"
	William J.	"	7				"
	Thomas A.	"	5				"
	Sarah A.	"	3				"
	Annie Vic	"	6/12				"

	Name		Age	Occupation	Real	Pers.	Birthplace
642	Hugh C.	KELSON	39	Carpenter		200	Tenn.
	Elizabeth	"	37				"
	William H.	"	15				"
	Jno. M.	"	13				"
	Jacob T.	"	11				"
	Margaret	"	5				"
643	Adam	MOWRY	45	Hatter		250	Tenn.
	Margaret	"	45				"
	Catharine	"	30				"
	Martha	"	17				"
	David	"	15				"
	Andrew	McKEE	16				"
644	James	COLLINS	23			100	S. C.
	Caroline M.	"	20				Tenn.
	Leonard B.	"	9/12				"
645	Patrick	McCLUNG	67	Farmer	3,000	4,400	Ga.
	Hannah G.	"	56				Tenn.
	John C.	"	19				"
	Patrick A.	"	16				"

Page 90   4 July 1860

	Name		Age	Occupation	Real	Pers.	Birthplace
	Isabella C.	DAVIS	16				Tenn.
646	James H.	McCLUNG	28	Farmer		2,300	Tenn.
	Rachel L.	"	24				"
	James T.	"	5				"
	Andrew B.	"	10/12				"
647	Stephen	BELT	61	Waggon Maker	1,800	500	N. C.
	Sally	"	64				"
	William	"	32				S. C.
648	Stephen K.	BELT	27	Farmer		200	S. C.
	Tempa	"	26				Tenn.
	William B.	"	2				"
	Mary E.	"	1				"
649	Robert B.	BELT	25	Farmer	600	600	S. C.
	Elizabeth J.	"	21				Tenn.
	James A.	"	2				"
	Sarah J.	"	7/12				"
650	Tobias	PETERSON	30	Farmer	600	550	Tenn.
	Nancy L.	"	30				S. C.
	John Y.	"	5				Tenn.
	Sally R.	"	2				"
651	William	BICKNELL	20	Laborer		500	Tenn.
	Evaline	"	19				"
	Ann Eliza	"	10/12				"
652	Robert	DAVIS	65	Cooper		100	Tenn.
	Elvira	POSTON	40				"
	William R.	"	18				"
	Peter E.	"	15				"
	Sarah T.	"	13				"

	Name		Age	Occupation	Real	Pers.	Birthplace
	John L.	"	11				"
	Edward N.	"	9				"
	Robert	"	7				"
	Catharine V. S. DAVIS		10				"
	Mary	"	37				"
653	Martha	HENRY	46			100	Tenn.
	Cyntha J.	"	25				"
	Sarah E.	"	22				"
	Elmira	"	16				"
	Rosanna	"	11				"
654	Phebe	McCOLLUM	45	Farmer	3,000	11,625	Tenn.
	Joseph B.	"	21				"

Page 91   4 July 1860

	Name		Age	Occupation	Real	Pers.	Birthplace
	James	McCOLLUM	18				Tenn.
	Sarah M.	"	14				"
655	William	CRAIG	45	Farmer	1,500	1,200	Tenn.
	Eliza	"	35				"
	Samuel H.	"	18				"
	James	"	15				"
	Mary E.	"	14				"
656	Hugh H.	CRAIG	24	Farmer	1,000	600	Tenn.
	Mary E.	"	23				"
	William G.	"	4				"
	James B.	"	2				"
	Ann Eliza	"	1/12				"
657	Albertus	BELT	28	Farmer		500	S. C.
	Mary A.	"	22				Tenn.
	James W.	"	4				"
	Sally	"	2				"
	Andfew A.	"	1				"
659	David K.	BEATY	67			250	N. C.
	Isabella	"	59				Tenn.
	Mary E.	"	31				"
	Sarah J.	"	24				"
	Martha E.	"	21				"
	Resetta L.	" (f)	18				"
	Russia A.	" (f)	13				"
660	H. A.	McCOLLUM	26	Farmer	2,500	700	Tenn.
	Isabella M.	"	26				"
	Hetty A.	"	2				"
	David A.	"	2/12				"
	N. A.	WARSHAM	9				"
661	Thomas O.	SARTAEN	23	Farmer		2,525	Tenn.
	Martha E.	"	22				"
	William A. R.	"	7				"
	John R.	"	6/12				"
	Sam J. L.	BAYLESS	20			1,047	"

	Name		Age	Occupation	Real	Pers.	Birthplace
662	John R.	BLACK	46	Farmer	1,400	4,300	Tenn.

<u>Page 92</u>   <u>4 July 1860</u>

	Name		Age	Occupation	Real	Pers.	Birthplace
	Elizabeth E.	BLACK	41				S. C.
	James A.	"	20				N. C.
	John S.	"	18				"
	Mary J.	"	16				"
	Nancy A.	"	14				"
	Pleasant T.	"	12				"
	Joseph M.	"	5				Tenn.
	William C.	"	2				"
	Mary	RHEA	64				S. C.
663	Wm. M.	BAYLESS (mwy)	49	Physician	1,200	3,075	Tenn.
	Sarah H.	"	33				"
	Benj. J.	"	18				"
	Joseph T.	"	16				"
	William R.	"	13				"
	Jabes H.	" (m)	8				"
	Andrew V.	"	4				"
	Alexander F.	"	1				"
	Nancy	HUGHS	68				"
664	John	KERR	44	Farmer	7,000	5,550	Tenn.
	Julia A.	"	42				"
	Jesse C.	"	20				"
	William N.	"	17				"
	Mary E.	"	14				"
	David M.	"	10				"
665	Lucinda	ELLEGE	45			200	Tenn.
	Polly C.	"	25				"
	James	"	23				"
666	James	TOWNSLEY	68	Farmer	1,000	1,400	Va.
	Jane	"	63				Tenn.
	Benj	BIRD	11				"
667	Jno. H.	NORWOOD	32	Farmer		500	Tenn.
	Margaret J.	"	33				"
	Barbara E.	"	1				"
668	C. W. C.	NORWOOD	66	Farmer	10,000	9,644	Tenn.
	Melinda	"	43				"
	Martha R.	"	6				"
669	Elizabeth	HOYL	37			100	N. C.
	William	"	9				Tenn.
	James	"	7				"
	Andrew	"	5				"

<u>Page 93</u>   <u>5 July 1860</u>

	Name		Age	Occupation	Real	Pers.	Birthplace
670	Samuel	CORN (mwy)	22	Laborer		100	N. C.
	Derotha	"	17				Tenn.

-211-

District 2   P.O.: Morganton

	Name		Age	Occupation	Real	Pers.	Birthplace
671	Barbara M.	PRICHARD	50	Farmer	2,000	800	Tenn.
	Phebe A. E.	BICKNELL	28				"
	Flora Albira	"	26				"
	George E.	"	16				"
672	Jesse	KERR, Sr.	69	Farmer	15,000	62,825	N. C.
	Phebe	"	34				Tenn.
673	General C. C.	KERR	34	Farmer	7,700	7,035	Tenn.
	Martha E.	"	32				"
	Jesse T.	"	12				"
	William H.	"	8				"
	Alabama T.	" (f)	7				"
	David M.	" (twins)	5				"
	John M.	"	5				"
	James B.	"	3				"
	General C. C.	"	1				"
674	Lyle	WILSON	44	Farmer	2,500	3,490	Tenn.
	Elizabeth	"	39				"
	John H.	"	18				"
	Sarah J.	"	12				"
	Jesse P.	"	7				"
	Andrew J.	"	4				"
675	Thomas	SANDERSON	44	Merchant	2,000	5,000	England Europe
	Helen H.	"	34				"
	Edward W.	"	16				"
	Barbara	"	14				"
	Anna	"	12				"
	Emmaline	WILLIS	35				"
676	Samuel D.	LAIN	32	Physician	2,000	3,000	Tenn.
	Martha L.	"	18				"
	No Name	" (m)	1/12				"
	Elizabeth	CALDWELL	16				"
	Robert	McCALL	21	Laborer			"
677	Gillespy	MONTGOMERY	44	Farmer	7,500	6,962	Tenn.
	Mary J.	"	35				Va.
	Samuel	"	12				Tenn.
	Robert	"	10				"
	James	"	7				"
	William	"	5				"

Page 94   District 2   P.O.: Brick Mill   5 July 1860

	Name		Age	Occupation	Real	Pers.	Birthplace
	Lirchfield(?)	MONTGOMERY	3				Tenn.
	Elizabeth M.	"	1				"
678	James M.	LAIN	41	Physician	6,000	7,330	Tenn.
	Eliza H.	"	25				"
	Clementine T.	"	9				"
	Mary E.	"	6				"
	Angeline V.	"	5				"
	Samuel H.	"	3				"
	Cordelia J.	"	1				"

District 2   P.O.: Brick Mill

	Name		Age	Occupation	Real	Pers.	Birthplace
679	William R.	HENRY	26	Farmer	10,800	5,550	Tenn.
	Narcissa	"	57			7,100	N. C.
680	Mary	CUMMING	49			150	Tenn.
	Rachel A.	"	21				"
	William H.	"	19				"
	Nancy J.	"	16				"
	Jasper	JONES	15				"
	Mary	CREGER	3/12				"
681	Ann E.	DUNN	38			300	Tenn.
	Cyntha E.	"	20				"
	Rhadamanthus H.	" (m)	18				"
	Robert T.	"	16				"
682	Robert	BOGLE	75	Farmer	6,000	1,350	Va.
	Montgomery	McTEER	40				Tenn.
	Martha	"	38				"
	Silliman	" (m)	21				"
	Cammilla	" (f)	10				"
683	Andrew	MILLER	73	Farmer	6,000	1,365	Tenn.
	Adaline	"	30				"
	Samantha	"	20				"
	John D.	"	27				"
684	Sellers	BIRDWELL	32	Farmer	1,000	810	Tenn.
	Lodora A.	"	23				"
	Samuel S.	"	5				"
	Harriet E.	"	3				"
	Mary A.	"	1				"
	Mary	"	72				N. C.
685	Elizabeth	JACKSON	54	Farmer	1,500	1,500	Va.
	James A.	"	27				Tenn.
	Samuel	"	18				"
	Harriet	"	16				"

Page 95   District 6   P.O.: Brick Mill   5 July 1860

	Name		Age	Occupation	Real	Pers.	Birthplace
	Everline	JACKSON	14				Tenn.
	George M.	"	10				"
686	Cyrus H.	COHORN	28	Farmer	2,500	675	Tenn.
	Caroline D.	"	25				"
	Alvira T.	"	3				"
	William R. J.	"	2				"
	Mary M. J.	"	4/12				"
687	Rufus	BIRDWELL	37			500	Tenn.
	Elizabeth	"	36				Va.
	Mary J.	"	12				Tenn.
	Dolly A.	"	10				"
	Amanda	"	8				"
	Joshua	"	6				"
	Susan	"	4				"
	Sarah C.	"	2				"
	Caroline	"	3/12				"

	Name		Age	Occupation	Real	Pers.	Birthplace
688	John	RUSSELL	74	Farmer		500	Tenn.
	Nancy	"	65				N. C.
	Robert P.	"	31				Tenn.
	Elizabeth	"	24				"
	Ann A.	"	8				"
689	James (Spix)	HENRY	57	Farmer	10,000	9,400	Tenn.
	Catharine	"	53				"
	Jane E.	"	31				"
	William G.	"	21				"
	Sarah E.	"	17				"
	Martha E.	"	16				"
	John F.	"	12				"
	Roma T. (?)	"	10				"
	Geo. W.	REAGAN	16				"
690	Ake	HENRY (mwy)	27			1,500	Tenn.
	Mary M.	"	21				"
691	Nathan	RICHARDS	33			200	Tenn.
	Ann E.	"	34				"
	Betsy J.	"	7				"
	Jesse L.	"	3				"
	Sarah C.	"	1				"
692	James A.	LOGAN	46	Farmer	10,000	7,700	Tenn.
	Martha C.	"	40				"
	John H.	"	12				"

Page 96   6 July 1860

	Name		Age	Occupation	Real	Pers.	Birthplace
	Michael R.	LOGAN	10				Tenn.
	Hugh L.	"	5				"
	Mary J.	"	4				"
	Martha M.	"	3				"
	Alexander W.	"	1				"
693	Edward R.	LAIN	35	Physician		500	Tenn.
	Sarah E.	"	25				Ga.
	James L.	"	6				"
	John L.	"	4				"
	William A.	"	2				"
694	John W.	MALCOM	50	Farmer	10,000	9,250	Tenn.
	Jane	"	42				"
	Margaret C.	"	21				"
	Samuel A.	"	19				"
	Nancy A.	"	14				"
	Eliza J.	"	12				"
	Elizabeth A.	"	8				"
	Lucinda C.	"	6				"
695	John C.	LOGAN	48	Farmer	4,500	2,975	Tenn.
	Lucinda	"	51				"
696	William G.	TAYLOR	55	Miller		1,500	Va.
	Margaret	"	51				Tenn.
	Mary	"	29				"
	Martha	"	27				"
	Elizabeth J.	"	24				"

	Name		Age	Occupation	Real	Pers.	Birthplace
	Rachel	"	22				"
	Margaret	"	20				"
	William	"	18				"
	Ann	"	16				"
	Thomas	"	14				"
	Caroline	"	12				"
697	James H.	McCONNELL	55	Farmer	3,500	6,330	Tenn.
	Ann M.	"	41				"
	John N.	"	20				"
	Ellen C.	REVELY	21				"
698	John A.	STEWARD	22	Blacksmith		300	Tenn.
	Elizabeth J.	"	21				"
	Ruhuma J.	" (f)	3				"
	James V.	"	1				"
	Margaret L.	"	17				"

Page 97   6 July 1860

	Name		Age	Occupation	Real	Pers.	Birthplace
699	James D.	DICKSON	26	Farmer	1,500	835	Tenn.
	Nancy	"	64				Va.
700	Benjamin	NOAH	45			100	N. C.
	Elizabeth	"	30				Ga.
701	George C.	GRIFFITTS	27	Farmer	6,000	3,000	Tenn.
	Margaret J.	"	22				"
	Mary A.	"	7/12				"
	James M.	"	29				"
702	James P.	ALLEN	57	Farmer	1,500	1,500	Tenn.
	Nancy	"	50				"
	John W.	"	20				"
	James L.	"	17				"
	William B.	"	16				"
	Samuel H.	"	14				"
	Nancy J.	"	12				"
	Francis M.	" (m)	10				"
	Mary E.	"	6				"
703	Geo. A.	McINTURF	28			300	Tenn.
	Sarah J.	"	22				Ga.
	Israel W.	"	8				Tenn.
	Alford C.	"	6				"
	Isabella	"	5				"
	Sarah E.	"	4				"
	Martha C.	"	1				"
704	Matthew H.	COHORN	29	Farmer	5,000	7,110	Tenn.
	Tersa	"	44				"
	Jane	"	40				"
	Martha	"	34				"
	Mary	"	32				"
	Nancy N.	"	25				"
	Esther A.	"	22				"
705	Lewis	HUTSELL	59	Farmer	1,000	850	Va.
	Nancy	"	48				Tenn.
	Alexander	SMITH	14				"

District 6   P.O.: Brick Mill

	Name		Age	Occupation	Real	Pers.	Birthplace
706	John	WALKER	50	Farmer	6,500	2,100	Tenn.
	Esther	"	44				"
	David C.	"	25				"
	Melinda E.	"	23				"
	William A.	"	19				"
	Alvira A.	"	15				"

Page 98   6 July 1860

	Name		Age	Occupation	Real	Pers.	Birthplace
	Francis P.	WALKER (M)	13				Tenn.
	Mary L.	"	11				"
	Hester M.	"	8				"
	John A.	"	4				"
707	James W.	LAIN	38	Laborer		50	Tenn.
	Sally D.	"	37				N. C.
	John S.	"	12				Tenn.
	Rachel E.	"	10				"
	James W.	"	5				"
	Sarah C.	"	2				"
	Mary A.	"	9/12				"
708	Kindrick	WILLIAMSON	28	Farmer		500	N. C.
	Lydia	"	29				"
	Martha	"	7				"
	Mary A.	"	4				"
	Bernice	"	1				"
709	Andrew	PORTER	51	Farmer	3,500	1,000	Va.
	Elizabeth	"	46				S. C.
	Mary A.	"	24				Tenn.
	Stephen	"	18				"
	Andrew J.	"	16				"
	Margaret M.	"	12				"
	Robert L.	"	10				"
	Nancy E.	"	7				"
	James	"	2				"
710	Wallace	EDMONSON	37	Farmer	6,000	1,400	Tenn.
	Mary E.	"	38				"
	Fatima	"	13				"
	Jennette A.	"	12				"
	William H.	"	11				"
	Andrew S.	"	9				"
	Joseph A.	"	7				"
	Sarah J.	"	6				"
	Lucina M.	"	3				"
	Jennette	"	82				Va.
711	William P.	LOGAN	49	Farmer	2,500	1,000	Tenn.
	Euturbe A.	"	47				Va.
	Samuel A. A.	"	23				Tenn.
	Rachel M.	"	21				"
	John A.	"	19				"

Page 99   7 July 1860

	Name		Age	Occupation	Real	Pers.	Birthplace
	James H.	LOGAN	17				Tenn.
	William D.	"	14				"

District 6   P.O.: Brick Mill

	Name		Age	Occupation	Real	Pers.	Birthplace
	Betsy J.	"	11				"
	Drusilla O.	"	6				"
712	George	LAMBERT (mwy)	24			500	Tenn.
	Nancy	"	14				
713	John	LAMBERT	63	Farmer			N. C.
	Mary	"	55				"
	Elmira	"	27				Tenn.
	Harriet	"	22				"
	Malinda	"	21				"
	Lee (m)	"	20				"
	Mary	"	17				"
	Nancy	"	15				"
	John	"	13				"
	Saphrona	"	11				"
	Martin	"	9				"
	Hannah	"	7				"
	Willie	"	5				"
714	James C.	HARBISON	30	Farmer		2,400	Tenn.
	Mary J.	"	27				"
	William A.	"	7				"
	Charles	BENDER (Bl)	31				"
715	Wm. H.	JENKINS	25	Farmer		700	Tenn.
	Mary E.	"	21				"
	James B.	"	3				"
	Samuel H.	"	1				"
716	Wyley	McADOO (Bl)	45			200	Tenn.
	Martha	" (Bl)	25				"
	Margaret	" (Bl)	3				"
	No Name (M)	" (Bl)	1/12				"
717	William	CONNER (Bl)	46	Farmer	220	13,137	Tenn.
	Rachel	" (Bl)	27				"
	James H.	" (Bl)	11				"
	Henrietta C.	" (Bl)	9				"
	Willis	" (Bl)	6				"
	William	" (Bl)	4				"
	Alexander	" (Bl)	1				"
	Michael	STERLING (Bl)	21				"
	John	" (Bl)	19				"

Page 100   9 July 1860

718	Leah	STERLING (Bl)	65			250	N. C.
	Catharine	BELL (Bl)	22				Tenn.
	Taylor	STERLING (Bl)	26				"
	Martha M.	" (Bl)	9				"
	David H.	BELL (Bl)	6				"
719	Jno. H.	EDMONSON	49	Farmer	6,300	2,800	Tenn.
	Margaret C.	"	48				"
	Jno. C.	"	22				"
	William H.	"	19				"
	James P.	"	15				"

District 6   P.O.: Brick Mill

	Name		Age	Occupation	Real	Pers.	Birthplace
	Matthew N.	"	10				"
	David L.	"	8				"
	Jno.	BLANKENSHIP (mwy)	21	Physician			"
	Sarah A.	"	17				"
720	Henry	STERLING	36	Farmer	1,400	850	Tenn.
	Sarah C.	"	35				"
	Andrew P.	"	9				"
	John H.	"	7				"
	William T.	"	5				"
	Samuel A.	"	4				"
	James S.	"	8/12				"
721	Samuel	THOMPSON	54	Farmer	200	350	Tenn.
	Dorcas	"	35				"
	Margaret A.	"	9				"
722	Robert W.	DUNLAP	23	Farmer	1,200	345	Tenn.
	Cyntha	"	18				"
723	Robert H.	SCOTT	45	Farmer	5,000	2,850	Tenn.
	Mary	"	48				"
	James E.	"	15				"
	Margaret J.	"	13				"
	William	HITCH	25	Laborer			"
	Henry S.	GOFF	22	"			"
	Margaret C.	SCOTT	22	Domestic			"
	Ezikiel B.	BIRD	4				"
724	H. H. C.	CARUTHERS	52	Farmer	1,500	1,100	Tenn.
	Nancy McC.	"	53				"
	James W.	McCULLY	2				"
725	James	RATLEGE	24	Laborer		50	Tenn.
	Elizabeth	"	19				"
	John	"	9/12				"

Page 101   9 July 1860

	Name		Age	Occupation	Real	Pers.	Birthplace
726	Elija B.	McKEEHAN	36	Farmer	1,200	1,025	Tenn.
	Susannah	"	29				"
	Elizabeth A.	McCULLY	26				"
727	Cornelius	McKENZIE	53	Shoe & Boot Maker	300	200	S. C.
	Martha	"	52				"
	Arcara	" (f)	23				Ala.
	Obadiah	"	21				Tenn.
	Angeline	"	17				"
	Direna	" (f)	14				"
	Louisa	"	9				"
728	Aaron	LOVE	41	Farmer	1,250	670	Tenn.
	Lucinda	"	31				"
	Nancy J.	"	8				"
	Robert H.	"	6				"
	William H.	"	4				"
	Mary A.		2				"
729	Robert S.	LOVE	39	Farmer	1,250	900	Tenn.
	Isabella C.	"	31				"

District 6 _____   P.O.: Brick Mill

	Name		Age	Occupation	Real	Pers.	Birthplace
	Samuel A.	"	11				"
	William D.	"	8				"
	Nancy C.	"	6				"
	Sarah J.	"	1				"
730	Josiah	GRASTON	67	Farmer	1,200	1,500	N. C.
	Ann	"	54				Va.
	John S.	"	19				Tenn.
	Huldah	"	17				"
	David E.	"	14				"
	Rebecca J.	HITCH	6				"
	Susan C.	"	4				"
731	Margaret	BRADLY	43			200	Tenn.
	Emaline	"	21				"
	Joseph	"	17				"
	Sarah	"	15				"
	Elizabeth	"	13				"
	Susan	"	11				"
	Mary N.	"	9				"
	Margaret	"	7				"
	Lewis	"	4				"
	Sapphrona	"	1				"
732	John	RATLEGE (mwy)	21	Laborer		150	Tenn.

Page 102   9 July 1860

	Name		Age	Occupation	Real	Pers.	Birthplace
	Sarah	RATLEGE (mwy)	20				Tenn.
733	James	FREW	58	Farmer	8,000	4,000	Tenn.
	Jane	"	54				Va.
	Robert A.	"	23				Tenn.
	Susan T.	" (mwy)	17				"
734	Abram H.	WALLACE	26	Farmer		850	Tenn.
	Margaret J.	"	26				"
	William S.	"	8				"
	Hester A.	"	2				"
	Dora A.	"	1				"
735	John	WALLACE	56	Farmer	2,500	2,300	Tenn.
	Hannah	"	51				"
	John L.	"	22				"
	Dililah A.	"	20				"
	Joshua L.	"	17				"
	Benj. A.	"	15				"
	Martha A.	"	9				"
	Julia A.	YOUNG	15				"
	Nancy	GAMBLE	75				Ky.
736	Eli	MYERS	39	Blacksmith	1,250	2,855	Tenn.
	Livena	"	38				"
	Washington W.	"	20				"
	Narcissa	"	15				"
	Philip P.	"	11				"
	Jacob T.		9				"
	Jasper T.	"	7				"
	Elizabeth C.	"	5				"

	Name		Age	Occupation	Real	Pers.	Birthplace
	Dorcas V.	"	2				"
	Baker	STALLIAN	21	Laborer			"
737	Barbara	BIRD	29			100	N. C.
	Susan C.	"	2				Tenn.
738	John	YEAROUT	65	Farmer		200	Va.
	Martha	"	62				"
	Edney	"	12				Tenn.
739	Wm. R.	YEAROUT	39		1,000	500	Tenn.
	Mira	"	30				"
	Mary	"	3				"
	Minerva J.	"	1				"
740	David J.	CARATHERS	47	Farmer	500	200	Tenn.
	Jane F.	"	59				Va.

Page 103   10 July 1860

	Name		Age	Occupation	Real	Pers.	Birthplace
741	Elizabeth	RUDD	35			75	N. C.
	Martin P.	"	15				Tenn.
	Robert H.	"	14				"
	Sarah C.	"	7				"
742	Mary V.	RUDD	70			30	N. C.
	Sinclair	"	25				Tenn.
	Lucinda	" (mwy)	18				"
743	George	RUDD	40	Farmer		50	Tenn.
	Barbara	"	30				"
	Mary E.	"	12				"
	Margaret J.	"	9				"
	Ascineth	" (f)	2				"
744	James	ABBOTT	26	Farmer		150	N. C.
	Mary J.	"	22				Tenn.
	Absiller	RUDD (f)	36				N. C.
745	James	REID	50	Farmer		250	N. C.
	Harriet E.	"	40				Va.
	Mary A.	"	21				Tenn.
	Alexander	"	18				"
	Ann	"	16				"
	James C.	"	15				"
	Nancy J.	"	8				"
	Laura A.	"	5				"
746	Elizabeth	McCOY	59		600	600	Tenn.
	Nancy	"	42				"
	Barbara	"	39				"
	Jane	"	37				"
	John C.	"	35	Cty. Ct. Clerk			"
	Henry	HARRISON	14				"
747	John	McCULLY	57	Farmer		1,000	Tenn.
	Martha F.	"	55				Va.
	Isaac A.	"	25				Tenn.
	Nancy A.	"	26				"
	Martha C.	"	6				"
	John M.	"	2				"
	William	CALDWELL	9				"

	Name		Age	Occupation	Real	Pers.	Birthplace
District 6 | | | | | | | P.O.: Brick Mill

	Name		Age	Occupation	Real	Pers.	Birthplace
748	John	STALLIAN	45	Farmer	300	500	N. C.
	Isabel	"	30				S. C.
	William A.	"	19				Tenn.
	Andrew J.	"	17				

Page 104 .... 10 July 1860

	Jno. M.	STALLIAN	15				Tenn.
	General Washington	"	13				"
	James F.	"	11				"
	Ellen	"	4				"
	Sarah A.	"	1				"
749	William W.	SHERRELL	29	Farmer		500	Tenn.
	Sarah M.	"	31				N. C.
	William R.	"	6				Tenn.
750	George	MORROW	25			500	N. C.
	Martha J.	"	23				Tenn.
	Sarah A.C.T.L.A.V.V.	"	1/12				"
751	William	MEANS	44	Farmer	2,000	2,000	Tenn.
	Cinda A.	"	39				"
	John N.	"	18				"
	Samuel A.	"	11				"
	Laura A. A.	"	5				"
	Sarah C.	"	1				"
	Mary S.	"	40				"
	Nancy	"	36				"
752	Jane	STRAIN	66	Farmer	1,000	1,125	Tenn.
	Mary	"	38				"
	Robert B.	"	35				"
	Cyrena	"	30				"
	Nancy J.	"	25				"
	James A.	"	4				"
	Mary J.	"	1				"
753	John	GARDNER	56	Wool Carder	2,000	2,000	Scotland
	Isabella	"	50				"
	John N.	"	25	Wool Carder			"
754	David GARDNER (mwy)		24	Machinist		500	"
	Margaret	"	23				Tenn.
	Mary j C.	"	10/12				"
755	Thomas	WILSON (Bl)	52	Farmer		400	Tenn.
	Polly	" (Bl)	24				"
	Alexander	" (Bl)	5				"
	James	" (Bl)	2				"
756	Samuel	MITCHELL	39	Farmer		450	Tenn.
	Susan	"	29				"
	Margaret	"	13				"
	Nancy S.	"	2				"

District 6   P.O.: Brick Mill

	Name		Age	Occupation	Real	Pers.	Birthplace
Page 105							11 July 1860
757	Charles	WILLIAMS	23	Laborer		150	Tenn.
	Sarah J.	"	19				"
	Mary T.	"	3/12				"
758	Elija	KING (Bl)	83			125	N. C.
	Nelly	" (Bl)	79				"
759	Thomas	DOWNY	50	Farmer		800	N. C.
	Matilda C.	"	45				"
	Rebecca A.	"	22				Tenn.
	William G.	"	18				"
	John A.	"	14				"
	Salina J.	"	9				"
	George T.	"	7				"
	William R.	"	1				"
760	Samuel L. (mwy	KERR (mwy)	25	Farmer	10,000	7,345	Tenn.
	Fanny A.	"	21				"
	John T.	"	13				"
	William	ROSS	24	Laborer			"
761	Mary	GARET	55	Farmer	7,000	2,925	Tenn.
	Margaret E.	"	29				"
	Mary L.	"	22				"
	Lemuel E.	"	19				"
	Samuel H.	"	17				"
762	Eliza	HENSLEY	40			150	Tenn.
	Elizabeth J.	"	20				"
	John S.	"	6				"
	William A.	"	1				"
763	Patrick W.	CULTON	77	Farmer	5,500	3,070	Va.
	Robert H.	"	43				Tenn.
	Margaret A.	"	34				"
	Mary C.	"	13				"
	James W.	"	10				"
	Margaret P.	"	2				"
764	George	PICKERING	34	Farmer	2,500	1,250	Tenn.
	Catharine C.	"	26				"
	George A. C.	"	7				"
	Mary A.	"	5				"
	Sarah E.	"	3				"
	Samuel H.	"	1				"
	Nancy J.	"	2/12				"
	Nancy	"	72				"
Page 106							11 July 1860
765	Samuel S.	STRANGE	27	Farmer		300	S. C.
	Hannah M.	"	22				Tenn.
	Mary S. C.	"	1/12				"
766	Archibald	GRISSUM	59	Farmer	2,500	1,795	Tenn.
	Mary M.	"	59				"
	Martha S.	"	23				"
	Archibald C.	"	20				"
	Mary E.	"	16				"

District 6   P.O.: Brick Mill

	Name		Age	Occupation	Real	Pers.	Birthplace
767	Edward	PEPLES	40	Farmer		1,300	Va.
	Susan S.	"	27				Tenn.
	Mary L.	"	16				Va.
	Reuben S.	"	14				"
	Susan S.	"	12				Tenn.
	Eliza M.	"	10				"
	Wm. H. R.	"	8				"
	Mary F.	"	8				"
	Cyrina J. A.T."		1				"
768	George E.T.	HAMILL	41	Farmer	1,500	1,100	Tenn.
	Margaret	"	40				"
	Hugh A.	"	14				"
	Mary C.	"	11				"
	Margaret E.	"	7				"
	Margaret	"	65				"
769	George W.	RUNION	54	Farmer	5,000	4,300	N. C.
	Margaret	"	58				"
	James A.	CULTON	48				Tenn.
	Mary J.	"	33				"
	Mary A.	"	17				"
	Margaret J.	"	15				"
	George P.W.	"	12				"
	Martha S.	"	9				"
	Robert L.	"	7				"
	James A.	"	4				"
	Amanda T.	"	1				"
770	A. Jefferson	CARTER	40	Laborer		100	N. C.
	Catharine	"	27				Tenn.
	Betsy A.	"	3				"
	William M.	"	2				"
	Thomas Jef.	"	9/12				"
771	Mark	WIMBERLY	44	Laborer		300	Tenn.

Page 107   11 July 1860

	Name		Age	Occupation	Real	Pers.	Birthplace
	Adaline	WIMBERLY	40				Tenn.
	Mary	"	17				"
	John	"	15				"
	Margaret	"	11				"
	Eliza	"	9				"
	Elizabeth	"	6				"
	Lusina	"	4				"
	Caroline	"	2				"
772	John	CUMMINGS	33			300	Tenn.
	Mary J.	"	26				"
	Bartley T.	"	6				"
	Andrew	HUX	14				"
	Zachariah T.	"	12				"
773	M. Leonidas	THOMPSON	34	Farmer	1,000	300	Tenn.
	Mary J.	"	24				"
774	Martin	MORGAN	66	Laborer		100	N. C.
	Agnes	"	64				"
	Kessiah	RICHARDS	49				Md.

District 6   P.O.: Brick Mill

	Name		Age	Occupation	Real	Pers.	Birthplace
775	William	McKAMY	68	Farmer	2,000	1,300	Tenn.
	Nancy	"	63				"
	Nancy	"	39				"
	John W.	"	29				"
	William	"	22				"
	Mary E.	"	19				"
776	Mary	McKAMY	70	Farmer	2,500	1,000	N. C.
	Nancy	"	35				Tenn.
	John C.	"	30				"
	Joseph	"	27				"
	Mary J.	"	23				"
777	William	SIMONS	65			2,500	N. C.
	Catharine	"	50				"
778	James M.	DOCKERY (mul)	27	Laborer		50	Tenn.
	Lusidda	"	32				Va.
	Susan E.	" (mul)	3				Tenn.
	Geo. Washington " (mul)		10/12				"
779	Abram C.	STEELE	61			250	N. C.
	Nancy M.	"	61				"
	Doctor Franklin	"	23				"

CLOSE OF DISTRICT 6

Page 108   District 7   P.O.: Maryville   11 July 1860

	Name		Age	Occupation	Real	Pers.	Birthplace
780	David A.	STEELE	34	Farmer		850	N. C.
	Lucretia	"	33				Tenn.
	John	"	17				"
	James T.	"	15				"
	Martha J.	"	10				"
	George N.	"	7				"
	Mary E.	"	4				"
781	Henry	HAMILL	59	Farmer	4,000	2,635	Tenn.
	Mary	"	53				"
	John A.	"	30				"
782	Robert	BRIANT	22	Laborer		100	N. C.
	Barbara J.	"	26				"
	Elizabeth E.	"	3/12				Tenn.
783	David	HAMILL	64	Farmer	2,000	4,135	Tenn.
	Nancy	"	60				"
	Archily (?)	ANDERSON	23				"
	Margaret	"	17				"
	Robert H.	"	1/12				"
784	John A.	HANNER	47	Farmer	3,000	1,300	Tenn.
	Margaret	"	46				"
	Isaac A.	"	15				"
	Mary J.	"	3				"
785	Joseph N.	HANNER	22	Carpenter		200	Tenn.
	Lutitia	"	21				Miss.

District 7   P.O.: Maryville

	Name		Age	Occupation	Real	Pers.	Birthplace
786	Jacob	BEST	44	Farmer	6,000	3,268	N. C.
	Nancy	"	36				Tenn.
	Susan E.	"	16				Mo.
	Rebecca A.M.	"	12				"
	Sarah C.	"	8				Tenn.
	Margaret L.	"	5				"
	Samuel J.	"	1				"
	Martha T.	"	2/12				"
787	Michael	HUFFSTUTLER	59	Farmer	2,000	1,600	N. C.
	Annamara	"	49				"
	Samuel J.	"	24				Tenn.
	Sarah A.	"	22				"
	Margaret C.	"	20				"
	George W.	"	17				"
	Mary J.	"	14				"
	David A.	"	13				"

Page 109   12 July 1860

	Name		Age	Occupation	Real	Pers.	Birthplace
	Martha F.	HUFFSTUTLER	10				Tenn.
788	Philip	COSNOR	44	Farmer	1,750	1,950	N. C.
	Mary	"	45				"
	David J.	"	21				Tenn.
	Martha A.	"	20				"
	John N.	"	18				"
	Hugh M.	"	16				"
	Samuel H.	"	14				"
	Henderson S.	"	12				"
	Margaret E.	"	9				"
	Philip A.	"	6				"
	William S.	"	2				"
	Martha J.	HAYS	20				"
789	James W.	ROSS	29	Farmer		600	Tenn.
	Margaret E.	"	26				"
	Lafayette A.	"	4				"
	Martha E.	"	2				"
	Sarah J.	"	1/12				"
790	Alford	CUNNINGHAM	53	Farmer	1,200	1,000	Tenn.
	Mary	"	40				"
	Margaret	"	14				"
	Moses	" (twins)	13				"
	Elijah	"	13				"
	William C.	"	8				"
	Martha J.	"	5				"
	Joseph R.	"	5/12				"
791	David	GIFFIN	39	Farmer	1,500	625	Tenn.
	Malvina	"	35				"
	Margaret	"	15				"
	Harriet M.	"	11				"
	Eliza E.	"	9				"
	Princeton	"	8				"
	James R.	"	5				"

	Name		Age	Occupation	Real	Pers.	Birthplace
	Caladonia	"	2				"
	Sarah A.	"	2/12				"
792	Sanders C.	HINTON	31	Farmer	1,000	725	Tenn.
	Dorcas	"	35				"
	Melinda J.	"	12				"
	Melissa A.	"	9				"
	Amanda M.	"	7				"

Page 110   11 July 1860

	Name		Age	Occupation	Real	Pers.	Birthplace
	Sanders C.	HINTON	6				Tenn.
	Henry C.	"	4				"
	Mary T.	"	1				"
	No Name (m)	"	1/12				"
793	Green B.	SAFFELL	56	Farmer	1,500	1,220	N. C.
	Jane	"	57				Tenn.
	Sarah M.	"	25				"
	Melissa E.	"	17				"
	William R.	"	14				"
	Green B.	"	9				"
	Elizabeth H.	SCRUGGS	38				"
794	Matthew H.	GARDNER	39	Farmer		300	Tenn.
	Elizabeth	"	38				"
	Decater L.	"	16				"
	Margaret C.	"	14				"
	Mariah J.	"	12				"
	Martha L.	"	10				"
	David N.	"	9				"
	Sarah T.	"	5				"
	George E.	"	3				"
795	George W.	HENRY	32	Farmer	15,000	18,200	Tenn.
	Isabella	"	24				"
	James D.	"	2				"
796	Abijah W.	EMMETT	44	Blacksmith	80	600	Tenn.
	John H.	"	20				"
	Alexander C.	"	12				"
	Hetty J.	"	11				"
	Mary C.	"	7				"
	Letty	CAMERON	38				"
797	George	KIZER	41	Farmer		600	N. C.
	Honor Emaline	"	45				"
	Margaret M.	"	17				Tenn.
	Mary E.	"	15				"
	John H.	"	13				"
	Dolly Ann	"	10				"
	Joseph H.	"	8				"
	George H.	"	3				"
	Samuel H.	"	1				"
798	Jno. W.	McGHEE	62	Farmer		700	N. C.
	Rosannah	"	46				Tenn.

District 7   P.O.: Maryville

	Name		Age	Occupation	Real	Pers.	Birthplace
Page 111							11 July 1860
	Evalina	McGHEE	17				Tenn.
799	Random M.	KEY	24	Laborer	.	400	Tenn.
	Margaret S.	"	22				"
	Marianetta	"	3				"
	Charles C.	"	1				"
	McKindree	"	5/12				"
800	Spencer	HENRY	54	Meth. Minister	6,000	1,280	Tenn.
	Elizabeth	"	53				"
	Catharine	"	30				"
	Samuel	"	25				"
	Dolly Ann	"	27				"
	Mary	"	23				"
	Adaline	"	19				"
	Spencer H.	"	17				"
	James P.	"	14				"
801	Josiah	TUCK	40	Laborer		500	Tenn.
	Elizabeth	"	32				"
	John	"	16				"
	Moses	"	15				"
	Tobias	"	13				"
	Mary E.	"	12				"
	Sarah S.	"	8				"
	Winny T.	"	1				"
802	David B.	MILLER	25	Farmer	2,000	1,000	Tenn.
	Robert B.	"	24				"
	Mary	"	20				"
	Thomas	"	16				"
	Elizabeth	"	29				"
803	Betsy A.	MEANS	42	Farmer	3,000	1,500	Tenn.
	Robert A.	"	16				"
	James S.	"	14				"
	John H.	"	12				"
804	Wilson	MAYS	42	Farmer		1,000	Tenn.
	Polly	"	45				"
	Sophia J.	"	5				"
	Houston S.	"	3				"
	John V.	"	19				"
	Emaline	" (mwy)	18				"
	Mary J.	SHERRELL	24				"
	William A.	"	5				"
Page 112							13 July 1860
805	James M.	HENRY	51	Farmer	7,000	7,070	Tenn.
	Ann	"	54				"
	Margaret I.	"	17				"
	Hetty J.	"	15				"
	Josiah N.	"	11				"
806	John	HOUSTON	63	Farmer	3,000	1,030	Tenn.
	Elinor	"	50				"
	Saml.	COLVILLE	6				"

	Name		Age	Occupation	Real	Pers.	Birthplace
807	Bartley	WILSON	20			500	Tenn.
	Mariah	"	19				"
	Martha A.	"	1				"
808	Alexander	RODDY	66				Tenn.
	William	"	27	Farmer	4,000	2,280	"
	Polly Ann	"	23				"
	Margaret	McELDRER	23				"
	John	HARGISS	11				"
809	Sam H.	SAFFELL	22			500	Tenn.
	Melissa A.	"	17				"
	John A.	"	1/12				"
810	Jonathan	THARP	70			350	Va.
	Sarah	"	69				Tenn.
811	Presley	BURNETT	62	Farmer		800	Tenn.
	Nancy	"	60				"
	Susan	"	29				"
	Campbell	"	25				"
	Melinda	"	20				"
812	A. Perry	CUNNINGHAM	26	Farmer		550	Tenn.
	Mary	"	23				"
	Cornelia	"	1				"
813	A. J.	WILSON	41	Farmer	5,000	3,200	Tenn.
	Sarah	"	37				"
	Jesse C.	"	17				"
	James L.	"	15				"
	Robert N.	"	13				"
	Mary L.	"	9				"
	Joseph L.	"	2				"
814	Alexander	COOK	67	Farmer	12,800	20,086	N. C.
	Levica	"	69				Md.
	Campbell W.	"	25				Tenn.
815	Calloway	MASHBURN	32	Laborer		50	N. C.

Page 113   13 July 1860

	Name		Age	Occupation	Real	Pers.	Birthplace
	Linda M.	MASHBURN	24				N. C.
	John	"	8				Tenn.
	Melissa	"	5				"
	William	"	3				N. C.
	Emaline	"	1				"
	John	PATE	74				"
816	Henderson	KERR	38	Farmer	2,500	2,000	Tenn.
	Mary J.	"	8				"
	Rachel J.	"	34				"
817	Joseph	SHELLY	69	Hammerman		350	N. C.
	Rebecca	"	57				"
	William	"	27				Tenn.
	Catharine	"	19				"
	John	"	18				"
	James	"	14				"

	Name		Age	Occupation	Real	Pers.	Birthplace
	William	"	7				"
	Amanda E.	"	2				"
818	Joab	WALDROP (mwy)	27	Stone Mason		300	N. C.
	Hannah E.	"	23				"
	Pinkney	HAMMONDS	17				"
819	Adrian	MARTIN	44	Farmer	3,000	2,100	Tenn.
	Sarah	"	40				"
	John H.	"	17				"
	Elizabeth	"	15				"
	Mary C.	"	13				"
	Sarah E.	"	10				"
	Jesse L.	"	7				"
	No Name	" (m)	2				"
820	Hiram	WALKER	38	Farmer	500	675	Tenn.
	Mariam	"	34				"
	Betsey	"	33				"
	Joanna	"	69				"
	James A.	"	12				"
	John	CRYE	11				"
821	Esther	McTEER	49		500	150	Tenn.
822	Wm.	TEFETELLER	25			100	Tenn.
	Rosanna	"	28				"
	Eliza J.H.	"	9				"
	William C.	"	8				"
	James H.	"	5				"

Page 114   13 July 1860

	Name		Age	Occupation	Real	Pers.	Birthplace
	Martha E.	TEFERTELLER	3				Tenn.
	Cyrina C.	"	10/12				"
823	Joseph	TEFERTELLER	65	Laborer		650	N. C.
	Elizabeth	"	63				"
	Anna J.	"	40				Tenn.
	Rachel S.	"	36				"
	Michael	"	21				"
	Jefferson H.	"	18				"
	Anderson	HODGE	18				"
	Henry	TEFERTELLER	12				"
	Eliza J.	"	8				"
824	Elizabeth	HAYS	68	Farmer	750	500	N. C.
	William	"	24				"
825	Gold	WILSON (mwy)	44	Farmer	2,500	1,075	Tenn.
	Tilitha C.	"	26				"
	Sarah E.	"	18				"
	Robert A.	"	16				"
	Mary J.	"	14				"
	James L.	"	12				"
	John N.	"	10				"
	Samuel C.	"	8				"
826	Elizabeth	GUY	62	Farmer	300	500	Tenn.
	Mary J.	"	28				"

District 7   P.O.: Maryville

	Name		Age	Occupation	Real	Pers.	Birthplace
827	Mary A.	McGHEE	50	Farmer	5,000	800	Tenn.
	Robert	"	22				"
	Margaret	"	20				"
	William	"	19				"
828	James M.	KERR	50	Farmer	5,000	2,565	Tenn.
	Elizabeth	"	50				"
	Polly A.	"	25				"
	Sarah C.	"	19				"
	Margaret L.	"	15				"
	William W.	"	6				"
	Martha E.	"	4				N. C.
	Adolphus	HIGDEN	17	Laborer			Tenn.
	Henry A.	BRIANT	14				"
829	Hugh	ROGERS	40	Laborer			N. C.
	Martha L.	"	27				"
	Joab L.	"	10				Ga.
	Simpson H.	"	8				"

Page 115   14 July 1860

	Name		Age	Occupation	Real	Pers.	Birthplace
	Benj. W.	RODGERS	5				Ga.
	William P.B.	"	2				Tenn.
	Sarah A.	"	11/12				"
830	James	McGHEE	26	Carpenter	1,000	500	Tenn.
	Elizabeth	"	31				"
	John M.	"	6				"
	Samuel L.	"	3				"
	No Name	" (f)	3/12				"
831	Moses	MARTIN	46	Farmer	1,000	950	Tenn.
	Celia	"	41				"
	David K.	"	19				"
	James H.	"	15				"
	William G.	"	14				"
	Dolly C.	"	12				"
	Adrian L.	"	10				"
	Rachel A.	"	9				"
	John W. A.	"	3				"
	Lucy L.	"	1				"
832	John	McGHEE	32	Farmer	1,000	500	Tenn.
	Margaret	"	34				"
	Nancy A.	"	10				"
	James B.	"	7				"
	Robert I.	"	2				"
	Nancy	CAMPBELL	66				"
833	Andrew B.	HANNER	27	Carpenter	500	800	Tenn.
	Mary	"	25				"
	Christopher C.	"	8				"
	Martha A.	"	2/12				"
	Margaret	TAYLOR	13				"

	Name		Age	Occupation	Real	Pers.	Birthplace
834	James	BALL	57			50	Tenn.
835	Nathaniel T.	SMALLEN	63	Farmer		200	Tenn.
	Elizabeth	"	61				"
	Matthew M.	"	25				"
	Mary	"	22				"
836	Elizabeth	PRATHER	49			150	Tenn.
	Eliza C.	"	8				"
837	Amos	RIDDLE	45	Laborer		100	Tenn.
	Nancy	"	40				"
	Elizabeth J.	"	18				"
	William M.	"	14				"

Page 116   14 July 1860

	Name		Age	Occupation	Real	Pers.	Birthplace
	Frank	RIDDLE	12				Tenn.
	Hugh	"	10				"
	Martha A.	"	6				"
	Irvin E.	"	4				"
	Mary E.	"	10/12				"
838	Eli	HUFFSTUTLER	28	Farmer	300	1,270	Tenn.
	Polly A.	"	24				"
	Samuel D.	"	5				"
	Isaac P.	"	3				"
	John T.	"	6/12				"
839	Caleb	BEST	40	Farmer	2,500	1,544	N. C.
	Polly	"	40				Tenn.
	Martin C.	"	17				"
	Matilda J.	"	15				"
	William D.	"	11				"
	Caleb	"	8				"
	Isaac A.	"	5				"
	Mary S.	"	2				"
840	Christopher	BEST	38	Farmer	1,200	1,260	N. C.
	Mary L.	"	26				Tenn.
	Martha A.	"	16				Mo.
	Caleb	MARTIN	7				Tenn.
841	Elizabeth	FARR	33			500	N. C.
	Elizabeth F.	"	16				Tenn.
	John H.	"	14				"
	Mary J.	"	12				"
	James H.	"	10				"
	William J.	"	8				"
	Martha N.	"	5				"
	Cornelia C.	" (twins)	10/12				"
	Cordelia E.	"	10/12				"
842	John M.	BEST	63	Farmer	7,000	2,765	N. C.
	Frances	"	59				"
	Andrew J.	"	21				Tenn.
	Sarah A.	"	17				"
	William R.	"	10/12				"
	John	WOODWARD	18	Laborer			"
	Nicholas	BLEVINS	11				"

District 7   P.O.: Maryville

	Name		Age	Occupation	Real	Pers.	Birthplace
843	James	THOMPSON	46	Farmer	300	600	Tenn.
	Margaret	"	47				Va.

<u>Page 117</u>   <u>14 July 1860</u>

	Name		Age	Occupation	Real	Pers.	Birthplace
	Wm. W.	THOMPSON	21				Tenn.
	Sarah E.	"	20				"
	George S.	"	18				"
	Mary E.	"	13				"
	Julia A. M.	"	11				"
	Asa W.	" (m)	8				"
	Robert G.	"	5				"
844	Darian	BLEVINS	21	Farmer		850	Tenn.
	Elizabeth	"	18				"
	Samuel A.	"	6/12				"
845	Thomas E.	SCOTT	28	Blacksmith	500	500	Tenn.
	Rebecca	"	27				"
	Martha E.	"	3				"
	John A.	"	1				"
846	Thomas	CARPENTER	69	Farmer	2,000	718	N. C.
	Polly	"	66				"
	Betsy A.	BEST	15				"
847	Nancy	CARPENTER	32		700	500	Tenn.
	Lucinda A.	"	5				"
	Sarah J.	"	3				"
848	Daniel	RAZOR	40	Blacksmith	1,500	875	Tenn.
	Sarah	"	36				""
	Alford W.	"	13				"
	Nancy J.	"	11				"
	Matilda	"	10				"
	Esther	"	8				"
	Peter	"	6				"
	Isaac T.	"	4				"
	William D.	"	2				"
	Emily	PETERS	28				"
849	Isaac	MOODY	53	Farmer		500	N. C.
	Elender	"	40				"
	Elizabeth	"	18				"
	Abner	"	15				"
	Margaret	"	13				"
	Nancy J.	"	11				"
	Sally L.	"	7				"
	Martha A.	"	5				Tenn.
	Thomas	"	1				"
850	Hiram	SELLERS	37	Farmer	1,000	500	N. C.

<u>Page 118</u>   <u>14 July 1860</u>

	Name		Age	Occupation	Real	Pers.	Birthplace
	Silena	SELLERS	34				N. C.
	Martha J.	"	15				"

1860 U. S. CENSUS OF BLOUNT COUNTY, TENNESSEE

District 7   P.O.: Maryville

	Name		Age	Occupation	Real	Pers.	Birthplace
	Mary S.	"	13				"
	Henry	"	6				Tenn.
	Gaither	"	4				"
	William	"	1				"
	Lucy	CARROLL	53				N. C.
851	Amos	THOMPSON	38	Farmer	400	300	Tenn.
852	Wm.	THOMPSON	51	Farmer	500	500	"
	Susan	"	16				"
	John	"	12				"
	Samuel	"	8				"
853	John	MORTON	62	Farmer	1,500	1,450	N. C.
	Mary	"	57				"
	Hetty A. E.	"	21				Tenn.
	Martha L.	"	19				"
	Mary W.	"	18				"
	John H.	"	26				"
854	John	KAGALA	23	Farmer	500	500	Tenn.
	Polly	"	41				Va.
	Stephen M.	"	1				Tenn.
	Susannah	"	53				Va.
855	James	McDANIEL	60	Laborer		200	N. C.
	Polly	"	45				"
	Alexander	"	4				Tenn.
856	Cain	SMALLEN	38	Laborer		300	Tenn.
	Jane	"	35				"
	Margaret T.	"	14				"
	William N.	"	10				"
	Safrina A.	"	5				"
	Martha A.	"	2				"
857	Samuel	CHAPMAN	23	Laborer		75	Tenn.
	Isabella	"	23				"
858	Henry H.	MORTON	41	Farmer		300	Tenn.
	Nancy C.	"	34				"
	Eliza J.	"	14				"
	Samuel C.	"	13				"
	Margaret A.	"	1				"
859	George	THOMPSON	53	Farmer	1,000	875	S. C.

Page 119   16 July 1860

	Name		Age	Occupation	Real	Pers.	Birthplace
	Polly	THOMPSON	48				Tenn.
	Nancy	"	24				"
	Martha	"	22				"
	Margaret	"	20				"
	Sam Wright	"	18				"
	Elizabeth	"	16				"
	Martin	"	14				"
	John	"	13				"
	Caroline	"	12				"
	George	"	6				"
	Stephen	BARNETT	69				England

	Name		Age	Occupation	Real	Pers.	Birthplace
860	James	TAYLOR	40	Farmer	1,000	965	Tenn.
	Catharine	"	35				"
	William T.	"	14				"
	Sophia L.	"	12				"
	Isaac W.	"	10				"
	Nancy E.	"	8				"
	Michael L.	"	6				"
	Martha C.	"	4				"
	David B.	"	6/12				"
861	William H.	MORTON	35	Farmer	250	500	Tenn.
	Celia	"	34				"
	Granville A.	"	12				"
	John D.	"	10				"
	Jeremiah T.	"	7				"
	Lucinda S.	"	4				"
862	William	GARDNER	39	Farmer	600	850	Tenn.
	Nancy	"	35				"
	Henry M.	"	20				"
	Andrew J.	"	18				"
	Matthew A.	"	17				"
	John C.	"	14				"
	Mary E.	"	12				"
	Robert B.	"	11				"
	Jane	THOMPSON	33				"
863	George	TAYLOR	67	Farmer	600	1,085	N. C.
	Sarah M.	"	42				Tenn.
	Samuel M.	"	16				"
	Rachel A.	"	15				"
	Nancy I.	"	14				"

Page 120   16 July 1860

	Name		Age	Occupation	Real	Pers.	Birthplace
	Isabella A.	TAYLOR	12				Tenn.
	Rebecca E.	"	10				"
	Benj. C.	"	9				"
	Margaret C.	"	7				"
	Emeline	"	5				"
	Hugh J.	"	2				"
	Julia A.	"	1				"
	Margaret	CHAPMAN	23				"
	Emeline	"	22				"
864	Robert	THOMPSON	35	Farmer		300	Tenn.
	Jane	"	37				"
	Thomas	"	14				"
	James	"	12				"
	Martha R.	"	10				"
	David	"	6				"
	Polly A.	"	3				"
	Samuel	"	1/12				"
865	Joseph	KAGALA	47	Farmer	1,500	1,850	Va.
	Mary	"	43				"
	Catharine	"	23				"
	Anna	"	19				

District 7   P.O.: Maryville

	Name		Age	Occupation	Real	Pers.	Birthplace
	Absalom	"	17				"
	Jane	"	15				"
	Missouri	" (f)	13				"
	William	"	9				"
	Joseph	"	7				Tenn.
	John	"	5				"
866	Jacob	BUMGARNER	69	Cooper	150	250	Va.
	Margaret	"	67				"
867	David	GARDNER	45	Blacksmith	600	875	Tenn.
	Nancy	"	39				"
	Elizabeth A.	"	17				"
	Thomas M.	"	16				"
	Margaret I.	"	14				"
	James R.	"	11				"
	John B.	"	9				"
	George R.	"	7				"
	Martha M.	"	5				"
	William S.	"	4				"
	Robert S.	"	2				"

Page 121   16 July 1860

	Name		Age	Occupation	Real	Pers.	Birthplace
868	Michael	GARDNER	74	Farmer	600	600	S. C.
	Elizabeth	"	74				Pa.
	Margaret	"	36				Tenn.
	Montgomery	"	11				"
869	Livena	KAGALA	40	Farmer	2,000	850	Va.
	Mary M.	"	18				"
	William S.	"	16				"
	Harriet C.	"	12				"
	Alford H. A.	"	8				"
	Soloman A.	"	6				Tenn.
870	Cooper Y.	BUMGARNER	26	Miller		150	Va.
	Rebecca A.	"	23				Tenn.
	James R.	"	3				"
	Jacob A.	"	1				"
871	Enoch F.	VINYARD (mwy)	20	Farmer		150	Tenn.
	Susan E.	"	17				"
872	Green W.	VINYARD	43	Farmer		790	Tenn.
	Mary	"	43				"
	Pleasant	"	22				"
	John	"	19				"
	William T.	"	17				"
	Martha J.	"	14				"
	Sarah C.	"	8				"
	Jordan C.	"	1				"
873	William	ROBBINS	58	Farmer		1,100	N. C.
	Nancy	"	54				"
	Thomas	"	26				"
	William F.	"	25				"
	Elizabeth	"	19				"

	Name		Age	Occupation	Real	Pers.	Birthplace
	Frances	" (f)	17				"
	Margaret	"	14				"
874	John	VAUGHT	51	Farmer	700	1,515	Tenn.
	Rebecca	"	36				"
	Andrew P.	"	17				"
	Melinda C.	"	15				"
	Lorenzo D.	"	13				"
	John C.	"	11				"
	Mary E.	"	8				"
	Hetty A.	"	5				"
	George A.	"	2				"

Page 122   17 July 1860

	Name		Age	Occupation	Real	Pers.	Birthplace
875	George	SMITH	29	Laborer		250	Tenn.
	Loretta	"	27				"
	Sarah C.	"	10				"
	Oma E.	"	9				"
	Hannah A.	"	6				"
	Henderson T.	"	3				"
	Elizabeth	MULVANY	65				"
876	Thomas H.	NEAL	64			100	N. C.
	Anna	"	64				"
	Alvira	"	14				Tenn.
877	Green B.	NEAL	35			75	Tenn.
	Sarah	"	23				"
878	William	PAYNE	45	Tanner		150	Tenn.
	Susan	"	46				"
	Fransina	"	20				"
	John W.	"	18				"
	Sarah	"	17				"
	Margaret	"	14				"
	Catharine	"	12				"
	Francis M.(m)	" (twins)	9				"
	Mary		9				"
	William	"	6				"
	Samuel	"	9/12				"
879	Allen	HALL	35	Carpenter	625	500	Va.
	Priscilla	"	28				N. C.
	Mary S.	"	6				Tenn.
	William B.	"	2				"
	John F.	"	10/12				"
880	Rufus M.	CREGER	35	Carpenter		500	Va.
	Martha P.	"	25				Tenn.
	Rachel	"	6				"
	Hester A.	"	3				"
	Eli A.	"	1				"
	No Name	" (f)	2/12				
881	Jesse	KERR Jr.	51	Farmer	15,000	22,850	Tenn.
	Mary A.	"	46				"
	William	"	22				"

	Name		Age	Occupation	Real	Pers.	Birthplace
	David C.	"	20				"
	Leonidas M.	"	18				"
	Eliza S.	"	11				"

Page 123   District 17   P.O.:Chilhowie   17 July 1860

	Name		Age	Occupation	Real	Pers.	Birthplace
	Alex F.	KERR	6				Tenn.
	Nancy E.E.	"	3				"
882	Signor	EVERETT	53	Sawyer	3,333	500	N. C.
	Catharine	"	48				Tenn.
	Nancy E.	"	19				"
	Hannah C.	"	16				"
	Cynthia S.	"	10				"
	James	"	6				"
	Daniel	"	4				"
883	Humes I.	DAVIS	30	Farmer		600	Tenn.
	Susannah	"	25				"
	Margaret N.	"	1				"
884	William S.	HUTTON	29	Sheriff	1,200	1,500	Tenn.
	Nancy C.	"	21				"
	Joseph A.	"	9/12				"
885	William G.	HOGUE	67	Farmer	300	300	N. C.
	Hollin	"	61				"
	James S.	"	23				"
	Lucinda	"	34				"
	George D.	EUSTICE	14				"
	Nancy	"	12				"
	William	"	10				"
	Edista	HOGUE (f)	7				"
	Henry	"	5				"
	James	"	3				"
	Hollin	" (f)	1				Tenn.
886	John S.	MOORE	50	Farmer		500	Tenn.
	Sarah	"	45				"
	Mahala	"	26				"
	Elizabeth	"	22				"
	Sarah	"	19				"
	William D.	"	17				"
	George W.	"	13				"
	Jesse B.	" (m)	10				"
	John G.	"	8				"
887	William	HOLLOWAY	54	Farmer	600	800	Tenn.
	Jane	"	54				S. C.
	Minten	" (m)	19				Tenn.
	Jacob	"	17				"
	Lucretia	"	20				"

Page 124   24 July 1860

	Name		Age	Occupation	Real	Pers.	Birthplace
	John	HOLLOWAY	13				Tenn.
888	Andrew B.	SHOWN	41	Farmer	700	300	Tenn.
	Saraphire	"	36				"
	William J.	"	14				"

District 17   P.O.: Chilhowie

	Name		Age	Occupation	Real	Pers.	Birthplace
	Madison T.	"	12				"
	Margaret	"	10				"
	Sarah J.	"	8				"
	James I. T.	"	6				"
	John S.	"	10/12				"
889	Thompson	BRIANT	79		1,500	700	Va.
	Catharine	"	65				N. C.
	Hannah M.	"	30				"
890	Richard	BRIANT	35	Laborer		300	N. C.
	Nancy	"	30				Tenn.
	James	"	7				"
	John	"	5				"
	Mary A.	"	3				"
891	John	BEST	43	Farmer	1,500	830	N. C.
	Catharine	"	39				Tenn.
	Polly Ann	"	19				Mo.
	Jacob C.	"	13				"
	Sam H.	"	9				Tenn.
	Frederic	"	6				"
	Sarah J.	"	2				"
892	Abraham	RIDGE	60	Distiller	250	200	N. C.
	Phebe	"	52				Tenn.
	David	"	18				"
893	Thomas	STEWARD	26	Farmer		200	Tenn.
	Mary A.	"	23				"
	John M.	"	2				"
	Mary J.	"	7/12				"
894	James	BEST	28	Farmer		250	Tenn.
	Susannah	"	23				"
	Phebe J.	"	4				"
	Young C.	"	2				"
895	Jacob	BORDON	52	Farmer	300	600	Tenn.
	Luvica	"	60				S. C.
	William	"	15				Tenn.
	Peter	KERR	6				"
896	John	RIDGE	24	Blacksmith		200	Tenn.

Page 125   24 July 1860

	Name		Age	Occupation	Real	Pers.	Birthplace
	Catharine	RIDGE	22				Tenn.
	John	"	3				"
	Jacob	"	2				"
	Luvica J.	"	1/12				"
	Jacob	BORDON	80		100		Va.
897	Elizabeth	CARVER	80			100	S. C.
	Cyntha	"	30				Tenn.
	Matilda	"	15				"
	Albert I.	"	12				"
	John M.	"	10				"
898	Susan	HEADRICK	59			100	Tenn.
	Sarah	"	33				"

District 17   P.O.: Chilhowie

	Name		Age	Occupation	Real	Pers.	Birthplace
	Susannah	"	19				"
	Levi	"	16				"
	Levina S.	"	8				"
	Vina C.	"	6				"
899	Pamela	GURGANUS	80			50	S. C.
	Margaret	ISBELL	60				"
900	Russell	JONES	52	Farmer	300	870	Ga.
	Jane	"	47				Tenn.
	John	"	22				"
	Francis M.	" (m)	20				"
	Elizabeth J.	"	19				"
	William J.	"	17				"
	Nancy A.	"	16				"
	Margaret M.	"	13				"
	Thomas J.	"	11				"
	James M.	"	14				"
	Andrew M.	"	9				"
	Irvin N.	"	7				"
	Riley	"	6				"
	Polly Ann	"	4				"
902	George W.	BROWN	31	Farmer		1,700	Tenn.
	Mary A.	"	27				"
	Robert B.	"	6				"
	Samuel S.	"	4				"
	William T.	"	3				"
	Laura A.	"	3/12				"
902	Leonidas	SPRADLIN	31	Farmer		687	Tenn.
	Sarah	"	25				"

Page 126   24 July 1860

	Name		Age	Occupation	Real	Pers.	Birthplace
	Mary	SPRADLIN	4				Tenn.
	Matilda	"	2				"
	No Name	" (f)	1/12				"
903	James	ANDERSON	58	Farmer	300	650	Tenn.
	Luvica	"	42				N. C.
	John A.	"	23				Tenn.
	William	"	21				"
	Elizabeth	"	20				"
	James M.	"	18				"
	David	"	16				"
	Larkin	"	14				"
	Nancy A.	"	12				"
	Isaac	"	10				"
	George	"	8				"
	Sally A.	"	6				"
	Columbus	"	4				"
	Mary J.	"	3				"
	Margaret	"	2/12				"
904	David	SPRADLIN	51	Farmer	1,000	800	Va.
	Matilda	"	51				Tenn.
	David	"	19				"
	Margaret	"	16				"

District 17   P.O.: Chilhowie

	Name		Age	Occupation	Real	Pers.	Birthplace
	Euphamfa	"	13				"
	Mildred	"	11				"
	John	"	10				"
905	Henry	DANIELS (mul)	24	Carpenter		100	Tenn.
	Nancy	" (mul)	18				"
906	Priscilla	McCULLY	62			150	Tenn.
	Mary E.	"	24				"
	Thomas J.	"	26				"
	David	"	21				"
	Martha J.	"	6				"
	John D.	"	1				"
907	James	LEMMONS	22	Laborer		100	N. C.
	Margaret	"	15				"
	Matilda J.	"	6/12				"
908	Alexander	AMBURN (mul)	38	Farmer	1,250	900	N. C.
	Mary Ann	"	30				Tenn.
	Franky	" (mul)	15				"
	Thomas	" (mul)	14				"

Page 127   24 July 1860

	Name		Age	Occupation	Real	Pers.	Birthplace
	Sarah	AMBURN (mul)	12				Tenn.
	Anna	" (mul)	10				"
	Gabriel	" (mul)	9				"
	Everline	" (mul)	7				"
	Alexander	" (mul)	5				"
	Mary Ann	" (mul)	3				"
	William	" (mul)	1/12				"
	Anna	" (mul)	32				"
909	Thomas M.	SPRADLIN	29	Farmer		400	Tenn.
	Caroline	"	28				"
	Mary Ann	"	1				"
910	Franky (f)	AMBURN (mul)	60	Farmer		605	N. C.
	Burnett (m)	" (mul)	24				Tenn.
	Isaac	BIRD	13				"
	Nathaniel	SPRADLIN	24				"
911	Uriah	AMBURN (mul)	21			200	Tenn.
	Betsy J.	"	23				"
	Mary C.	" (mul)	1				"
912	Mary	PHILIPS	63	Farmer	250	200	Va.
	Betsy A.	SMITH	31				Tenn.
	Sarah J.	"	10				"
	Margaret C.	"	8				"
	Polly Ann	"	5				"
913	Thomas	CARVER	55	Farmer	1,000	1,100	Ky.
	Margaret	"	53				Tenn.
914	Rebecca	BIRD	69			50	N. C.
	Lucretia J.	"	26				Tenn.
	James T.	"	8				"
	George W.	"	1				"

District 17   P.O.: Chilhowie

	Name		Age	Occupation	Real	Pers.	Birthplace
915	Rebecca	BLEDSOE	30			50	Tenn.
	Grigsby R.	"	10				"
	Columbus W.	"	7				"
	Sarah J.	"	5				"
	Nancy E.	"	1				"
	Nancy	"	66				"
916	Charles	CHAMBERS	33			100	Tenn.
	Sarah	"	28				"
	Lafayette A.	"	11				"
	George W.	"	8				"
	Mary J.	"	6				"

Page 128   25 July 1860

	Name		Age	Occupation	Real	Pers.	Birthplace
	Ruth A.	CHAMBERS	4				Tenn.
	Nancy E.	"	1				"
917	Absolom	BORING	26	Carpenter		250	Tenn.
	Nancy J.	"	20				"
	James M.	"	3/12				"
918	Louisa	HARRISON	27	Farmer	600	500	Tenn.
	Martha	"	7				"
	Matilda C.	"	5				"
	Mary C.	"	3				"
919	Edmond	McELDRER	60	Farmer	500	600	Tenn.
	Hester	"	55				"
	Caroline	"	21				N. C.
	Modina	"	19				"
	Henry	"	17				"
	Alford	"	15				"
	Martha	"	13				"
920	Wm.	McELDRER	25	Laborer		150	N. C.
	Mary	"	27				Tenn.
	Matilda	"	3/12				"
921	James	GOODIN	24	Farmer		150	Tenn.
	Margaret S.	"	27				"
	Thomas J.	"	3				"
	No Name	" (m)	1				"
922	Samuel	CHARLES	56	Farmer	300	400	Tenn.
	Priscilla	"	49				"
	Arminda	"	9				"
923	John	SMITH	48	Carpenter	100	200	S. C.
	Rachel	"	44				Tenn.
	Sarah J.	"	25				"
	Allen	"	21				"
	James	"	19				"
	Joseph	"	16				"
	Elizabeth C.	"	13				"
	Nancy J.	"	10				"
	John	"	8				"
	Lewis	"	6				"
	Blankenship B.	"	4				"

District 17 | | | | P.O.: Chilhowie

	Name		Age	Occupation	Real	Pers.	Birthplace
924	Robert R.	WRIGHT	25	Farmer		250	Tenn.
	Mary	"	19				"
925	Harvey S.	BRIGHT	45	Farmer	4,000	2,800	Tenn.

Page 129 | | | | | | | 25 July 1860

	Name		Age	Occupation	Real	Pers.	Birthplace
	Elizabeth J.	BRIGHT	30				"
	Wm. M.	"	9				
	Nancy A.	"	5				
	John H.	"	1				
	Jesse	" (m)	76			4,700	Va.
	Nancy	GHORMLY	63			300	Tenn.
926	Samuel	ELLIOTT	24	Laborer		100	N. C.
	Mary	"	25				Tenn.
	William T.	"	7				"
	Eliza M.	"	1				"
927	William	DONLEY	29	Farmer		1,800	Tenn.
	Adria	"	35				N. C.
	Martha C.	"	12				Tenn.
	Mary J.	"	10				
	John J.	"	7				
	Margaret N.	"	4				
	Nancy A.	"	2				
928	Eppy	EVERETT	28	Farmer		1,000	Tenn.
	Mary E.	"	23				"
	John H.	"	2				"
929	Samuel	GHORMLEY	43	Physician			Tenn.
	Anne	"	32				England
	William H.	"	4				Tenn.
	Fanny J.	"	3				"
	Nancy E.	"	1				"
930	Jesse A.	KLINE	55	Farmer	300	850	N. C.
	Adaline	"	40				"
	David V. L.	"	20				"
	Marion P.	" (m)	19				"
	Carsada	"	16				"
	William	"	14				"
	James K. P.	"	12				"
	Edwina	"	10				"
	Daniel Dallas	"	8				"
	Doctor Pierce	"	7				Tenn.
	Scottia	"	6				"
	Sarah	"	4				"
	David	"	84				N. C.
	Iredell	RHEA	60				Tenn.
	Sarah	WRIGHT	27				"

Page 130 | | | | | | | 25 July 1860

	Name		Age	Occupation	Real	Pers.	Birthplace
931	Moses Y.	BIRCHFIELD	49	Blacksmith		315	N. C.
	Ruth	"	52				"
	William A.	"	16				Tenn.
	Temperance A.	"	13				"

	Name		Age	Occupation	Real	Pers.	Birthplace
	Harriet C.	"	12				"
	Robert J.	"	8				"
	Ozina A. A.	" (f)	5				"
932	John	BIRCHFIELD	27			100	N. C.
	Mary	"	24				Scotland
	Jane	"	6				Tenn.
	John	"	4				"
	Agnes C.	"	2				"
933	George J.	WARD	44	Den. Sur & Physician			N. C.
	Martha J.	"	34				"
	Disdimonia	"	17				"
	David	"	4				"
934	David	CULVERSON	77	Farmer	4,000	670	N. C.
	Martha	"	63				"
	Houston	" (Bl)	16				"
935	Alford	DEAL	35	Farmer	300	1,000	N. C.
	Mary E.	"	33				"
	Martha M.	"	6				"
	William M.	"	2				"
936	Francis	NICHOLS (m)	39			50	S. C.
	Nancy	"	38				N. C.
937	Hannah	NICHOLS	32			50	N. C.
	Houston W.	"	8				"
	Albert N.	"	6				"
	No Name	" (f)	1/12				Tenn.
938	Russell	WELCH	51	Farmer		475	Tenn.
	Fanny	"	42				S. C.
	Thomas J.	"	23				N. C.
	Betsy J.	"	21				"
	Eda A.	"	18				"
	Nancy L.	"	16				"
	John M.	"	13				"
	Daniel R.	"	10				"
	William A.	"	9				"
	Fanny L.	"	6				"
	James W.	"	4				"

Page 131   26 July 1860

	Name		Age	Occupation	Real	Pers.	Birthplace
	Jemima C.	WELCH	1				N. C.
939	John	HUGGINS	35	Laborer		150	N. C.
	Frances	" (f)	30				"
	Jane	"	9				"
	Nancy	"	8				"
	Mary	"	6				"
	Georgia	"	4				"
	Hollin	" (m)	1				"
940	Carson	DAVIS	50	Farmer	1,000	1,345	N. C.
	Hagra	"	50				"
	Elmira A.	"	22				"
	John F.	"	18				

	Name		Age	Occupation	Real	Pers.	Birthplace
	Charles N.	"	15				
	Nancy E.	"	12				Ga.
							"
941	Isaac	ELLIOTT	32			300	Tenn.
	Ruth	"	31				N. C.
	Martha J.	"	11				"
	Mary A.	"	8				Tenn.
	Candais	"	7				"
	William H.	"	5				"
	Mira M.	"	3				"
	John B.	"	11/12				"
942	Daniel	ANDERSON	31	Farmer		300	Tenn.
	Martha	"	25				"
	William R.	"	7				N. C.
	Mary A.	"	5				"
	Sarah J.	"	3				Tenn.
	Martha A.	"	3/12				"
943	Perry	JOHNSON	35	Gate Keeper	400	300	Tenn.
	Martha	"	8				"
	Jemima	"	5				"
	Mary	"	3				"
944	Nathan C.	CULVERSON	42	Farmer		500	N. C.
	Mary	"	41				"
	Martha L.	"	21				"
	Nioma E.	"	19				"
	Nathan W.	"	17				"
	Nancy C.	"	16				"
	Aletha	"	14				"
	Mary	"	12				Ga.

Page 132   26 July 1860

	Name		Age	Occupation	Real	Pers.	Birthplace
	David F.	CULVERSON	9				Ga.
	Jason A.	"	4				N. C.
945	Daniel	TEFERTELLER	53	Laborer		50	N. C.
	Wilson	"	20				Tenn.
	Vina	"	16				"
	James	"	10				"
	Missouri	" (f)	9				"
946	David	HAMILTON	48	Farmer		300	Tenn.
	Catharine A.	"	46				"
	Churchwell	"	19				"
	William	"	15				"
	Elizabeth	"	12				"
	Sarah	"	9				"
	Everline	"	5				"
947	James	HARRISON	54	Farmer	6,000	1,120	Tenn.
	Anna	"	39				Ga.
	Louisa	"	16				Tenn.
	Ellen	"	14				"
	Sarah A.	"	12				"
	James C.	"	10				"

District 17   P.O.: Chilhowie

	Name		Age	Occupation	Real	Pers.	Birthplace
	Mary	"	8				"
	Elizabeth C.	"	5				"
	Winniford C.	"	4				"
	Henry	" (twins)	2/12				"
	Peggy Ann	" (twins)	2/12				"
	Caleb	LOWRY	48				Ga.
948	Ellen J.	CLARK (mul)	32				N. C.
	Betsy A.	" (mul)	17				"
	Lucinda	" (mul)	14				Tenn.
	Martha J.	" (mul)	12				"
	James A.	" (mul)	7				"
	Eliza S.	" (mul)	1				"
949	Ephraim	CLARK	60			50	Tenn.
	Lucretia	"	23				"
	Nancy J.	"	8/12				"
	Polly	LEE	53				S. C.
	Jackson	"	18				Tenn.
	Sarah A.	"	13				"
950	Elizabeth	RAGAN	43			75	Ga.
	George W.	"	19				Tenn.

Page 133   26 July 1860

	Name		Age	Occupation	Real	Pers.	Birthplace
	Dolly J.	RAGAN	18				Tenn.
	John L.	"	14				"
	Sarah M.	"	8				"
	Mary E.	"	1				"
951	Robert	BRIANT	65			500	Tenn.
	Elizabeth	"	63				"
	Henry	"	15				"
	Modina	"	13				"
	Pouza	" (m)	12				"
	Hervey	"	9				"
	Lanta	" (m)	8				"
	Thomas	"	7				"
952	David L.	HARGISS	31			200	Tenn.
	Sarah A.	"	30				"
	William	"	12				"
	John	"	10				"
	Mary E.	"	7				"
	Catharine J.	"	6				"
953	Rebecca	HARGIS	71			400	S. C.
	William W.	"	23				Tenn.
	Elizabeth	"	22				"
	John T.	"	42	Com. S. Teacher	500		"
954	Samuel T.	HARGIS	20			350	Tenn.
	Mary S.	"	19				"
	Robert	"	1				"
	Isaac M.	"	2/12				"
955	Henry	STOUT	76			300	Va.

District 17   P.O.: Chilhowie

	Name		Age	Occupation	Real	Pers.	Birthplace
956	Henry	ELLIOTT	22	Laborer		100	Tenn.
	Mary	"	32				"
	Godfrey	"	8				"
	John J.	"	4				"
	William H.	"	1				"
957	Nich.	HOWARD	35	Farmer		500	Tenn.
	Elizabeth	"	30				"
	Clara J.	"	12				"
	Nancy C.	"	7				"
	Hawkins P.	"	4				"
	Joseph	"	2				"
958	John	HOWARD	61	Farmer	2,500	400	Tenn.
	Katy Catharine	"	56				"

Page 134   District 1   P.O.: Brick Mill   27 July 1860

	Name		Age	Occupation	Real	Pers.	Birthplace
	Mary A.	HOWARD	18				Tenn.
	Nioma	"	17				"
	Sarah C.	"	15				"
959	Samuel	HOWARD	38	Farmer		400	Tenn.
	Anna	"	38				"
	John M.	"	14				"
	Sarah	"	12				"
	Hannah C.	"	10				"
	James	"	6				"
	Mary J.	"	2				"
960	Alexander	NEAL	30			100	N. C.
	Lukinza	"					Tenn.
	William J.	"					"
	John	"					"
	Sarah E.	"					"
	Sam Lane						"
961	William	GOIN	43			75	N. C.
	Susannah	"	18				Tenn.
	Stephen A.	"	20				"
	Hugh	"	16				"
	Lucinda J.	"	14				"
	William H.	"	6				"
	Ann D.	"	6/12				"
962	Wm. J. D.	PUGH	29	Farmer	2,000	2,235	Tenn.
963	William B.	BINGHAM	55	Farmer	2,500	1,250	N. C.
	Lafrey	"	53				Tenn.
	Jemima	"	22				"
	William P.	"	21				"
	Josiah M.	"	18				"
	John H.	"	15				"
	Samuel S.	"	12				"
	Mary	"	9				"
	Glaphrey	" (f)	7				"
	Elizabeth D.	PUGH	58				N.C.

District 17   P.O.: Chilhowee

	Name		Age	Occupation	Real	Pers.	Birthplace
964	Robert S.	PARSONS	59	Farmer	1,600	800	Tenn.
	Nancy	"	60				"
	John C.	"	25				"
	Isaham C.	"	20				"
	Adam C.	SHANKS	55				"
	Sarah	"	46				"

Page 135   District 1   P.O.: Brick Mill   27 July 1860

	Name		Age	Occupation	Real	Pers.	Birthplace
965	James H.	WALKER	41	Farmer	3,000	1,725	Tenn.
	Mary	"	40				"
	Martha C.	"	18				"
	Gilbert R.	"	17				"
	James A.	"	15				"
	Lewis T.	"	12				"
	Abner R.	"	10				"
	Mary E.	"	8				"
	Joseph	"	5				"
	William H.	"	3				"
	No Name	" (m)	5/12				"
966	James K.	PARSONS	35	Farmer	1,000	400	Tenn.
	Sarah M.	"	32				"
	Alford S.	"	6				"
	John C.	"	4				"
967	Saml. T.	WOODS	33	Farmer	4,200	3,830	Tenn.
	Margaret	"	29				"
	Christopher A.	"	4				"
	William H.	"	4/12				"
	Jane	"	53				"
968	Wesley	KIRBY	46	Farmer	1,600	1,200	Tenn.
	Margaret	"	44				"
	James R.	"	17				"
	Wesley S.	"	15				"
	Saml. H.	"	13				"
	William F.	"	11				"
	Joseph P.	"	9				"
	Linsay L.	"	6				"
	John A.	"	3				"
	Sarah A.	LOVELY	24				S. C.
969	Samuel	McCALL	35	Farmer		1,000	Tenn.
	Mary J.	"	38				"
	Samuel H.	"	21				"
	William A.	"	18				"
	John S.	"	12				"
	Polly A.	"	10				"
	James	"	3				"
	Eliza J.	"	3/12				"
	Mary	HENRY	60				"
970	John	HOYL	42	Farmer		800	N. C.

Page 136   28 July 1860

	Name		Age	Occupation	Real	Pers.	Birthplace
	Margaret	HOYL	40				Tenn.
	George	"	17				"

District 1   P.O.: Brick Mill

	Name		Age	Occupation	Real	Pers.	Birthplace
	William	"	15				"
	Samuel	"	12				"
	James M.	"	10				"
	Dorothy E.	"	8				"
	Hetty A.	"	4				"
	Ambrose D.	"	2				"
971	Samuel D.	BEST	31	Farmer	300	1,490	Tenn.
	Sarah A.	"	24				"
	Frederic	"	5				"
	Florentine	"	3				"
	George W.	"	1				"
972	Frederic	BEST	52	Miller	2,500	1,000	Tenn.
	Susannah	"	45				"
973	William	TUCKER	33			100	Tenn.
	Jemima	"	28				"
	Caroline	"	9				"
	Eliza J.	"	7				"
	Rebecca A.	"	3				"
	Francis E.	" (f)	1				"
974	Felix	DEWBERRY	56	Farmer		300	S. C.
	Rachel	"	60				N. C.
	William	"	21				Tenn.
975	Jacob	BEST	55	Farmer	2,500	1,000	N. C.
	Mary	"	55				Tenn.
	Sarah A.	"	25				"
	Lucinda	"	23				"
	Martin V.	"	21				"
	Elizabeth	"	19				"
976	Frederic D.	BEST	26	Farmer		500	Tenn.
	Sarah	"	21				"
	Mary J.	"	4				"
	Samuel M.	"	1				"
977	John S.	CRYE	31	Farmer	1,800	888	Tenn.
	Sarah C.	"	22				"
	George H.	"	1				"
	Josephine	"	21				"
978	George	BEST	49	Farmer	11,000	1,400	Tenn.
	Jane A.	"	42				"

Page 137   28 July 1860

	Name		Age	Occupation	Real	Pers.	Birthplace
	William R.	BEST	21				Tenn.
	Daniel	"	20				"
	John F.	"	18				"
	James M.	"	16				"
	Henry A.	"	14				"
	Mary J.	"	11				"
	Dolly A.	"	6				"
	Catharine	"	4				"
979	Alexr.	WILLIAMSON	50	Farmer	3,000	1,460	Tenn.
	Mary	"	44				"

District 1   P.O.: Brick Mill

	Name		Age	Occupation	Real	Pers.	Birthplace
	Lafayette S.	"	22				"
	William H.	"	18				"
	Mary A.	"	10				"
	Martha	HAMILL	22				"
980	John	BEST	62	Farmer	3,500	1,260	N. C.
	Elizabeth	"	43				Tenn.
	Henry	"	21				"
	Isaac	"	14				"
	George M. Dallas	"	12				"
	Pierce	"	5				"
	Elizabeth	"	14				"
	Caroline	"	11				"
	Malinda	"	9				"
981	Lanty M.	ARMSTRONG	37	Farmer	2,000	2,245	Tenn.
	Jane	"	29				"
	Eliza	"	51				"
	Samuel H.	"	21				"
	Robert L.	"	14				"
982	George M.	BRIAN (mwy)	20			200	Tenn.
	Amanda	"	27				"
983	Elizabeth	KITE	62			150	Tenn.
	John	"	27				"
	Caroline	"	23				"
	Henry H.	"	19				"
	Malvina	"	17				"
	Martha	"	14				"
984	Henry F.	McTEER	29	Blacksmith	1,000	875	Tenn.
	Sarah	"	33				"
	Millard F.	"	4				"
	Nancy E.	"	2				"

Page 138   28 July 1860

	Name		Age	Occupation	Real	Pers.	Birthplace
985	John F.	GARNER	40	Farmer	5,000	2,850	Tenn.
	Rachel E.	"	4				
986	Joseph	GRAY	34			600	Tenn.
	Rachel	"	40				"
	William R.	"	11				"
	Samuel B.	"	6				"
	Ralph W.	"	3				"
987	William	HEADRICK	30			400	Tenn.
	Nancy	"	28				"
	John R.	"	6				"
	Jane T.	"	4				"
	Samuel S.	"	3/12				"
988	Nancy	GARNER (mul)	22			100	Tenn.
	Margaret	" (mul)	4				"
	John B.	" (mul)	2				"
	William	" (mul)	9/12				"
989	John	HALL	58	Farmer		500	Va.
	Jane	"	54				"

District 1   P.O.: Brick Mill

	Name		Age	Occupation	Real	Pers.	Birthplace
	Susan	"	32				"
	Elizabeth J.	"	20				"
	Margaret S.	"	17				"
	William ·	"	5				Tenn.
	John	"	4				"
990	James B.	BRIANT	47			200	N. C.
	Mary A.	"	41				"
	Henry A.	"	17				Tenn.
	Isaac J.	"	11				"
	Salina A.	"	10				"
	William R.	"	7				"
	Hannah S.	"	3				"
	Caroline	"	21				"
991	George	SMITH	38	Laborer		100	Va.
	Elizabeth	"	34				Tenn.
	Eliza J.	"	10				"
	Louisa W.	"	9				"
	Sarah	"	6				"
	John M.	"	3				"
	Frederic D.	"	2				"
992	Adaline	QUIETT	28			50	Tenn.
	Minerva J.	"	5				"

Page 139   30 July 1860

	Name		Age	Occupation	Real	Pers.	Birthplace
	Wm. F.	QUIETT	3				Tenn.
993	Wm. W.	HOWARD	45	Farmer	16,000	8,165	N. C.
	Martha A.	"	34				"
	Mary N.	"	12				Tenn.
	John H.	"	10				"
	Joseph S.	"	3				"
	No Name	" (m)	3/12				"
994	Saml. D.	BEST	30	Farmer	1,500	640	Tenn.
	Elizabeth	"	31				"
	Thomas	"	7				"
	John H.	"	6				"
	Margaret A.	"	5				"
	Rebecca J.	"	2				"
995	Elias	CRYE	32	Farmer	1,500	875	Tenn.
	Nancy J.	"	24				"
	John A.	"	5				"
	William A.	"	2				"
996	David	MELSON	47	Laborer		125	N. C.
	Lucinda	"	41				Tenn.
	Nathaniel	"	17				"
	Isabella	"	13				"
	Andrew A.	"	10				"
	William H.	"	6				"
	Ransom	"	4				"
	James W.	"	1				"

District 1   P.O.: Brick Mill

	Name		Age	Occupation	Real	Pers.	Birthplace
997	Peter	HEADRICK	22	Laborer		100	Tenn.
	Mary J.	"	20				"
	Jacob	"	1				"
998	Mary A.	SPRADLIN	30	Farmer	,2500	2,260	Ala.
	Franklin B.	THOMPSON	13				Tenn.
	Green T.	"	11				"
	Samuel E.	"	10				"
	Keturah W.	" (f)	8				"
	Mahala	HAMONTREE	30				"
999	Mary	TULLOCH	40	Farmer	3,000	1,175	Tenn.
	John M.	"	22			150	"
	Samuel S.	"	20				"
	William H.	"	18				"
	Andrew V.	"	15				"
	George H.	"	13				"

Page 140   30 July 1860

	Name		Age	Occupation	Real	Pers.	Birthplace
	Eliza J.	TULLOCH	7				"
	James C.	"	5				"
	Mary A. C.	"	1				"
1000	Samuel	TULLOCH	54	Farmer	2,000	5,500	Tenn.
	Catharine M.	"	49				"
	James M.	"	26				"
	Elizabeth	"	24				"
	John C.	"	22				"
	Mary	"	20				"
	Hetty A.	"	16				"
	William S.	"	12				"
	Caroline	"	10				"
1001	Jesse A.	WELLS	44	Laborer		250	N. C.
	Artimisa	"	50				Tenn.
	James M.	"	21				"
	Nancy C.	"	17				"
	Margaret A.	"	15				"
	Melinda J.	"	13				"
	Henry I.	"	12				"
	Mary E.	"	10				"
	Minerva J.	"	6				"
1002	Elizabeth B.	BELK	47			100	Tenn.
	Nancy J.	"	13				"
	Allen D.	ALEXANDER	18				"
	Sarah E.	"	16				"
1003	Alford	DAVIS	45	Farmer		250	Tenn.
	Susan	"	36				"
	Sarah J.	"	11				"
	Mary M.	"	10				"
	McLin	" (m)	6				"
	William G.	"	5				"
	Alford	"	3				"
	Martha S.	"	2				"
	Arvagina	" (f)	2/12				"

	Name		Age	Occupation	Real	Pers.	Birthplace
1004	James	KAYLOR	30	Farmer	800	565	Tenn.
	Nancy	"	31				"
	George	"	13				"
	Martha J.	"	12				"
	William	"	8				"
	Mary C.	"	6				"

Page 141   30 July 1860

	Name		Age	Occupation	Real	Pers.	Birthplace
	Sydney A.	KAYLOR	4				Tenn.
1005	James	HEADRICK	30	Laborer		100	Tenn.
	Jane	"	30				"
	William	"	8				"
	James	"	6				"
	John	"	4				"
	Elizabeth	"	2				"
	Thomas	"	6/12				"
1006	Eli	JOHNSON	56	Farmer	1,000	900	S. C.
	Moriah	"	34				Tenn.
	Mary M.	"	23				"
	Sarah A.	"	20				"
	Thomas M.	"	18				"
	Richard H.	"	15				"
1007	William S.	LOGAN	34	Farmer	300	500	Tenn.
	Nancy J.	"	34				"
	Joseph W.	"	6				"
	Samuel R.	"	3				"
	Martha C.	"	4/12				"
1008	Eleanor	DELANEY	41		100	250	Tenn.
	Eliza J.	"	19				"
	Joseph R.	"	16				"
	William D.	"	14				"
	Nancy A.	"	10				"
	Mary A.	"	6				"
	Jim Henry	"	2				"
	David C. McK.	"	1				"
1009	Jno. C.	CALDWELL	38	Blacksmith	1,000	450	Tenn.
	Margaretta	"	42				Va.
	John S.	"	12				Tenn.
1010	Robt. B.	CALDWELL	45	Farmer		550	Tenn.
	William	"	17				"
	Sarah J.	"	15				"
1011	Daniel H.	DELANEY	29	Farmer		550	Tenn.
	Minerva	"	20				"
	Melissa M.	"	5				"
	Mary J.	"	1				"
1012	David	VAUGHT	53	Cooper & Waggon Mk.		650	Tenn.
	Sarah	"	55				N. C.
	Nancy S.	"	20				Tenn.

District 1   P.O.: Brick Mill

	Name		Age	Occupation	Real	Pers.	Birthplace
Page 142							31 July 1860
	Jno. P.	Vaught	24				Tenn.
	Richard H.	"	21				
	William L.	"	17				
	Mary R. D.	"	15				
1013	Robert	EAKIN	30	Laborer		100	Tenn.
	Nancy S.	"	16				"
	Mary T.	"	9/12				"
1014	Legman J.	RYAN	31	Farmer	500	500	N. C.
	Evaline H.	"	25				Tenn.
	John B.	"	8				"
	Caroline	"	4				"
	Monroe M.	"	1				"
1015	Alford B.	HOWARD	50	Farmer	12,000	5,655	N. C.
	Euphania	"	44				Tenn.
	George W.	"	23		600	1,500	"
	Ruth E.	"	21				"
	James C.	"	20				"
	Mary E.	"	15				"
	William B.	"	14				"
	Margaret S.	"	11				"
	John R.	"	9				"
	Caswell B.	"	8				"
	Samuel	"	5				"
1016	Zachariah	COLLINS	29	Miller & Sawyer		75	Tenn.
	Rebecca J.	"	26				"
	John	"	7				"
	Margaret S.	"	6				"
	Robert F.	"	3				"
	Sarah J.	"	3/12				"
1017	Philip	COPE	40	Laborer		50	Tenn.
	Tempy	"	35				"
	Mary	"	19				"
	Catharine	"	14				"
	Peter	"	12				"
	Harriet	"	10				"
	Jane	"	8				"
	Josephine	"	6				"
	John	"	4				
1018	Samuel	UNDERWOOD	36	Laborer		100	Tenn.
	Lydia	"	34				
Page 143							31 July 1860
	James	UNDERWOOD	2				Tenn.
1019	Doctor F.	GENTRY	33	Laborer		75	Tenn.
	Angeline W.	"	27				"
	Laura J.	"	6				"
	Charles A.	"	3				"
	John M. F.	"	5/12				

District 1   P.O.: Brick Mill

	Name		Age	Occupation	Real	Pers.	Birthplace
1020	John	MONTGOMERY	40	Farmer	8,000	7,600	Tenn.
	Sarah A.	"	35				"
	Samuel	"	14				"
	Elizabeth E.	"	12				"
	James W.	"	10				"
	Virginia	"	8				"
	Mary C.	"	6				"
	John A.	"	4				"
	Charles McG.	"	1				"
1021	George B.	ERWIN	75	Miller		200	S. C.
	Nancy C.	"	31				Tenn.
	Andrew J.	"	18				
	Elizabeth	"	13				
1022	John	CURTIS	29	Distiller		500	S. C.
	Frances C.	"	28				Tenn.
	Susan E.	"	7				"
	Willis G.	"	5				"
	Sarah S.	"	2				"
	Emaline	"	3/12				"
1023	Jane	HIX	46			150	Tenn.
	Elizabeth	"	27				"
	Ann E.	"	1				"
1024	James H.	MONTGOMERY	50	Farmer	8,000	6,035	Tenn.
	Sarah B.	"	39				"
	Mary E.	"	11				"
	Jane	"	8				"
	Margaret	"	6				"
	Sarah	"	3				"
	William	HIX	18				"
1025	Ann	SMITH	55	Farmer		500	Tenn.
	Andrew V.	"	21				"
	Alvira A.	"	17				"
	Arthur S.	"	15				"
1026	David C.	THOMPSON	30	Farmer		1,230	Tenn.

Page 144   1 Aug. 1860

	Name		Age	Occupation	Real	Pers.	Birthplace
	Lucinda A.	THOMPSON	30				Tenn.
	Lorenzo A.	"	5				"
	Nancy J.	"	2				"
	Mary A.	"	1				"
1027	Allen D.	HAWKINS	22	Farmer		150	Tenn.
	Mary C.	"	21				N. C.
	Eliza J.	ODUM	19				"
1028	Richard	HAWKINS	77			175	N. C.
	Jane	"	33				Tenn.
	Richard	"	23				"
	Mildred	"	14				"
	Rosannah	"	10				"
	Samuel	"	8				"

	Name		Age	Occupation	Real	Pers.	Birthplace
1029	Jacob	COPE	29	Laborer		50	Tenn.
	Rebecca A.	"	28				"
1030	John	HAMONTREE	40	Farmer	1,000	575	Tenn.
	Eliza J.	"	30				"
	Mitchell	"	9				"
	Mary S.	"	7				"
	Ruth A.	"	5				"
	Amanda J.	"	2				"
1031	James & Mary	WOOD	56/54			400	N.C./N.C.
	Elizabeth C.	"	29				"
	William King	"	20				"
	Jesse Green(m)	" (twins)	20				"
1032	Arthur	GREER	43	Farmer	1,500	1,325	Tenn.
	Almira E.	"	27				"
	James M.	"	18				"
	John N.	"	16				"
	Joseph C.	"	6				"
	Samuel C.	"	2				"
	David	"	1				"
	Jane	"	80				"
1033	Robert G.	ARMSTRONG	45	Farmer	600	900	Tenn.
	Martha	"	46				"
	John M.	"	11				"
	Mary A. E.	"	5				"
1034	John C.	TAYLOR	50	Farmer		600	Tenn.
	Elizabeth	"	50				"
	Margaret M.	"	21				"

	Name		Age	Occupation	Real	Pers.	Birthplace
	William M.	TAYLOR	18				Tenn.
	Joseph S.	"	15				"
	Andrew H.	"	13				"
	Martha A.	"	9				"
1035	William	KING	80	Farmer	500	700	N. C.
	Elizabeth	"	58				Va.
	William	"	45				N. C.
1036	Ephraim C.	KING	24			250	Tenn.
	Melinda T.	"	25				"
	Samuel S.	"	3				"
	Sarah M.	"	1				"
1037	Edward	PASS	19			100	Tenn.
	Mary K.	" (mwy)	19				"
	Melinda T.	"	1/12				"
1038	Archibald	DICKSON	38	Farmer		675	Tenn.
	Eliza J.	"	35				"
	Margaret E.	"	13				"
	William C.	"	10				"
	Elizabeth J.	"	8				"
	James P.	"	6				"

District 1   P.O.: Brick Mill

	Name		Age	Occupation	Real	Pers.	Birthplace
	Andrew J.	"	4				"
	Joseph	"	1/12				"
1039	Pleasant M.	ALEXANDER	52	Miller		150	S.C.
	Eliza J.	"	51				"
	Columbus B.	"	17				Tenn.
	Druscilla	"	15				"
	Eliza	"	12				"
	Lucinda E.	"	5				"
1040	Harriet C. SPARKS (mul)		22	Laborer		.25	N. C.
	Sarah S.	" (mul)	3				Tenn.
	James R.	" (mul)	6/12				"
1041	James L.	SPARKS	52	Laborer		300	N. C.
	Nancy	"	43				"
	Margaret M.	"	17				"
	Hannah S.	"	15				"
	James M.	"	13				"
	Nancy J.	"	11				"
	Huldah M.	"	7				"
	Martha P.	"	5				"
	William H.	"	3				"

Page 146   1 Aug. 1860

	Name		Age	Occupation	Real	Pers.	Birthplace
	Alcia H. M.	SPARKS	6/12				Tenn.
1042	James	ARMSTRONG	42	Farmer	500	300	Tenn.
	Sam	"	12				"
	William	"	14				"
	Robert	"	16				"
1043	Joseph M.	MOORE	27	Farmer	200	500	Tenn.
	Rebecca J.	"	27				"
	John H.	"	1				"
	Mary E.	"	2/12				"
	Ellen C.	"	28		100		"
	Catharine M.	"	24		100		"
1044	Elizabeth	SHIPLEY	53	Farmer		400	Tenn.
	Martha E.	"	23				"
	Mahala M.	"	21				"
	Washington V.	"	18				"
1045	John	HUGHS	48	Laborer		300	N. C.
	Winniford	"	45				Tenn.
	Sarah	"	25				"
	Jane	"	23				"
	Eliza	"	17				"
	Andrew J.	"	27				"
1046	Wade H. K.	SWAN	38	Painter	4,000	100	France
	Sarah M.	"	38				Tenn.
	Franklin M.	"	4				"
1047	Thomas	CALDWELL	41	Farmer	500	600	Tenn.
	Mary J.	"	34				"
	Joseph M.	"	3				"
	John S.	"	8/12				"
	William S.	"	8				"

District 1   P.O.: Brick Hill

	Name		Age	Occupation	Real	Pers.	Birthplace
1048	Thomas	ANDERSON	24	Farmer		740	Tenn.
	Mahala C.	"	28				"
	John A.	"	1				"
1049	Hugh S. W. JOHNSON (mwy)		29	Farmer	250	665	Tenn.
	Mary A.	"	27				"
	Clarissa A.	CALDWELL	69				"
	Sarah J.	"	34		250		"
	Nancy J.	"	30		250		"
1050	Samuel H.	GARNER	33	Farmer	5,000	1,500	Tenn.
	Rebecca J.	"	21				"
	James D.	"	3				"

Page 147   1 Aug. 1860

	Name		Age	Occupation	Real	Pers.	Birthplace
	Mary E.	GARNER	1				Tenn.
1051	Wm.	WILLIAMSON	81	Farmer	2,000	960	N. C.
	Rebecca	"	64				"
	Nancy A.	RUDD	19				Tenn.
1052	William H.	GARNER	35	Farmer	1,500	1,555	Tenn.
	Mary	"	24				"
	William F.	"	6				"
	John A.	"	4				"
	Polly J.	"	2				"
	Pryor S.	"	1/12				"
1053	Jane F.	HAMILL	44		1,000	200	Tenn.
1054	Margaret	RHYNE	51			250	N. C.
	Eli	"	21				Tenn.
	Lettitia T.	"	17				"
	John P.	"	15				"
	Martin A.	"	13				"
	Elish W.	"	10				"
1055	Matthew W.	PRIVETT	27	Laborer		100	Tenn.
	Elizabeth	"	28				"
1056	Levi H.	BRIANT	36	Farmer		150	N. C.
	Elizabeth	"	35				Tenn.
	John M.	"	16				"
	Dolly C.	"	14				"
	Mary A.	"	10				"
	Martha C.	"	7				"
	Sarah J.	"	4				"
	William R.	"	9/12				"
	Catharine	RHYNE	74				N. C.
1057	Jane	HALE	63	Farmer	1,500	1,000	Ga.
	John C.	"	20				Tenn.
1058	Nancy	HENRY	63	Farmer	10,000	8,650	S. C.
	Samuel	"	33		2,500	3,700	Tenn.
1059	Alexander	HALE	91	Farmer	8,000	7,000	Md.
	Sarah A.	HALE	49		1,500	5,880	Tenn.
	Sarah J.	"	20				"

District 1   P.O.: Brick Mill

	Name		Age	Occupation	Real	Pers.	Birthplace
1060	James A.	McKANY	33	Merchant		1,500	Tenn.
1061	Lucrita	PUGH	56	Farmer	2,500	2,300	Tenn.
	Lafayette	"	20	Com. S. Teacher			"
1062	Elizabeth	HUTTON	47	Farmer	3,300	2,800	Tenn.
	Josiah C.	"	22				"

Page 148   2 Aug. 1860

	Name		Age	Occupation	Real	Pers.	Birthplace
	John N.	HUTTON	20				Tenn.
	Thomas S.	"	17				"
	James C.	"	15				"
	Harvey A.	"	13				"
	George D.	"	10				"
	Sarah	BROWN	22				"
1063	James L.	SAFFELL	32	Farmer	625	650	Tenn.
	Elizabeth A.	"	36				"
	Sarah S.	"	10				"
	Florence C.	"	6				"
	Margaret E.	"	1				"
1064	Josiah D.	PUGH	48	Farmer	3,500	9,666	Tenn.
	Mary P.	"	36				"
	Joseph S.	"	22				"
	Samuel J.	"	21				"
	Martha A.	"	19				"
	Virginia G.	"	18				"
	Dickinson	MORRIS	72				Va.
	Nancy	"	68				"
1065	Luther	RAGSDALE	27	Blacksmith		500	Tenn.
	Mary A.	"	33				"
	Sarah A.	"	4				"
	Nancy F.	"	2				"
	Margaret R.	"	3/12				"
1066	Richard	McQUIN	28	Ditcher			Ireland
	James	"	23	"		500	"
1067	James	MALONE	26	"			"

1860 BLOUNT COUNTY MORTALITY SCHEDULE

The 1860 Mortality Schedule was taken along with the 1860 census. It was to include the individuals who died one year prior to June 1, 1860.

Each entry lists the name, age, sex (f=female, m=male), whether married, race, month died, occupation, cause of death and how long sick before death. Since the majority of the persons listed were white, to save space we have listed the race only for blacks and mulattoes. All others are white.

Every effort has been made to be accurate. However, some of the names were faded and very hard to read. If you have any questions, you should consult the original on microfilm.

Page 1

1. Rose Cox, 27, f, married, mulatto, slave, S.C., May, consumption, 6 mos.
2. No name Nipper, 1/12, m, Tn., Oct., typhoid fever, 10 days.
3. Amanda J. Daltiny (Dolling?), 32, f, married, Tn., March, consumption, 5 mos.
4. Sarah J. Tedford, 15, f, mulatto, free, TN, Oct., consumption, 3 mos.
5. Lisa Cox, 13, f, black, slave, TN, Aug., inflammation of bowels, 1 day.
6. Nancy Cox, 1, f, black, slave, TN, Oct., bronchitus, 2 mos.
7. Melinda Terry, 1/12, f, TN, June, unknown, 3 wks.
8. John B. McLin, 75, male, widower, PA, April, cabinet maker, unknown, 4 days.
9. Frank Cox, 1, male, black, slave, TN, Jan., pneumonia, 10 days.
10. Jim Cox, 1, male, mulatto, slave, TN, Oct., croup, 10 days.
11. Sarah M. Whittenberg, 6/12, f, TN, March, croup, 3 days.
12. James F. Talbot, 1, m, TN, June, inflammation of bowels, 1 wk.
13. Joseph M. Brown, 22, m, TN, Apr., farmer, typhoid fever, 4 wks.
14. Faraba Gourley, 1, f, black, slave, TN, Jan., croup, 2 days.
15. No name Prater, 1/12, male, black, slave, TN, Jan., croup, 2 days.
16. James Taliaferro, 26, m, black, slave, NC, Nov., drowned, sudden.
17. Jane Ish, 2, f, black, slave, TN, July, croup, 2 days.
18. Elizabeth Richards, 73, f, widow, VA, Feb., unknown, 4 wks.
19. Joel Stone, 69, m, NC, Dec., painter, tetanus, 12 days.
20. John I. Meiser, 3, male, TN, Nov., unknown, 1 wk.
21. Elizabeth Allen, 16, f, TN, Oct., typhoid fever, 4 wks.
22. Samuel Jones, 84, male, married, NC, Sept., farmer, dibility, 6 mos.
23. William Philips, 1/12, m, TN, Jan., croup, 2 wks.
24. Pleasant H. Philips, 36, m, married, TN, Feb., farmer, consumption, 2 yrs.
25. Elizabeth G. Moore, 1, f, TN, Oct., croup, 3 wks.
26. John F. Cochran, 2, m, TN, March, typhoid fever, 1 wk.
27. Wm. L. Burnham, 1, m, TN, June, chlorea infantum, 1 day.
28 William Dunlap, 47, m, married, NC, Oct., farmer, unknown, 3 wks.
29. Nancy E. Hackney, 4, f, TN, May, typhoid fever, 3 wks.
30. Margaret Hamill, 1, f, TN, June, inflammation of brain, 6 wks.
31. Charles Leeper, 66, m, mulatto, slave, GA, July, cholera, 23 hrs.
32. Cepha French, 5, m, TN, June, typhoid fever, 16 days.
33. Josephine H. Lingenfelter, 3, f, TN, Nov., croup, 5 days.
34. Molly Hackney, 10/12, f, TN, Aug., inflammation of brain, 3 wks.
35. Mary Ann Dawson, 9/12, f, TN, July, croup, 2 wks.

Page 2

1. Lorenzo D. Jackson, 12, m, black, slave, TN, Jan., dropsy, 4 mos.
2. Lucinda Caston, 91, f, widow, VA, July, unknown, 5 wks.
3. Polly Ann Hammer, 27, f, TN, May, consumption, 2 yrs.

4. Jesse Hammer, 9/12, m, TN, June, cold, 2 mos.
5. Sarah Brooks, 68, f, widow, VA, Aug., dropsy, 3 wks.
6. Charles Wayman, 1/12, m, TN, May, unknown, 3 days.
7. Sarah Griffitts, 4/12, female, black, slave, TN, April, enlargement of brain, 3 w
8. Sam Jackson, 1, m, black, slave, TN, March, croup, 3 wks.
9. Jim Jackson, 35, m, black, slave, TN, March, consumption, 5 mo.
10. James Jackson, 2/12, m, black, slave, TN, March, unknown, 1 mo.
11. Mary E. Waddle, 7/12, f, TN, June, cold, 3 mos.
12. Ann Kizer, 57, f, widow, unknown, Nov., chills, 6 wks.
13. Alexander Conner, 2/12, m, TN, Oct., sore throat, 1 wk.
14. Margaret Conner, 87, f, widow, Ireland, Feb., old age, 5 mos.
15. Margaret M. M'Connell, 12, f, TN, July, measles, 2 wks.
16. Elizabeth Montgomery, 70, f, widow, PA, July, dibility, 5 wks.
17. Ann Eliza Wilson, 1, f, TN, June, flux, 6 days.
18. Charles Kerr, 1/12, m, black, slave, TN, Nov., diseased liver, 1 wk.
19. Missouri Wilson, 1, f, black, slave, TN, June, flux, 2 wks.
20. Matthew Phinney, 5/12, m, TN, March, inflammation of brain, 11 days.
21. John F. Cohorn, 2, male, TN, Feb., typhoid fever, 2 wks.
22. Burton Logan, 11/12, m, black, slave, TN, Jan., croup, 1 day.
23. Mary J. Edmondson, 21, f, TN, Feb., bronchitus, 1 yr.
24. John M'Keehan, 1/12, m, TN, April, unknown, sudden.
25. Apsley Stallion, 55, f, NC, Feb., consumption, 3 wks.
26. John Gaut, 63, m, married, TN, July, farmer, unknown, sudden.
27. Mary Culton, 78, f, married, PA, June, diseased bowels, 13 days.
28. Sarah E. Grissume, 12, f, TN, Dec., unknown, 2 mos.
29. John M. Hamull, 16, m, TN, May, diseased liver, 1 yr..
30. Elizabeth Thompson, 6/12, f, TN, Oct., diseased liver, 5 days.
31. Leander H. Cunningham, 2, m, TN, Jan., worms, 3 wks.
32. William A. Gardner, 6, m, TN, June, inflammation of brain, 3 days.
33. Eliza Henry, 3/12, f, black, slave, TN, June, cold,
34. Betty Ann Emmett, 49, f, married, TN, Nov., consumption, 6 mos.
35. Naomi Kerr, 9, f, TN, Aug., inflammation of brain, 1 day.

Page 3

1. William C. Prather, 44, m, married, ALA, June, shoemaker, typhoid fever, 16 dys.
2. Lusidna M. Prather, 12, f, TN, July, typhoid fever, 2 wks.
3. James Farr, 36, m, married, TN, Sept., farmer, billious fever, 3 wks.
4. Samuel G. Farr, 2, m, TN, June, flux, 10 days.
5. John A. Hanner, 9/12, m, TN, Aug., croup, 5 days.
6. Martha Crye, 67, f, widow, TN, Aug., old age, 1 mo.
7. Joseph M. Chapman, 2, m, TN, June, flux, 3 wks.
8. John Thompson, 56, m, married, TN, March, laborer, intemperance, sudden.
9. Sarah Stout, 74, f, married, VA, March, unknown, sudden.
10. William N. Parsons, 1, m, TN, Sept., thrash, 2 mos.
11. Saml T. Hoyl, 1/12, m, TN, May, unknown, 2 days.
12. William Garner, 87, m, widower, NC, May, dropsy, 5 mos.
13. Elizabeth Garner, 4, TN, June, consumption, 6 mos.
14. William P. Spradlin, 1/12, m, TN, Oct., unknown, 2 wks.
15. Theophilus Odum, 49, m, NC, Feb., laborer, pneumonia, 12 days.
16. Sarah Hammontree, 83, f, widow, NC, Feb., old age, 1 mo.

Page 4

1. William McNabb, 73, m, married, SC, May, threadbaler, consumption, 4 mos.
2. Sam Houston Kidd, 1/12, m, TN, Sept, unknown
3. infant, 1/12, f, black, slave, unknown
4. Margaret Hicks, 60, f, NC, widow, Jan., nurse, pneumonia, 3 wks.

5. Betsy A. Haddox, 9, f, TN, March, tenant child, putrid sore throat, 7 days.
6. James N. Haddox, 4, m, _____
7. Augustine Haddox, 1, m, _____
8. Negro infant, 1/12, f, black, slave, Aug., unknown
9. Penelope Rankin, 11, f, Oct., farmer's child, putrid sore throat, 5 days.
10. Moses Thompson, 11/12, m, Nov., 4 days.
11. Mary Moss, 26, f, VA, Sept., factory hand, cancer in breast, 9 mos.
12. Mary Swaggerty, 5/12. f, TN, Aug., tenant child, unknown, 2 mos.
13. Eleanor Harris, 75, f, widow, VA, May, farmer's widow, palsey (with age) 4 mos.
14. Narcissa Kerby, 43, f, married, TN, Sept., farmer's wife, consumption, 6 mos.
15. Infant of Kerby, stillborn
16. William Mitchel, 20, m, Aug., tenant son, pneumonia, 3 wks.
17. Infant, stillborn
18. James Morton, 59, married, NC, July, farmer, typhoid fever, 7 wks.
19. Richmond (Deadney?), 21, m, TN, Sept., 19 days.
20. John (Simms?), 12, m, Feb., congestive fever, 5 days.
21. Will C. Gillispie, 44, married, March, intemperance, 2 wks.
22. Tolbert Wesley, 2/12, m, July, bowel complaint, 1 mo.
23. Infant, 4/12, f, _____
24. Infant, stillborn
25. Martha Davis, 28, f, VA, consumption, 12 mos.
26. Infant, TN, Jan., stillborn
27. Telano Gillespie, 9/12, f, Sept., TN, inflammation of brain, 5 days.
28. Infant, 1, f, TN, Nov., 4 wks.
29. Elizabeth Easley, 3, f, June, flux, 16 days.
30. Clementine McClure, 23, f, TN, married, May, tenant wife, inflammatory fever, 14 days.
31. Isaack, 1, m, black, slave, Oct., sore throat, 5 days.
32. Jane Cowan, 70, f, widow, June, farmer, bilous fever, 3 wks.
33. Mary Clark, 24, f, married, Oct., farmer's wife, consumption, 12 mos.
34. Abe Fancher, 24, m, mulatto, slave, secrofula?, 6 mos.
35. Mary Raulston, 10/12, f, Nov., dropsy of brain, 5 wks.

1. Margaret McGinly, 26, f, Married, TN, Aug., attorneys wife, consumption,
2. John Montgomery, 48, m, TN, Jan, laborer, intemperance, 1 day.
3. Andrew Blackburn, 31, m, married, TN, Aug., N. S. Pres., consumption, 7 mos.
4. Sally Blackburn, 1, f, TN, April, inflammation of lungs, 9 mos.
5. Infant, Aug., stillborn
6. Leonard Rhea, 55, married, NC, Jan., miller, consumption, 3 mos.
7. William Toole, 69, m, married, TN, May, saddler, old age, 6 mos.
8. William Hicks, 61, m, married, NC, April, shoemaker, congestive chills, 2 wks.
9. Sarah Anderson, 28, f, TN, married, Jan., farmer, typhoid fever, 8 days.
10. Peter Grindstaff, 9, m, TN, Feb. 2 wks.
11. George Rawlston, 79, m, married, VA, Sept., rheumatism, 8 yrs.
12. Lucy Whitehead, 11, f, TN, March, clothes caught fire, 6 hrs.
13. Infant, 3/12, m, TN, June.
14. Mary Johnson, 19, f, TN, Sept., nuralgia, 1 wk.
15. Isaack Simerly, 9/12, m, Jan., disease of head.
16. Robert McClain, 8, m, TN, March, tonsilitis, 4 days.
17. Margaret McClain, 4, f, March, 20 days.
18. Jesse Britt, 45, m, VA, Sept., tenant, pleurisy, 3 days.
19. Jordan Steel, 1, m, TN, June, disease of head, 2 wks.
20. Polly M. McCauley, 1/12, f, TN, March, 2 days.
21. Eliza Everitt, 29, f, married, VA, Feb., farmer's wife, consumption, 3 mos.
22. Patrick Carney, 45, m, married, Ireland, Jan., stonecutter, inflammation of brain, 14 days.

23. Ebenezer McGinley, 51, m, married, TN, June, farmer, consumption, 6 mos.
24. Margaret Henry, 29, f, married, TN, March, farmer's wife, consumption, r mos.
25. Lorenzo Wilson 6, m, TN, Oct., smith's son, 4 mos.
26. John Clampet, 40, m, married, May, laborer, typhoid fever, 3 wks.
27. Thomas Dunlapp, 37, m, married, TN, May, farmer, typhoid fever, 2 wks.
28. Infant, stillborn , Sept.
29. Margaret Murrey, 28, f, married, NC, Aug., tenant's wife, consumption, 3 mos.
30. Teuar. 45, f, black, slave, TN, June, dropsy, 1 mo.
31. Sarah, 1, f, black, slave, TN, June, unknown, 1 day.
32. James, 1, m, June, worms, 4 days.
33. Martha Rogers, 29, f, married, Oct., fits, 4 days.
34. George Blasey, 85, m, married, butcher, Ireland, liver complaint, 2 wks.
35. Infant, Aug., stillborn.

1. John Brakebill, 61, m, married, Oct., farmer, enysipilas, 13 days.
2. John, 1, male, mulatto, slave, April, clothes caught fire, 17 hrs.
3. Malindy Davis, 24, f, TN, April, breast complaint, 12 mos.
4. William Johnson, 1/12, m, Jan., hives, 2 days.
5. Crowron? Barns, 3, m, Dec., sore throat, 3 days.
6. Thomas Henry, 1/12, m, May, unknown, 2 days.

1860 U. S. CENSUS OF BLOUNT COUNTY, TENNESSEE

INDEX

Numbers refer to the page number. The page number will be listed only once
for a given surname, though there may be many families of the same surname
on the page.

- S -

SAFFELL 49, 139, 140, 141, 193, 226, 228, 258

SANDERSON 212

SARTAIN 210

SARTEN 100

SAUL 202

SCOTT 55, 56, 127, 201, 218, 232

SCRIBNER 8

SCROGGS 66

SCRUGGS 65, 141, 202, 226

SEATON 83

SEIBER 39

SELLERS 232

SEMPSON 184

SESLER 45

SHADDAN 178

SHADDEN 104, 106

SHANKS 247

SHARP 20, 22, 26, 163

SHAVER 84, 104, 135

SHAVERLY 140

SHEAY 51

SHEDDAN 205, 206

SHEFFER 22

SHELLY 228

SHERREL(L) 25, 84, 221

SHERRILL 227

SHIELDS 129

SHINAT 152

SHIPLEY 186, 256

SHIRLEY 192

SHOEMAKER 135

SHOFFNER 2

SHOWN 237

SIMERLY 61, 64, 66, 69

SIMMONS 89

SIMMS 19, 24, 28

SIMONS 224

SIMPSON 191

SINGLETON 6, 11, 136, 137, 140, 141, 144

SISEMORE 109

SKINNER 196

SKIPRETH 178

SLOAN 43

SMALLEN 231, 233

SMITH 31, 38, 44, 45, 46, 47, 65, 118, 135, 142, 162, 163, 164, 174, 176, 184, 214, 236, 240, 241, 250, 254

SNEED 71

SNIDER 56, 117, 118, 201, 218, 232

SOUTHERLAND 139

SPARKS 130, 163, 201, 256

SPEARS 157

SPILIMAN 137

SPRADLIN 19, 204, 239, 240, 251

STAFFORD 101

STALEY 188

STALLIAN 220, 221

STANFIELD 178

STANSBERRY 3, 178

STEELE(E) 73, 78, 79, 80, 136, 156, 224

STEPHENS 2, 36, 151, 207

STERLING 49, 217, 218

STEWARD 13, 215, 238

STEWART 185

STINNET(T) 31, 144

STONE 26, 42, 58, 90, 135, 157, 159, 165, 186, 208

STOOPS 15

STOUT 204, 245

STRAIN 221

STRANG 33

www.ingramcontent.com/pod-product-compliance
Lightning Source LLC
Chambersburg PA
CBHW081431270326
41932CB00019B/3161